KARL MARX
AND THE PHILOSOPHY
OF PRAXIS

For Bob

with very best wishes

Gavin Kitching

May 1988

KARL MARX AND THE PHILOSOPHY OF PRAXIS

Gavin Kitching

ROUTLEDGE
London and New York

First published in 1988 by
Routledge
11 New Fetter Lane, London EC4P 4EE

Published in the USA by
Routledge
in association with Routledge, Chapman and Hall, Inc.
29 West 35th Street, New York NY 10001

Printed in Great Britain by
Richard Clay Ltd, Bungay, Suffolk

British Library Cataloguing in Publication Data
Kitching, G.N.
   Karl Marx and the philosophy of Praxis.
   1. Marx, Karl, *1818–1883*   2. Wittgenstein,
   Ludwig   3. Social sciences ——
   Philosophy
   I. Title
   300′.92′2   B3305.M74

   ISBN 0–415–00713–5
   ISBN 0–415–00714–3 Pbk

Library of Congress Cataloging in Publication Data
Kitching, G.N.
   Karl Marx and the philosophy of praxis: an
   introduction and critique / Gavin Kitching.
   p. cm.
   Bibliography: p.
   Includes index.
   ISBN 0–415–00713–5
   ISBN 0–415–00714–3 (pbk.)
   1. Marx, Karl, 1818–1883.   I. Title.
   B3305.M74K523   1988
   335.4′092′4——dc19

For Pamela and Ewan

'Philosophy is a battle against the bewitchment of our intelligence by means of language.' Ludwig Wittgenstein, *Philosophical Investigations*

'Labour is the living, form giving fire; it is the transitoriness of things, their temporality, as their formation by living time.' Karl Marx, *Grundrisse*

'Can I move? Will you just let me move?!' Sundance to Butch in *Butch Cassidy and the Sundance Kid*

CONTENTS

PREFACE

Introductions to the thought of Karl Marx now abound and are just one product of the positive explosion in Marxist scholarship which has taken place in the west over the last fifteen to twenty years. However, such texts divide fairly clearly into two groups. On the one hand are introductions to Marx's 'social and political thought' concentrating on such topics as his theories of history, class struggle, the state, ideology, and his views on revolution and socialism. On the other hand – and somewhat less abundant – are introductions to Marx's economics, dealing with his theories of value, exploitation, capital accumulation, etc. Brief and readable texts which attempt to encompass both these dimensions are much rarer, and rarer still are texts which attempt to evaluate as well as present Marx's ideas across this range.

The rarity of texts which do attempt those tasks, and the even greater rarity of those which attempt to do it briefly, may well be a sign of wisdom. Marx's scholarship, like that of many of his great nineteenth-century contemporaries, encompassed a range of concerns transgressing the boundaries of modern-day academic specialisms. There are therefore very few modern commentators who have the confidence – or perhaps the foolhardiness – to deal with his thought in its entirety. To do that, and to attempt a critique, may be both arrogant and naive – certainly it is extremely risky.

But there are also risks in not at least attempting such a task on behalf of the modern reader. For Marx did regard his thought – or at least the thought of his mature years – as a unity. For example, he would, I am sure, have regarded discussion of his social or political ideas which proceeded in abstraction from his economic theories as misleading to the point of travesty, and yet this has been done often enough. On the other hand however, he was not an 'economist' in the modern sense (despite numerous attempts to reclaim his as such), precisely because he insisted that economic issues – of value, price, production, consumption, profit – could not be adequately grasped unless seen in a social and historical context.

How far Marx's thought actually *was* a seamless unity, how far he actually succeeded in an integration of his philosophical, historical, and economic ideas is of course a moot point, and one to which I devote considerable attention in what follows. As will become apparent, I am now quite sceptical about his achievements in this regard. None the less, such an integration was his aspiration, his project, and if we are to grasp that project and to evaluate it properly we must take it seriously and deal with it as a totality. Marx was not a philosopher, he was not an historian, he was not a sociologist, he was not a political scientist, he was not an economist. Rather, in an intellectual world which did not know these distinctions, he was both something of all these things and more than any one of them. So we are confronted by an invidious choice. We can either bowdlerize his thought by coralling it into the particular discipline in which we have been trained and feel confident, or we can risk making fools of ourselves by attempting to follow him in his total project. I have taken the latter risk.

I have been supported in taking that risk by a number of other people to whom I must give thanks. Two cohorts of sociology students at the Polytechnic of North London have borne my lectures and seminars on Marx with fortitude and have given me valuable feedback which has helped shape this book. Geoffrey Hawthorn and John Harriss gave me astute comments and stout support when I needed both greatly, as did my friend John Harrison, whose tolerance and sympathetic criticism of ideas with which he profoundly disagrees is a mark of that personal liberalism from which the whole left could benefit. Finally my thanks to all my colleagues in the Department of Sociology at the Polytechnic of North London who have provided space and time for this book to be written in an environment in which both are in increasingly short supply, and most especially to Jennie Somerville, whose comments on my original draft manuscript were often lengthy, occasionally acerbic, but always acute, and without whose efforts this book would certainly have been the worse.

Gavin Kitching
June 1987

EDITIONS OF THE WORKS OF MARX AND ENGELS REFERRED TO IN THIS BOOK

MESW   Karl Marx and Frederick Engels, *Selected Works in One Volume* (London, Lawrence & Wishart, 1970).

MESC   Karl Marx and Frederick Engels, *Selected Correspondence* (Moscow, Progress Publishers, 1955).

MECW   Karl Marx and Frederick Engels, *Collected Works* (London, Lawrence & Wishart, 1975 onwards).

GI   Karl Marx and Frederick Engels, *The German Ideology* (Part One, with selections from Parts Two and Three). Edited with an introduction by C.J. Arthur (London, Lawrence & Wishart, 1970).

PP   Karl Marx, *The Poverty of Philosophy*, with an introduction by Frederick Engels (New York, International Publishers, 1963).

Karl Marx, *Capital: A Critical Analysis of Capitalist Production*, vol. I, translated from the third German edition by Samuel Moore and Edward Aveling (Moscow, Progress Publishers, 1965).

Karl Marx, *Capital: A Critique of Political Economy*, vol. III (Moscow, Progress Publishers, 1971).

TSV   Karl Marx, *Theories of Surplus Value*, Parts 1, 2, and 3 (London, Lawrence & Wishart, 1968, 1969, and 1972).

Grundrisse   Karl Marx, *Grundrisse: Foundations of the Critique of Political Economy (Rough Draft)*. Translated with a Foreword by Martin Nicolaus (Harmondsworth, Penguin, 1973).

INTRODUCTION

This book began life as a series of introductory lectures on Marx
delivered to a class of undergraduate Sociology and Applied
Social Studies students at the Polytechnic of North London.
Thus, when I decided to convert these lectures into a single
manuscript I at first imagined that I would simply write an
introductory textbook on Marx.

Although such textbooks now abound, I felt emboldened to
supply the market with another by complimentary remarks by
both students and colleagues on the clarity and originality of
the original lectures. In particular I felt that the introductory
literature on Marx is still lacking in works which endeavour to
present his thought as a whole and to criticize it as a whole, and
is especially lacking in works which present and criticize his
economic theories clearly and in a short space. Thus, I felt
that beginning students and others interested in Marx, but
intimidated by the scope and difficulty both of his own work
and of most of the secondary literature, might still benefit from
this further addition to the already voluminous writings on
Marx and Marxism.

However, as this work progressed I found my original project
cross-fertilizing with another. I have been engaged for some
time on a study of the later philosophy of Ludwig Wittgenstein,
with the aim of writing a book on the implications of that
philosophy for social and political theory in general. Thus, as
this short book took shape, I found it gradually turning, not into
a Wittgensteinian critique of Marx, but into a presentation and
evaluation of Marx's thought from a perspective drawn from
Wittgenstein's later philosophy. Moreover, I found that the use
of this perspective enabled me both to draw out some interesting implications from Marx's own earlier philosophy, and to
use those implications in a productive way to shed what I hope

is some fresh light on the ideas and theories of the mature Marx.

However, while I have found this cross-fertilization both helpful and clarifying of my analysis, it has made it altogether more difficult for me to describe or classify the final outcome of my efforts. For on the one hand this book is clearly something more than an introductory text on Marx, and its final two chapters in particular take the reader into overtly philosophical terrain which those merely seeking an introduction to Marx's own ideas may find somewhat exotic. On the other hand however, it is not an advanced treatise in philosophy and an interested and thoughtful reader of it is certainly not required to have any knowledge of Wittgenstein or of Wittgensteinian philosophy to enjoy it or to find it illuminating. S/he has simply to be interested in Marx and in finding out about Marx. For though this is a Wittgensteinian book about Marx, it is still a book about Marx, not about Wittgenstein.

However, the introductory student in particular should, in fairness, be forewarned that this is a book on Marx informed by a particular philosophical perspective, and one reason for this Introduction, and for a large number of notes and the annotated bibliography at the end of the book, is to allow the reader to investigate this perspective further if it excites curiosity. Indeed, I hope and believe that this is a book in which the notes are more than usually worth reading, and this is particularly true of the notes to chapters 1, 6 and 7, in which extensive reference is made both to Wittgenstein's own work and to Wittgensteinian literature in general.

For those readers of this book who are not beginners in Marxism, in social theory, or in the philosophy of social science, two further introductory remarks are perhaps in order.

Firstly, it will be obvious, both by the occasional explicit avowal and by the implications of the entire analysis which follows, that this work presents a staunchly anti-realist interpretation of Marx. To that extent it runs against the grain of what has been the dominant philosophical approach to Marxism in contemporary social theory. Indeed I believe that the current, and widely admitted, crisis in contemporary Marxist theory is due, in part at least, to the fundamental shortcomings of realism as a philosophy of social science. Also – and to attach one final philosophical banner to the masthead – this work not only presents an anti-realist account of Marx, it also relies on a strongly pragmatist reading of Wittgenstein in order to develop that account. Its particular debt to the work of Richard Rorty will be obvious. Perhaps less obvious (because they are less well known and appreciated in Britain) but just as worthy of mention, is its debt to Hanna Pitkin's *Wittgenstein and Justice* (University of California Press, 1972) and to David Rubinstein's *Marx and Wittgenstein* (Routledge & Kegan Paul, 1981).

However, the philosophically aware reader will also note that though this work does take up an anti-realist position, that position is, as I have said, only occasionally avowed and is never explicitly defended.[1] Though some Wittgensteinian philosophers, and some of Wittgenstein's fiercest critics, would see this inexplicit approach as wholly in the spirit of the master, I have to say that this omission in no way marks a mystical cult of the ineffable. Nor does it betoken any allegiance on the part of this author to the view that what is wrong with realism can be 'shown' but not 'said'. It is simply that an explicit defence of the largely implicit positions adopted in this book is a project still in hand and to be completed in a later work. My failure to include any explicit critique of realism also derives from my desire to give priority, in this work, to the exposition and critique of Marx which is its primary purpose.

Secondly, and for Marxist readers of this book in particular, it is perhaps important to say that the writing of it, and the reading and thought upon which it was based, have been part of a long process through which I have finally come to break with a particular picture of society and of reality, a picture which usually goes under the title of 'historical materialism'. The final chapter of this work attempts to outline that picture, to account for its compelling force (both for Marxists and others) and to say what is wrong with it. In fact the writing of this book represents my partial 'settling of accounts' with Marxism, the resolving, at least to my own satisfaction, of certain puzzles and dilemmas which are built into it as an intellectual tradition, puzzles by which my own intellectual work has been perennially marked, and which Althusserian and other realist renderings of Marx always seemed to me to exacerbate rather than resolve.

In a word, I cannot now accept any account of Marxism which presents it as any kind of absolutely privileged discourse. In particular I cannot now accept the view that Marxism equips one with some 'scientific' understanding of the world by which other 'ideological' or otherwise partial understandings can be 'stripped away', and an indubitable 'reality' revealed. Indeed I have been convinced that there was something wrong with this account of Marxism for a considerable time. My problem was to say what precisely was wrong with it, and to find an alternative way of thinking about Marxism which did not involve a collapse either into a radical subjectivism or into a kind of atheoretical positivism.

I think that Wittgenstein has helped me to construct such an account, or at least to begin its construction, but it should be noted that the Wittgensteinian rendering of Marx has one consequence which many Marxists will, I am sure, find uncongenial. For it introduces a strong, indeed central, reflexive element into Marxism. In other words, it asks, indeed requires, Marxists to pay far greater attention to themselves, to their reasons for wanting to know about the world, and in particular to their reasons for wanting to act in the world as Marxists.[2]

A good deal of the secondary literature on Wittgenstein has drawn attention to the affinity between his later thought and some varieties of existentialism.[3] To the extent that Wittgenstein's later philosophy stresses the inescapable responsibility we bear for any and all knowledge claims we make, and the inability of 'science' or anything else to obviate that human responsibility, this parallel appears to have some force. However, the later Wittgenstein also stresses that (a) this 'responsibility' for knowledge is a 'species' or (in some cases) a 'community' responsibility and not an individual responsibility and (b) his later philosophy also aims to undermine, radically, any asocial notion of 'selfhood' or 'self-identity', i.e. it aims to 'deconstruct' the self (to use a trendy term). Thus his reflexive approach to knowledge can also avoid a radical subjectivism or 'petty-bourgeois individualism' (as some Marxists would undoubtedly term it).

In short, the later Wittgenstein would want Marxists to see and understand themselves as a community, as a community of identity, as a community of knowers, as, to a degree, a language community, and above all as a community of people committed to the achievement of certain ends or goals. As such a community, they are engaged in a constant struggle, to increase their numbers, to have their knowledge claims more widely accepted, and above all to see their ends or goals achieved. As such a community, Marxists are also a part of wider communities of meaning (both individual human societies and the human species as a whole), in which their knowledge claims are at least potentially comprehensible and acceptable, their 'language game' and the practices in which it is embodied are linked to other human language games and practices, and their ends or goals are both acceptable and rejectable by other people (because understandable by them). Thus, as an epistemological and political community Marxists have a continuous and multi-dimensional fight on their hands which they may win or lose. What, from a Marxist point of view, is wrong with that? *A luta continua*.

One can only think that there is something wrong with it if one is wedded to an essentially nineteenth-century notion of science which takes the identity of the scientist to be a totally irrelevant datum in the assessment of the knowledge claims which he or she makes.[4] I think that for historical reasons many Marxists are wedded to such a notion of science, a naïve notion, which continually drives them back and forth between two (equally naïve) conceptions of knowledge – absolute 'objectivity' on the one hand and radical 'subjectivism' on the other. Because their notion of science does lead Marxists to think that they must choose between these equally false conceptions of knowledge, they should not, I believe, remain wedded to it. This book begins a critique of it (though it by no means completes the task) through its stress on the inherently reflexive nature of all knowledge claims, including scientific ones. One conclusion of this book is that Marxists may, if they wish, go on thinking of themselves as scientists, but that in order to do so they must have a very different conception of scientific practice from that which they have (predominantly) embraced.

I hope therefore, and in short, that the curiously hybrid plant which I have produced below will stimulate and instruct the beginning student, intrigue (if also enrage) the experienced Marxist, and also interest the knowing devotee of social theory and philosophy. Certainly I have found it enormously instructive and enjoyable to write and I hope that others will find it similarly enjoyable to read. If it leads only one reader to open, or reopen, the pages of the *Philosophical Investigations* I shall feel more than adequately rewarded.

A NOTE ON QUOTATIONS

The reader will find extensive quotations from the works of Marx and Engels throughout this book, sometimes single quotations, sometimes several, numbered in series. In all cases these quotations are followed by my own summaries and analyses of them, which may suggest, to some readers at least, that they themselves are redundant. However, there are several reasons why I believe their presence to be essential:

1. For readers new to the works of Marx it is important to see his thought expressed in his own words. Marx made great efforts to write clearly and stylishly and, in my view at least, he often succeeded. In general then he speaks better for himself than any commentator could ever speak for him and one is only showing due respect to his thought in allowing him to do so.

2. All the quotations from Marx and Engels in this book are there for an analytical purpose, i.e. I use them to show what I believe to be important aspects of Marx's thought, sometimes important continuities between his earlier and later thought, sometimes apparent contradictions, sometimes what I believe to be real contradictions and weaknesses in his thought. In other words, I use all the quotations in this book to make analytical claims of my own, both claims about Marx's intellectual achievements and criticisms of his failings. Given that this is so, it is important that readers have the quotations presented to them so that they make their own judgement about whether my analytical claims are justified.

3. Perhaps most importantly, exposure to the Wittgensteinian tradition in philosophy teaches one the importance of close textual analysis. It teaches one to pay close attention to the way in which language is used, to the way in which phrases, sentences, paragraphs are constructed, to the nouns and verbs chosen, to the metaphors, similes, and analogies employed. It also makes one profoundly sceptical of the distinction between 'form' and 'content' in writing, for it suggests very strongly that *how* something is said, is an integral part of *what* is said. Thus a Wittgensteinian book about Marx, which this claims to be, must make extensive use of quotations as the basis of such analysis. What can be achieved by such methods is, I think, most clearly demonstrated in the seventh and final chapter of this book.

CHAPTER 1

MARX, HEGEL, FEUERBACH, AND THE PHILOSOPHY OF PRAXIS

INTRODUCTION

It was Lenin who first suggested that Marx's work could be seen as a compound of three elements, German philosophy, English political economy, and French socialism.[1] I think that this is a broadly accurate characterization and I have followed it in the construction of this book.

Thus, this first chapter deals with the influence of German philosophy, especially that of Hegel and Feuerbach, on Marx's thought. Chapter 2 then examines Marx's theory of history upon which the influence of Hegel in particular was profound. Chapters 3 and 4 are concerned with Marx's economic theories. These are presented in chapter 3 and criticized in chapter 4. However, I also try to show in these chapters that Marx's economic theories were themselves profoundly influenced by his philosophical views and that the principal problems in his economic theory derive from his having viewed classical political economy through the prism of what I call his 'philosophy of praxis'. Chapter 5 analyses Marx's views on revolution and communism and demonstrates that his philosophy of praxis continued to influence his conception of communism until the end of his life. This is true even though his study of classical political economy introduced a greater element of apparent 'realism' into his later writings on this subject.

Chapter 6 is concerned with Marx's views on class, on the state, and on ideology and contrasts his approach to these subjects with that of more modern Marxist literature. It is suggested that the latter is often seriously defective, mainly because it has departed from the philosophy of praxis which gave Marx's own writing on these subjects its power and purpose. The final chapter (chapter 7) analyses what I believe to have been Marx's most important intellectual legacy, his ontology, or what I call his 'picture of reality'. This picture is shown to be seriously misleading in some ways, in that it often serves to weaken or undermine Marx's own accounts of dynamic historical processes, and, more particularly, has implications or connotations which are directly at odds with the philosophy of praxis.

In short, Marx's philosophy of praxis – which I introduce and analyse in this first chapter – provides the guiding thread of interpretation and criticism of this entire book and is, I believe, illuminating both of the most profound strengths and of the most serious weaknesses in Marx's thought.

Overall then, although the order of treatment of Marx's ideas in this book follows Lenin's prescription, I have not given equal weight to all three of the elements within it. On balance this book devotes somewhat more space to the presentation and analysis of Marx's economic and philosophical ideas than to the political or sociological aspects of his thought. This is because I believe that it is Marx's philosophical views, rather than his political commitments, which provide the clue to the most profound continuities in his lifetime's work, and in addition my experience of teaching Marx has led me to the view that most students find his economic theories particularly difficult to grasp and even more difficult to criticize. One of my hopes for this book, in fact, is that it will lead to a wider comprehension of Marx's economic theories (especially among non-economists) and that it will also provide a brief and comprehensible account of their major weaknesses. I am also of the view that much Marxist sociology is neither very good Marxism nor very good sociology, and chapter 6 in particular tries to say why I believe this, and why I believe that sociology students in particular are prone to the most profound misapprehensions about Marx (even, perhaps especially, when they consider themselves his most enthusiastic devotees!). Putting this somewhat polemically, I would want to insist that Marx was not a sociologist and that he is often most profoundly misunderstood when he is considered as such.

There is one further introductory point before we proceed to the main business of this chapter. It is frequently said, by commentators both friendly and hostile to Marx, that he was one of the great intellectual 'system builders'; that he, along with his life-long friend and collaborator Friedrich Engels, erected a massive system of thought, perfectly finished, perfectly – indeed rigidly – coherent and 'scientific', and to be accepted or rejected as a whole because of that monolithic internal coherence.

This is not the Karl Marx that readers will meet in this book. To be sure, as I said in the Preface, Marx *aspired* to an integration of philosophical, historical and socio-economic perspectives on the world, and to that extent the thought of his mature years forms a unity. But when close analysis is made of Marx's more specific formulations, when attention is directed to his specific philosophical and methodological prescriptions and to his explanations of specific historical, political, and economic phenomena, then any sense of a monolithic system disappears. In its place a close encounter with Marx reveals a thinker who was a magnificently fertile, but somewhat chaotic spinner of ideas, theories, and insights. Karl Marx sometimes contradicted himself, continually changed explanatory emphasis in different contexts and different moments in his life, and above all continually revised and criticized his own ideas in the light of both changing circumstances in the world and of his own deepening understanding.

Marx would not have liked that characterization of himself. As we shall see in chapter 3, he thought of himself as a scientist who *had* erected a scientific system of thought, and he also showed a rather unfortunate tendency to change his mind while pretending he had not done so. Or, to be a little more generous, Marx was the kind of thinker who always presented his ideas in a forceful, even dogmatic manner, a manner which often disguised the fact that what was being dogmatically asserted at one moment was precisely what had been dogmatically denied at an earlier time.

None the less, and despite this tendency, Marx's favourite motto was *de omnibus dubitandum* ('doubt everything')[2] and it seems clear, at least to me, that he applied that motto conscientiously to his own work. Indeed one could wish that subsequent generations of Marxists had applied it as conscientiously as he did both to their own work and to his. For, as I shall try to show in what follows, I do not believe that intellectual consistency is always a virtue or that intellectual inconsistency is always a vice. On the contrary, it is the tensions, inconsistencies, even point-blank contradictions, in Marx's thought which make it so exciting to read, even today. For a rich and diverse world merely becomes pallid and grey if processed mechanically through some rigidly coherent intellectual system. Absolute coherence and consistency can usually only be purchased at the cost of extreme simplification of ideas. Marx was never willing to pay this price. Faced with a choice between acknowledging and trying to do justice to the complexity of human society, or ignoring or denying that complexity in order to make it fit his theory, Marx always opted for the first alternative. He was always closely attentive to new empirical findings about the world, always willing to change or adapt his ideas in the light of new evidence. What this means of course is that Marx was constantly reformulating many of his ideas, constantly revising them, qualifying them, shifting emphasis within them.

Thus, when that lifetime of intellectual exploration and reformulation is laid 'end to end', when we look at it, or try to look at it, as a whole, then of course we find inconsistencies, even contradictions. As I shall also try to show, some of these contradictions are merely apparent and disappear once they are seen in historical or political context. Others however are real enough and point to intractable difficulties and weaknesses in Marx's thought. Later in this book I shall be especially concerned with some fundamental contradictions and weaknesses in Marx's economic thought, but even here I shall show how it is possible to use some of Marx's economic ideas to reveal the flaws in others. Indeed, like all truly great thinkers, Marx himself often provides one with the intellectual tools with which to criticize his own ideas. And this is a part – an important part – of what I meant by saying earlier that consistency is not always a virtue nor inconsistency always a vice. For it is through the very analysis of the inconsistencies and contradictions in Marx that one can both see the limitations of his ideas and see how to amend and develop those ideas to deal with changed historical times.

MARX'S PHILOSOPHICAL FORMATION

From the time that he enrolled as a student at the University of Bonn in 1835 (when he was 17 years old) until he went into political exile in Brussels in 1845, there is no doubt that the most powerful intellectual influence on Marx was the philosopher Georg Wilhelm Friedrich Hegel and some of his followers (the so-called 'Young' or 'Left' Hegelians). In fact, as a young man in Germany, from his late teens until his late twenties Marx is best described as an Hegelian intellectual. He was engaged in a strenuous attempt to grasp Hegel's very difficult philosophy, to apply it – especially in a critique of religion and religious belief – and then to reformulate it in ways more acceptable to his own developing ideas. This last clause is vital, for it captures what Marx did – he *reformulated* Hegel's philosophical ideas. He did not by any means totally abandon them, and in fact once reformulated 'materialistically' (to use Marx's own word) they continued to influence his thought profoundly from the late 1840s until his death nearly forty years later.

In a famous 'Afterword' to the second German edition of Volume 1 of his great book *Capital*, written in 1873, Marx said:

> My dialectic method is not only different from the Hegelian but is its direct opposite. To Hegel, the life process of the human brain, i.e. the process of thinking (which under the name of 'the Idea' he even transforms into an independent subject) is the demiurgos[3] of the real world, and the real world is only the external, phenomenal form of 'the Idea'. With me, on the contrary, the idea is nothing else than the material world reflected by the human mind and translated into forms of thought.
>
> The mystifying side of the Hegelian dialectic I criticised nearly 30 years ago, at a time when it was still the fashion.

And Marx goes on to say:

> The mystification which dialectic suffers in Hegel's hands by no means prevents him from being the first to present its general form of working in a comprehensive and conscious manner. With him it is standing on its head. It must be turned right side up again, if you would discover the rational kernel within the mystical shell.[4]

So Hegel (that 'mighty thinker' as Marx calls him) developed, according to Marx, a mode of analysis, or a method, which has a 'rational kernel' but which Hegel himself presented in a 'mystical' or 'mystified' form. That method or mode of analysis is 'the dialectic' or 'the dialectical method'. Thus, if we are to understand Marx we must understand Hegel, and also the critique of Hegel made by another of his youthful followers, Ludwig Feuerbach. For Marx's own critique of Hegel was deeply influenced by Feuerbach's, though going beyond it in important ways.

HEGEL

G.W.F. Hegel (1770–1831), a lecturer and professor of philosophy at the Universities of Jena, Heidelberg and Berlin, is one of the most difficult of all philosophers to understand. His most important works are *The Phenomenology of Spirit* (1807), *The Science of Logic* (1812), *The Philosophy of Right* (1821) and *The Philosophy of History* (1830–1). He invented a whole philosophical language of his own which is hard to follow even in German and reads even more strangely in translation. For this reason, as much as any other, his work has been subject to the most conflicting interpretations. Indeed such conflicts began even before his death, for he was influential among both conservative and radical intellectuals in the Germany of his day, with conservatives emphasizing some aspects of his thought and radicals others. Given this difficulty, I have chosen not to include long quotations from Hegel in an introductory text of this sort, but to provide a summary of Hegel's central philosophical ideas, especially those which most influenced Karl Marx and the other 'Young Hegelians' in the Germany of the 1820s and 1830s.[5]

Hegel is usually termed an 'idealist' philosopher, indeed he is often considered the greatest, or at least the most extreme, idealist philosopher. In its philosophical use the adjective 'idealist' (and the noun 'idealism') derive from 'idea' not from 'ideal' (as in the most common modern English usage). Thus, an idealist philosopher holds to some version of the view that the world is known through the mind, through *ideas*.

According to this view then, all the objects in the world (chairs, tables, clouds) are objects of perception. They are known to human beings only through their minds. Perhaps, if human beings had the capacity to metamorphose their atoms and molecules and *become* chairs, tables, or clouds this might not be the case. Perhaps then human beings could 'know' a chair by actually becoming a chair (although this itself is a rather confusing idea, in that chairs cannot be said to 'know' that they are chairs!). But in any event, since such a metamorphosis is not possible, since human beings cannot do this, the only world they know, the only world they can know is the-world-known-through-the-mind. Indeed the known world is, by definition, the world that *human beings* know, since, arguably, human beings are the only living entities which engage in the practice or activity called 'knowing'. But if this is true (says the idealist philosopher) then what is the distinction between 'the world' and 'the (human) mind'? If I say 'I know the world through my mind', it sounds as if there is something separate from my mind – the world – which I know. But if I cannot know anything about the world except through my mind, then it follows that what my mind tells me about the world *is* what the world is. 'Mind' and 'world' are one.

There was however another tradition of philosophy (to which the seventeenth-century English philosopher, John Locke, and the great 'Scottish Enlightenment' philosopher, David Hume, belonged) which seemed to have a reply to all this. This alternative tradition, which is still very much alive, is generally called 'empiricism' and its counter-position to idealism runs broadly as follows.

'All this stuff about "the mind"', said the empiricists, 'is just so much unscientific nonsense. All you mean by "the mind" – all you *can* mean – is the human brain, and the brain, just like any other object in nature is investigable scientifically. We can find out how the brain works.' 'Moreover', said Locke and others, 'the brain *is* connected to the world by something palpable and understandable, the human sense organs – the eye, ear, nose, sense of touch etc.' Thus Locke argued that it is through their senses that human beings obtain the basis of all their knowledge of the world.

At the beginning of life, the human brain is like a large blank screen or sheet of paper. As life commences that screen or that blank sheet of paper begins to be filled by what Locke called 'sense impressions' or sense data (colours, sounds, shapes, smells). Then, through a process of childhood learning, human beings begin to 'associate' these sense impressions both with one another and with certain objects in the world. Once they have acquired, through these sense impressions, a basic core of simple words corresponding to simple objects, they then gradually build up more complex sets of ideas and concepts by combining and contrasting these more simple ones. This learning is shown in the expansion of the vocabulary of nearly every human being from more simple to more complex words as they grow up.

Thus empiricist philosophy, in contrast to idealism, claims that there *is* a connection between mind and world, a connection via sense impressions and their impact upon the brain, an impact which is scientifically investigatable and understandable. According to this view then, human knowledge of the world is knowledge of something external to the mind. 'Mind' and 'world' are not one, are not inseparable. Human beings are not trapped, as it were, inside their minds.[6]

In the seventeenth century this view seemed to carry the day among intellectuals and in some ways it underpinned the seventeenth- and eighteenth-century faith in 'science' and 'reason' which was such a hallmark of that European intellectual movement which is generally referred to as 'the Enlightenment'. However, in the late eighteenth century it was called fundamentally into question by the great German philosopher Immanuel Kant. Kant was in turn perhaps the greatest single inspirer of Hegel's philosophy.

To simplify greatly, Kant pointed out that the empiricist account of knowledge was obscure and vague in one crucial respect – in its account of how simple sense impressions become 'associated' or 'combined' into more complex ideas and concepts. For example, one could see how sense impressions could 'give' one the idea of blue, green, yellow, brown, etc., but how, in themselves, could they ever 'give' one the idea of colour? For there is no sense impression which is 'colour'. Moreover, said Kant, there are other even more fundamental concepts for human beings (he mentioned especially the concepts of time and space) which are not derivable by association, contrast, or anything else, from sense impressions.

Kant therefore concluded that the human mind is not a *tabula rasa*, not a blank sheet ready, at birth, to be filled with sense impressions. On the contrary, in order to make sense of – to use – sense impressions, the human mind must *already* at birth be possessed of certain basic organizing categories or frames of reference into which those sense impressions are fitted or through which they are filtered. These organizing categories or frames of reference are often called 'innate ideas', 'innate' because they precede any individual human being's experience of life. They come with all human beings 'out of the womb', as it were. We are born with them, they are part of our heritage as members of the species *homo sapiens*. These categories constitute in fact the core of our faculty of *reason*, which, for Kant, was the central faculty distinguishing human beings from all other animals.[7]

Kant therefore laid the groundwork for Hegel's philosophy, because he restated and refurbished the 'idealist' view of mind and world against the empiricist attack. Hegel, convinced by Kant that the basic idealist position did hold, that mind and world were one, that there was no defensible way of distinguishing them, went on to build a vast theory of human knowledge and human history on this basis, a theory which took him well beyond Kant.

We may now turn to Hegel's philosophy itself. The two central concepts in that philosophy are 'Spirit' (*Geist*) and 'the Idea' (*Idee*). Taking something of a risk, I shall translate Hegel's *Geist* as 'the human spirit or essence' and *Idee* as 'thought or reason'. For Hegel these two concepts were intimately connected, because what for him distinguished human beings, what was their 'spirit' or 'essence' *was* their capacity for thought or reason.

However, Hegel's major development of idealist philosophy after Kant lay in his insistence that both spirit and thought or reason – 'the Idea' – have a *history*. The human capacity for reason, the human understanding, grows and expands, deepens, through time. Indeed human history, for Hegel, is the history of that development of reason. And he went further. For in Hegel's philosophy we not only find the view that mind and world are one (in the sense that there is nothing which can be known of the world except through the mind). We also find the view *that mind actually creates the world*. For Hegel this is true in two senses:

1. Since for Hegel 'the world' = 'knowledge of the world', then as knowledge changes (i.e. as mind develops) so the world changes.

2. Since human beings act in the world on the basis of their knowledge of it, the world becomes increasingly shaped and dominated by reason through human-activity-conducted-on-the-basis-of-reason, a form of activity which becomes increasingly predominant among human beings as their species progresses.

A simple, if somewhat extreme example might make this second point clearer. In the city of London, and indeed in every other city in the world, people travel to work and to their other destinations by fixed roadways and by other fixed means of communication, such as railways and (in London) the underground system. But why do we have this kind of organization?

Why do we not, for example, operate a system whereby every individual is supplied with a large bulldozer or tank. Then each person could make their way to work by the most direct possible route, rather than along fixed routes. Every morning teams of workers would stand by to bury the dead who had been killed as bulldozing commuters crashed through their houses, while other teams of workers stood ready to erect new – presumably prefabricated – buildings to replace those destroyed. Each morning this process would recommence.

Why do we not do this? The answer is so obvious as hardly to need stating. We do not have the latter system of urban transportation because it would not be a 'rational' or 'reasonable' system to have. It would be so wasteful and destructive in every way as to be hardly conceivable except by a madman (or by an academic trying to make a point!). In other words, the physical organization of our towns and cities, the pattern of fixed transport routes with houses and other buildings arranged 'safely' around them, is a reasonable or a rational system. The physical organization of a city is the embodiment, the physical expression (actually just one of millions of physical expressions) of human reason at work. Indeed one can think of all human artifacts, from the most humble (pens, pencils, tables, chairs, spoons) to the most grand (dams, road and rail systems, airports, telecommunication systems) as just such embodiments or 'objectifications' of human reason. As we shall see, this was a very important concept in Hegel's philosophy and influenced Marx profoundly.

However, there is a respect in which I have expressed everything above in a very unHegelian way. Because in Hegel's pure philosophy, and especially in his most influential work, *The Phenomenology of Spirit*, human beings, actual human subjects, hardly appear at all. This is because, for Hegel, what all human beings have in common – what makes them human – is 'mind' (reason, thought). Moreover, the categories of thought are the same for all human minds. Hence in Hegel the world becomes the creation, the product, of these universal categories of thought. Thus, for example, Hegel would say that the private life of a citizen was the product of (or the 'embodiment' of, as we tend to say in English) *the idea* of 'privacy'. Similarly, a bureaucracy, for Hegel, would be the product or embodiment of *the idea* of 'public spiritedness' or of 'rational objectivity in the general interest'.

Hegel had a particular way of speaking about all this which involved the use of two of his most important concepts – *objectification* and *alienation*. According to Hegel, all human history is a process whereby ideas objectify themselves in material reality. Thus, the idea of 'shelter' is objectified into houses, the ideas of 'communication' and 'transport' are objectified into roads, railways, buses, cars, telegraph wires, etc. And in the political sphere the idea of a 'general interest of society' is objectified into the institutions of the state. However, this process of objectification is also, for Hegel, a process of alienation. Because as mind objectifies itself into innumerable different material products and social and political institutions (the family, the occupational group, the state) it *fails to grasp*, as it were, that these things *are* its products, its embodiments, its manifold objectifications. Hence it treats them as things separate ('alien') from itself. In fact this was how Hegel explained empiricism, empiricism was the expression, in the realm of philosophy, of mind's alienation from itself.

The linked concepts of objectification and alienation bring us to the heart of Hegel's philosophy of history. For Hegel, human history is the process by which mind first alienates itself through objectification and then, gradually and in stages, recognizes these objectifications as its own products and comes, therefore, to understand these objectifications and its own achievements and potential. In Hegel, the overcoming of alienation – which is the end, the goal, the culmination of history – consists in mind's total self-understanding, mind's total unimpeded self-consciousness both of itself and thus (simultaneously) of the world. Mind's total self-understanding – the final triumph of reason one might say – is simultaneously mind's total understanding of, and mastery over, the world.

One particular application of the Hegelian idea of alienation is particularly important in understanding Marx. Hegel's own philosophy was highly theological, for ultimately Hegel thought 'spirit' and 'mind' an expression of God, and conservative Hegelians in early nineteenth-century Germany were usually religious. But the young 'left Hegelians', especially Ludwig Feuerbach and David Strauss,[8] rejected this aspect of Hegel's philosophy, and actually turned Hegel's concepts of objectification and alienation into tools of atheistic thought.

For the left Hegelians – with whom both the young Karl Marx and the young Friedrich Engels identified – religious belief was a classical and particularly crippling form of mind's self-alienation. For in religion some of the most sublime products of the human mind – moral values, notions of justice and injustice, of beauty and of truth – are objectified into predicates or characteristics of alien super-human beings (gods or a God) who are then both separated from the human realm and placed, by the mind, in domination over that realm. In fact in many religions a God or gods are worshipped as the actual creators of the world. But according to the left Hegelians, this was simply a stage in the historical development of mind. For when mind recognizes that notions of morality, justice, truth, etc. *are* its creations, it will simultaneously recognize that God or gods are its 'objectifications', its creations too, and will then reappropriate these sublime categories as part of its own being. Or put more simply, in the left Hegelian conception atheism is an important stage on the road to the human mind's overcoming of its own alienation. Marx remained an atheist throughout his life because he never abandoned this left Hegelian conception of religion as alienation which he had learnt in his youth.

MARX

We can now return to Marx. Earlier in this chapter I said that in the late 1840s, after ten or so years of studying Hegel, Marx 'reformulated' Hegel's philosophical ideas in important ways, but that there were central features of that philosophy which he never abandoned. I can now say more precisely what I meant by this. Part of this reformulation Marx shared in common with other left Hegelians, notably Feuerbach; other parts were original to him. I shall try to make clear which was which.

In common with Feuerbach, Marx reintroduced actual thinking, acting human subjects into Hegel's philosophy of history, but – and also like Feuerbach – he maintained Hegel's basic vision of the historical process and of historical progress. In other words, like nearly all the other left Hegelians, the young Marx accepted Hegel's view that human liberation would consist in human beings attaining 'complete' understanding of and 'complete' mastery over both their own nature (which, following Hegel, he sees as essentially rational) and over nature, or the world, as a whole.[9]

However, and again in common with Feuerbach, Marx rejected

the view that this liberation could occur simply in the realm of thought or reason, in the realm of 'mind'. On the contrary, for Marx, since human enslavement was a product of human activity, human liberation required a fundamental change in that activity, and that implied (and here Marx began to break with Feuerbach and other left Hegelians) a fundamental change in human society. One can perhaps best understand these differing conceptions of enslavement and liberation in Hegel and Marx by examining Marx's particular adaptation of the Hegelian concepts of objectification and alienation.

'OBJECTIFICATION' AND 'ALIENATION' IN MARX'S PHILOSOPHY

Marx borrowed both these terms from Hegel, but his use of them is very different. Whereas in Hegel objectification and alienation are states of 'the Idea', are conceived as products of 'mind', forms or stages of the self-development of mind in history, for Marx, as for Feuerbach, alienation and objectification are products of human *activity*. Human beings alienate themselves in the very process of filling the world with innumerable objectifications of their activity and creativity. Thus in his 1844 manuscript on 'Alienated Labour' Marx says:

> What then constitutes the alienation of labour? First, in the fact that labour is external to the worker, that is, that it does not belong to his essential being; that in his work, therefore, he does not affirm himself but denies himself, does not feel well but unhappy, does not freely develop his physical and mental energy, but mortifies his body and ruins his mind. The worker, therefore, feels himself only outside his work, and feels beside himself in his work. He is at home when he is not working, and when he is working he is not at home. His work therefore is not voluntary but coerced; it is *forced labour*. It is therefore not the satisfaction of a need, but only a means for satisfying needs external to it. Its alien character emerges clearly in the fact that labour is shunned like the plague as soon as there is no physical or other compulsion. External labour, labour in which man is externalised, is labour of self sacrifice, of mortification. Finally, the external nature of labour for the worker appears in the fact that it is not his own,

but someone else's, that it does not belong to him, that in that labour he does not belong to himself but to someone else. Just as in religion the spontaneous activity of human imagination, of the human brain and the human heart, operates independently of the individual, i.e. as alien divine or diabolical activity, so the worker's activity is not his spontaneous activity. It belongs to another, it is the loss of self . . .

His creation, through practice, of an *objective world*, his *working upon* inorganic nature, is the proof that man is a conscious species being, that is, a being which is related to the species as its own essence, or to itself as a species being. To be sure, animals also produce. They build themselves nests, dwelling places, as the bees, beavers, ants etc. do. But the animal produces . . . under the domination of direct physical need, while man produces even when he is free from physical need and produces truly only in freedom from need. An animal produces only itself, while man reproduces the whole of nature. The animal's product is directly part of its physical body, while man steps out freely to confront his product. The animal builds only according to the standard and the need of the species to which it belongs, while man knows how to apply the intrinsic standards of the laws of beauty.

It is precisely in his working over of the objective world therefore, that man proves himself to be really a species being. This production is his active species life. In and through such production, nature appears as *his* work and reality. The object of labour, therefore, is the *objectification* of the species life of man for man duplicates himself not only intellectually, as in consciousness, but also actively in reality, and therefore contemplates himself in a world that he has created. In so far as alienated labour tears away from him his species being, his actual objectivity as a member of the species . . .

Similarly, in degrading spontaneous activity, free activity, to the level of a means, alienated labour makes man's species life a means for his physical existence . . .

Alienated labour therefore makes:

. . . man's species being, his nature as well as his generic intellectual activity, into an existence alien to him, into a means to his individual existence. It alienates from man his own body, as well as nature outside him, as well as his spiritual being, his *human* being.

. . . A direct consequence of man's alienation from the product of his labour, from his life activity, from his species being, is the *alienation of man from man*. When man confronts himself, he confronts *another* man. What is true of man's relationship to his work, to the product of his work, and to himself, is also true of man's relationship to the other man, and to that man's labour and the object of his labour.

Generally, the proposition that man's species being is alienated from him means that one man is alienated from another, just as each of them is alienated from human nature.[10]

So Marx is here arguing that what makes people people, what makes human beings human – what is, in Marx's terminology, their 'species being' – is their capacity for conscious creative activity. It is of the essence of human beings, for Marx, that through such creative activity they both transform inanimate nature and they create and transform their own nature. (For Marx, people *are* what they do.) Moreover, since this conscious creative activity is natural to human beings, since it is in their nature to be creative, they do not need any physical compulsion to do it. Thus, although human beings, like other animals, will do what they need to do in order to acquire a basic subsistence, in order to stay alive, unlike other animals they will continue to create, to produce, even when their basic material needs are satisfied. Indeed Marx argues, as we see above, that 'man ... produces truly' only when he is free from physical need. For when freed from such physical pressures human beings will produce not only those things which are useful, they will also produce what is beautiful, what satisfies human aesthetic standards. Indeed for Marx only human beings have aesthetic standards. Concepts of beauty and ugliness are *themselves* part of what human beings have created through their activity.

It is thus absolutely vital to understand that when Marx speaks of 'production' in these early philosophical manuscripts, he is *not* referring only to material production, to the production of material objects. For Marx it is of the essence of human beings that they are creative producers, of material objects of course, but also of ideas, of social institutions and values and indeed of language. So Marx would say that human beings have 'produced', among other things, language, the family, government, beauty, ugliness, truth, falsehood, justice, injustice, houses, roads, music, electricity, fashion, time, space, books, religion, paintings, humour, tragedy, dance, mime, face powder, hair driers, hydrogen bombs, racial prejudice, cork tiles, anti-Semitism, gas cookers, psychotherapy, word processors, and long sentences consisting of exemplary nouns. And this productive faculty of human beings, this conscious creative activity which is unique to them as a form of life, is what is wonderful for Marx about people, and it is this wonder that informs the whole of his early philosophical humanism.

However, while the innumerable material and ideal 'objectifications' of conscious human activity make Marx wonder at human beings as a species, he also argues, as we can see above, that in a society of 'private property' this creativity takes alienated forms. For the creative human essence is not realized, or at any rate not fully realized, in any society in which (a) people have to work in order to live, rather than living in order to create, and (b) the products of human activity do not belong to their producers, but to others, and (c) people are compelled to compete against each other, rather than working for each other.

In short, in the world of 'private property' which Marx saw around him in the 1840s, human beings, the creative productive species, had been reduced, in the main, to impoverished wage slaves, forced to put their creativity into monotonous, boring, and often physically and mentally crippling wage labour in order to obtain a pittance for themselves and to make wealth for others who owned the 'means of production'.

In later developments of Marx's thought, developments heavily influenced both by his study of classical political economy and by his own political involvements, the society of alienated labour becomes 'capitalism' rather than simply the society of 'private property', and the alienated labourers become the 'working class' or 'proletariat' rather than all human beings in general. But none the less Marx's conception of the human essence – as conscious creative activity – remained unchanged throughout his life, as did his conception of the world as *objectification* of that activity and of capitalism as the form of society in which the human essence is *alienated*. It follows that for Marx communist society would be the form of society in which such alienation would be ended and human beings set free to give full expression to their creativity in a positive way. As we shall see later (pp. 131–4) this is indeed the case in Marx's 'early' and 'late' conceptions of communism.

To give some indication of the continuity of Marx's thought in this regard, there follow three quotations, the first from *The*

German Ideology of 1846, the second from the fourth notebook of Marx's *Grundrisse*, written in January 1858, and the third from Marx's *Capital* of 1867.

The way in which men produce their means of subsistence depends first of all on the nature of the actual means of subsistence they find in existence and have to reproduce. *This mode of production must not be considered simply as being the production of the physical existence of the individuals*. Rather it is a definite *form of activity* of these individuals, a definite form of expressing their life, a definite *mode of life* on their part. As individuals express their life, so they are. What they are therefore, coincides with their production, both of what they produce and with how they produce. The nature of individuals thus depends on the material conditions determining their production.[11]

The worker emerges not only richer, but emerges rather poorer from the process than he entered. For not only has he produced the conditions of necessary labour as conditions belonging to capital; but also the value creating possibility . . . which . . . lies within him, now exists as surplus value, surplus product, in a word as capital, as master over living labour capacity, as value endowed with its own might and will, confronting him in his abstract, objectless, purely subjective poverty. He has produced not only the alien wealth and his own poverty, but also the relation of this wealth as independent, self-sufficient wealth . . . All this arose from the act of exchange, in which he exchanged his living labour capacity for an amount of objectified labour, except that this objectified labour . . . now appears as posited by himself, as his own product, as his own self-objectification as well as the objectification of himself as a power independent of himself, which moreover rules over him, rules over him through his own actions. In *surplus labour*, all moments are products of *alien labour – alien surplus labour* transformed into capital. . . .[12]

A commodity is therefore a mysterious thing, simply because in it the social character of men's labour appears to them as an objective character stamped upon the product of that labour; because the relation of the producers to the sum total of their own labour is presented to them as a social relation, existing not between themselves but between the products of their labour. *This is the reason why the products of labour become commodities, social things whose qualities are at the same time perceptible and imperceptible by the senses.* In the same way the light from an object is perceived by us not as the subjective excitation of our optic nerve, but as the objective form of something outside the eye itself. But, in the act of seeing, there is at all events, an actual passage of light from one thing to another, from the external object to the eye. *But it is different with commodities. There the existence of the things quâ commodities, and the value relation between the products of labour which stamps them as commodities, have absolutely no connexion with their physical properties and with the material relations arising therefrom.* There it is a definite social relation between men, that assumes in their eyes, the fantastic form of a relation between things. In order, therefore, to find an analogy, we must have recourse to the mist enveloped regions of the religious world. In that world the productions of the human brain appear as independent beings endowed with life, and entering into relation both with one another and the human race. So it is in the world of commodities with the products of men's hands. This I call the Fetishism which attaches itself to the products of labour, so soon as they are produced as commodities, and which is therefore inseparable from the production of commodities.[13]

There are two particularly important points to note about these quotations:

In the first quotation, from *The German Ideology*, Marx makes it clear that a mode of production is not simply a mode of 'physical' or 'material' production. Rather it is, he says 'a definite form of activity' of individuals, 'a definite form of expressing their life'. It would therefore follow that in a given mode of production people would produce 'definite forms' of ideas, values, social institutions, as well as – and at the same time as – producing a 'definite form' of material subsistence. We also see this broader conception of production in the second quotation from the *Grundrisse*, where we find the worker 'producing' 'his own poverty' as well as 'alien wealth' and also producing 'the relation of this wealth as independent, self-sufficient wealth'.

Unfortunately however Marx did not always stick to this broader, more inclusive concept of production, but, under the influence of classical political economy, narrowed it down to mean precisely physical or material production. Thus in Marx's 1859 Preface to his *Contribution to a Critique of Political Economy* (see chapter 2) one finds a formulation like 'the mode of production of material life *conditions* the social, political and intellectual life process in general', and elsewhere we find him writing that 'the handmill gives you society with the feudal lord, the steammill, society with the industrial capitalist' (*PP*, p. 109).

This narrowing of 'production' to physical or material production is unfortunate because, in conjunction with propositions about the 'conditioning' of social, political and intellectual life processes by the 'mode of production of material life', it gave rise to endless debates about 'economic reductionism' in Marx's thought. On the other hand, a much broader notion of production which makes it coextensive with a particular *way or 'mode' of life* avoids this reductionist interpretation and the philosophical problems to which it leads. These problems are discussed at length in chapters 2 and 7.

The third quotation – from Marx's *Capital* – has a most interesting philosophical implication. It will be noted that in this quotation Marx is saying that the 'value relations' of commodities are not perceptible through the senses. Commodities are of course physical products, and the physical processes of their production, exchange, and utilization are, therefore, perceptible through the senses. But the 'social' characteristics of commodities – their 'value relations' – the ways in which they constitute social relations between people (between people in the past and people in the present, and between people in the present) these things are *not*, according to Marx, perceptible through the senses. They cannot be seen, heard, touched, smelt. This opens up the question of how such relations *are* perceived, if not through the senses, and I will return to this issue in chapter 4 when analysing Marx's economic theory. But for the moment the reader should simply note this point, for it will become of considerable significance later in this work.

We should also note, by way of conclusion to this section, that Marx's 'materialization' of Hegel's concepts of objectification and alienation – their conversion into states of human beings rather than of 'the Idea' – was one of the most important results of the influence of Ludwig Feuerbach on the young Karl Marx. For in essence Feuerbach simply restated the empiricist ('sense impressions') philosophy as an Hegelian critique of Hegel. Feuerbach argued that Hegel had taken as the *subjects* of the historical process categories of the human mind ('simplicity', 'complexity', 'generality', 'specificity', 'public', 'private') what were simply *objects* produced by the thinking of actual, material human subjects.[14]

However, while Marx accepted Feuerbach's materialist inversion of Hegel, he did not remain content with it. For, as I have already implied in the account of objectification and alienation above, in his own philosophy, developed from 1845–6 or so, Marx declined to separate 'thinking' from 'life'. In fact by 1845–6 Marx had formulated a philosophy – which I have termed a philosophy of praxis – in which he refused either to derive life from thought (as in Hegel) or to derive thought from life (as in Locke and Feuerbach). For Marx, what made human beings different from any other species of animate life was their capacity for conscious creative activity – for practice or praxis as he called it – a concept which he used to embrace both thought and life. Since in my view this conception is at the centre of the whole of Marx's thought from the 1840s onwards, and its full significance has been underestimated and misunderstood, even by many Marxists, I wish now to outline it explicitly and in detail.

THE PHILOSOPHY OF PRAXIS IN MARX

In his famous *Theses on Feuerbach* of 1845 Marx pointed out that Hegelian idealism and Feuerbachian – or Lockean – materialism shared a common fault. For both treated human beings as if they were simply thinking creatures. In Hegel's case, he took the rational categories which he believed that all human minds shared and made them the prime movers of history. In the case of Feuerbachian materialism, an account of brains receiving sense impressions is offered as a sufficient account of how human beings think. But by the mid-1840s Marx had come to the conclusion that both these philosophies were inadequate because human beings were not simply thinking creatures, they were active creatures.

Human beings do all sorts of things (running, jumping, building, destroying, fighting, negotiating, making, repairing, loving, hating) and thinking is therefore just one of the things they do. Or, to put it in an altogether better way, thinking is intertwined with, as an integral part of, everything they do. In

short, thinking is an integral part of the active life, of the practice
(in German *praxis*) of an active purposeful creature.[15] Indeed it is
the presence of thought which makes an act an act and not (for
example) a reflex response. What makes sticking one's left hand
out a 'left-turn signal' and not a nervous tic, is (a) the circumstances in which it is done (e.g. while one is riding a bicycle and
approaching a junction) and (b) the thought or intention with
which it is done. Marx was to put it very well many years later,
and in regard to a totally different matter.

> A spider conducts operations that resemble those of a weaver,
> and a bee puts to shame many an architect in the construction
> of her cells. But what distinguishes the worst of architects
> from the best of bees is this, that the architect raises his
> structure in imagination before he erects it in reality. At
> the end of every labour process we get a result that already
> existed in the imagination of the labourer at its commence-
> ment. He not only effects a change of form in the material on
> which he works, but he also realises a purpose of his own.[16]

For Marx then, a focus on the total of human activity was a way
to escape both Hegelian idealism (since if one does not start
by defining human beings as those creatures which think one
does not end up obsessed by the categories of thought) and
Feuerbachian materialism (since human beings do not, as it
were, 'sit around' passively receiving sense impressions and
combining them into ideas and concepts). In so far as they do
this 'combining' – and note that this too is an act – they do it
only as part of actively doing other things. So, if Marx had to
pick an essential definition of human beings it would not be
'those creatures which think' but 'those creatures which act'.[17]

We are now in a position to understand these points as they
were expressed in Marx's own words, the *Theses on Feuerbach* of
1845. The first, second, and eighth theses are, I think, the ones
most relevant to reinforce the points made above.

Thesis I
The chief defect of all hitherto existing materialism (that of
Feuerbach included) is that the thing, reality, sensuousness,
is conceived only in the form of the *object, or of contemplation*,
but not as *sensuous human activity, practice*, not subjectively.
Hence in contradistinction to materialism the *active* side
was developed abstractly by idealism – which of course does

not know real, sensuous activity as such. Feuerbach wants sensuous objects, really distinct from the thought objects, but he does not conceive human activity as itself an *objective* activity.

Thesis II
The question whether objective truth can be attributed to human thinking is not a question of theory but is a *practical question*. It is in practice that man must prove the truth, the this-sidedness of his thinking. The dispute over the reality or non-reality of thinking that is isolated from practice is a purely *scholastic* question.

Thesis VIII
All social life is essentially *practical*. All mysteries which lead theory to mysticism find their rational solution in human practice and in the comprehension of this practice.[18]

In understanding these three theses a number of points should be borne in mind. Firstly, when Marx speaks of 'sensuous objects' in the first thesis he means 'objects of sense' or 'objects known through the senses'. Secondly, when he speaks of 'human activity as . . . an objective activity', he means 'an activity directed towards objects'. In other words, Marx is saying here that Feuerbach sees human ('sensuous') perception of objects as a passive or contemplative process, not as an active one. But for Marx, it does not make any sense to conceive 'sense objects', as Feuerbach does, as if they were simply 'there' in reality. On the contrary, they only *become* 'sense objects', objects known to human beings, when such beings actively appropriate them as part of their purposive life.

Finally, in the second and eighth theses it should be noted that when Marx speaks of 'objective truth' as a 'practical question', and of 'social life' as 'essentially practical', he is not naïvely juxtaposing 'practical' to 'theoretical', nor is he juxtaposing 'practical' activity to 'impractical' thinking (as we often do in English). Rather he is saying – as already noted – that all human thought is inextricably part of human *activity*. Marx is saying that the problem with Hegel, and with much Hegelian philosophy (both radical and conservative) in early nineteenth-century Germany, is that it first abstracts thought from other human activities and then asks how 'thought', so conceived, is related to the world. But for Marx this is first to create a problem and then to claim credit for solving it (or at least for discovering it!). For in Marx's view, 'thought' and 'world', 'thought' and 'reality' are 'already' and 'always' connected *through human activity*. It is human activity which, as it were, 'joins' thought to the world. Conversely, it is speculating about 'thinking' and 'thought' in abstraction from practice, from activity, which creates nearly all philosophical puzzles.

It is in this context that we must see the most famous of all the *Theses on Feuerbach*, the eleventh and final one:

> Philosophers have only *interpreted* the world in various ways, the point however is to *change* it.

Here Marx is taking 'philosophers' to task, not for interpreting the world, but for *only* interpreting the world. He is saying that since all interpretations of the world are themselves part of various activities in the world, the point is consciously to link one's interpretation to such an activity. Marx wants an interpretation of the world which is consciously and purposively linked to, or part of, an attempt to change the world, and he set out to create such an interpretation in his great book *Capital*. (Changing the world is of course only one possible activity in the world, another one would be trying to stop it changing – conservatism – and it too would have its linked 'interpretations'.)

There is one particular implication of this philosophy of praxis which is of immense importance. Indeed I believe that if its importance were grasped a great many debates in contemporary Marxism would cease overnight. From this perspective a question such as 'is it the way in which people produce which determines how they think, or is it the way in which they think which determines how they produce?' is a question unworthy of an answer because it is senseless. In this philosophy 'a way of producing' material products *is* simultaneously 'a way of thinking' (about such production), and 'a way of thinking' is something which is as much 'produced' as a table, a chair, or a nuclear power station.

Of course the *type* or *form* of production is different in each case, and there is frequently a point or purpose in distinguishing these forms by calling one 'material' or 'physical' and the other 'mental' or 'intellectual'. But both forms of production are human acts, both are expressions or embodiments of human activity. For Marx, who says 'act' says 'thought', and that some acts are physical and others mental is a distinction which sometimes, for some purposes, is useful and sometimes is not. In

Marx's conception of the human essence it is *not* useful, and in understanding human society it can often be misleading. In particular it is important to note that what we call 'mental' or 'intellectual' acts also have a physicality (they occur in human brains) while – more obviously and less frequently forgotten – every physical act, to *be* an act, must also be mental. Thus to speak of relations of 'determination' holding between (for example) 'a form of material production' and 'a form of thought' is also senseless because it involves positing a separation as two 'things' (so that one 'thing' can determine the other 'thing') of what are just different forms or expressions of human activity.

In a given society at a given time human beings are engaged in creative activity. Sometimes this takes the form of building windmills, digging canals, or designing aeroplanes. Sometimes it takes the form of writing books, acting plays and painting murals. If we are to speak of 'determination' at all, it is the determination of *all* these things by human activity – the creative force. At a given period in history, in a given society, all of that activity will have a certain character, a certain stamp, a certain form, which we can characterize as a particular 'mode of production' or 'mode of life'.

However, that a society has such a character, form or stamp, is not a characteristic of *it*, as it were. It is rather a characterization of it in thought. And a society is given (actively given) such a character, as a distinct 'mode of production', by being compared (this itself is an act) with societies which have preceded it or followed it. Such comparisons can focus on economic production, on social structure, on intellectual life, or on any combination of these things. From such comparisons different forms of society, or social formations, can be delineated. But this is always a retrospective act, and whether particular attention is given to the process of material production in making such retrospective distinctions depends on the purposes of the thinker making them, on the purposes which inform his/her actions as a thinker.[19]

Thus, there are purposes from which it makes perfect sense to consider (another act) the process of material production as more important than anything else in characterizing or classifying different societies. But that Marx did so, and Marxists do so, is a characteristic of their activity as Marxists. It is not a characteristic of material production itself. In itself material production is neither 'central' nor 'marginal', 'important' nor 'unimportant' in characterizing different forms of society. It is *made* important or unimportant through a human cognitive act – in this case Marx's cognitive act. Does this mean then that it was just a 'subjective preference' on his part? No it does not. Or rather, calling it a subjective preference would not be a useful way of characterizing Marx's activity here, mainly because he shared (and shares) the purposes from which he gave priority to material production with other people. But this is an issue which is taken up at length in the last two chapters of this book, so I will not elaborate upon it here.

However, while I think that Marx's creation of what might be called an 'activist materialism', a philosophy of praxis, out of a synthesis of Hegelian idealism with Feuerbachian materialism did represent a major intellectual achievement, I also think that Marx did not fully capitalize upon this achievement in his later work. In fact in some ways he actually retreated from it.

For firstly, Marx should perhaps have seen some implications of his philosophy of praxis which he apparently missed. In particular, if thought about the world *is* inextricably a part of practice or activity in the world, this implies that in a complex society, with a complex social structure and division of labour, there may be many different 'interpretations' of the world forming part of many different practices. People who live in different places, in different kinds of houses, who have different kinds of education, different kinds of neighbours and different kinds of jobs, may have very different interpretations of the world, or at any rate interpretations which differ in many important respects. Thus doctors and solicitors may see the world differently from business executives and civil servants, and the latter may in turn see it differently from car workers or shop assistants. Men may see the world differently from women, children differently from adults, black people differently from whites. And, following Marx, the precise ways in which they see it differently will be an integral part of the precise ways in which the praxis – the whole life activity – of these groups is different. Children *do* different things from adults, women *do* different things from men, solicitors *do* different things from shop workers, etc.

In short, what this kind of extrapolation from Marx's philosophy of praxis does, is to make problematic Marx's own tendency, in his later work, to think that the only kinds of practice or activity differences which are relevant to explaining differences in 'social consciousness' are differences in class practices. In his later work Marx came to concentrate almost exclusively on differences in class practices in society, to the exclusion of almost all other social divisions. This concentration on class divisions is not entailed by the philosophy of praxis, and is due, I think, almost entirely to other influences on Marx. In particular, it was due to the influence of classical political economy on his later thought about society (see chapters 3 and 4), and to the fact that he came to engage in one particular social practice – political agitation among industrial workers – to the exclusion of almost all others. If his own philosophy of praxis was right, one would expect that this particular type of political practice would be bound up with a particular kind of thought, would lead to particular emphases in Marx's thought, and, as we shall see, it did.

Unfortunately, the fact that Marx's own later thought is a perfect demonstration of the validity of his early philosophy, does not prevent the former from being flawed in important ways. For if, for example, differences in class practices are only some of the differences in practices which divide people in society, then it cannot be assumed, as Marx tended to do, that those class differences will always be more important to individual human beings than those other differences. Thus, for example, the different life activities of black people and white people, or of women and men, may in certain circumstances be more important in forming the social consciousness of those people than class differences. Whether they are more important or not is an empirical question to be investigated at any given point in human history. But the later Marx was a little too prone to substitute assumption for investigation in this matter.

Secondly, in Marx's later work, and especially in his work on political economy, we tend to find him taking up implicit philosophical positions which may not seem very consistent with his earlier philosophy of praxis. In particular in *Capital*, Marx takes up a position on science, which appears, at first sight, somewhat at odds with this philosophy. Marx claimed that *Capital* was a scientific work, and, as I shall argue in chapter 3, this means that he would have wished the truth or falsity of the theory put forward in that work to be established by the normal criteria applied to a work of science or scholarship. These criteria include logical consistency, verification or falsification by empirical evidence, reasonableness of premises and conclusions, etc. But the continuity of this approach to science with Marx's earlier philosophy lies in the fact that while these criteria may establish the *truth or falsity* of a theory, they cannot establish its *significance*. The philosophy of praxis by contrast is centrally concerned with significance or meaning, and it suggests that a scientific theory is significant if its truth or falsity makes some difference to human practices or activities outside it. Thus, to establish whether a theory is significant or not, one asks such questions as 'what purposes is this theory meant to serve?', 'what is meant to be achieved by it?', 'what is this theory for, what is one meant to do with it?'[20]

Asking any or all of these questions does not imply that one first decides what purposes a theory is serving and then judges it true or false depending upon whether one approves of these particular purposes or not. It is rather that a logically prior question to 'is this (any) theory true or false?' is the question 'what is at stake in deciding whether it is true or false?' Or, in other words, what follows, what difference does it make in the world if a theory is true or if it is false? For obviously, if nothing is at stake, if nothing follows, if a theory's being true or false makes no difference to anything outside itself then, quite simply it does not matter whether it is true or false, and we may as well save ourselves the intellectual energy necessary to find out. In the case of Marx's economic theory, however, its aim or purpose *is* clear; it is to show that 'capital accumulation occurs solely through the exploitation of the working class'. If the theory is true then that proposition is true, if the theory is false then that proposition may well be false. And of course if it is true that 'capital accumulation occurs solely through the exploitation of the working class' then this may have many implications for other practices and activities in the world, for example, political practices towards that class and by that class.

This is what I meant in stating earlier that Marx believed he had created a 'change-linked' interpretation of the world in *Capital*. But the problem is that in his later concentration on political economy and on political agitation and propaganda, Marx tended to take this 'background' philosophical position for granted, to rely silently upon it, but not to articulate it. Instead he concentrated on trying to establish that his theory *was* true, and so gave greater attention to such issues as: the nature of the concepts with which *Capital* is constructed, the logical consistency of the propositions in which those concepts are employed, the explanatory and descriptive power of his theory in relation to empirical evidence about capitalism, etc. These are certainly vitally important issues, absolutely central to establishing the truth or falsity of Marx's economic theory. But unfortunately many later generations of Marxists came to think that they were the only philosophical or epistemological issues of any importance in Marxism, that the significance as well as the truth of Marxism depended solely on its claimed ability to explain or describe the world better than any other theory.[21] The problem with this however is that concepts of 'explaining the world' or 'describing the world' left in this unqualified form are simply incoherent. (If you are in any doubt about this, think how you would react to an unqualified request to 'give a complete description of London' or to 'provide a complete explanation of money'.)[22]

The net result, in fact, of not asking the logically prior question about the *significance* of a theory (the implications for other practices or activities in the world of its being true or false) can be to produce an arid formalism, often combined with an equally arid positivism. That is to say, many contemporary Marxists think that they can prove that 'superiority' of Marxism by showing either (a) that it 'fits' or 'explains' the facts better than any other theory and/or (b) that it is more logically consistent than any other theory. And the problem here is not that either of these criteria are irrelevant or unimportant, but that, whether taken singly or together, if they are treated in abstraction from Marx's purposes they give one no determinate answer about overall 'superiority' or 'inferiority', although they may give one determinate answers about truth or falsity of particular propositions or sets of propositions.

For what application of these criteria reveals in fact is that Marx's theory certainly 'fits' or 'explains' some of the facts he adduces, but fails to explain others. But this is also true of other theories which deny that capital accumulation occurs solely (or at all) through the exploitation of the working class. They also reveal (as we shall see) that Marx's theory manifests both logical consistency and inconsistency. But this too is true of other theories which deny that capital accumulation occurs solely through the exploitation of the working class.

Thus, asking only about faithfulness to the evidence (or 'descriptive accuracy') or only about logical consistency can very easily lead to a situation in which one is battling valiantly with tools which can only tell one about truth or falsehood in order to try and demonstrate 'superiority' or 'inferiority'. But issues about the 'superiority' or 'inferiority' of theories, while they deeply involve issues of truth and falsehood (in the sense that no false theory or part of a theory can be judged 'superior') are not exhausted by, or reducible to simple questions of truth or falsity. For theories are also the creative products of theorists and thus judgements of them are also judgements of those theorists, of their purposes and activities in the world, and of the role of their theories in that wider life activity. Thus if one judges the purposes of a theorist valid, or if, more simply, one *shares* those purposes, but finds his or her theories false or mistaken in some way, one's reaction to that (what one will *do* about it) will be very different from one's reaction if one does not share those purposes. I hope that what I mean by that will become clearer as this book proceeds, for in a sense it is what this book is about. It is about what a Marxist *does* intellectually and politically if s/he finds considerable parts of Marx's theory false. It is a book which does not treat questions about the significance, the meaning, the superiority of Marxism as questions simply about the truth of Marxism, and is therefore a book written (I hope) in the spirit of the philosophy of praxis.

The reduction of Marxism's significance or meaning to a question only about its truth or falsity, the departure of Marxists from the philosophy of praxis, is itself the principal result or symptom of the academicization of Marxism. As Marxism becomes just one school of academic thought among others, so Marxists themselves come to think that 'whether objective truth can be attributed to human thinking' *is* (purely) 'a question of theory' and asking themselves 'purely scholastic questions' they get, of course 'purely scholastic' (and indeterminate) answers. Thus, in a supreme historical irony, Marxism itself is reduced to 'simply' or 'only' an *interpretation* of the world and in being so reduced it loses not only its political bite (a point often enough made and true) but, more fundamentally, it loses its philosophical soul and force. It loses touch with a profound epistemological and anthropological insight (an insight I have called the 'philosophy of praxis') which gave it such strength and saved it from scholastic aridity for so long.

CHAPTER 2

MARX'S THEORY OF HISTORY

In the social production of their existence, men inevitably enter into definite relations, which are independent of their will, namely relations of production which correspond to a given stage in the development of their material forces of production. The totality of these relations of production constitutes the economic structure of society, the real foundation upon which arises a legal and political superstructure and to which correspond definite forms of social consciousness. The mode of production of material life conditions the general process of social, political, and intellectual life. It is not the consciousness of men that determines their existence but their social existence that determines their consciousness.

At a certain stage of their development, the material forces of production in society come in conflict with existing relations of production, or – what is but a legal expression for the same thing – with the property relations within the framework of which they have operated hitherto. From forms of the development of the productive forces these relations turn into their fetters. Then begins an epoch of social revolution. The changes in the economic foundation lead sooner or later to the transformation of the whole immense superstructure.

These two paragraphs are from Marx's *Preface to the Critique of Political Economy* written in January 1859.[1] They are perhaps the most famous paragraphs of a famous text (famous anyway in Marxist scholarship). Whole books have been written both to attack and defend them, and they have been, and continue to be, endlessly debated.[2] This is because the 1859 Preface is taken to be, and was taken by Marx to be, his most considered and authoritative statement of both his method of analysis of society and of his approach to history.

Broadly speaking debate about these passages has centred on the following questions:

1. Do these passages show Marx to be some kind of 'deterministic' thinker, and if so, what kind of determinist do they show him to be?[3]

2. Is the mechanism of historical change which Marx outlines here – the 'relations of production' becoming a 'fetter' on the 'forces of production' and producing a 'social revolution' – meant to be a 'law' of historical development? Closely bound up with these two questions has been a third:

3. What precisely does Marx mean by the crucial terms in these paragraphs? What does he mean by 'mode of production' (of material life)? What does he mean by 'forces of production'? What does he mean by the 'economic structure' of society which is the 'foundation' for a legal and political 'superstructure', etc.

This third question, or set of questions, is important because it turns out that what one takes Marx to mean by these crucial terms deeply affects one's answers to the first and second questions. Also, finding out what he means by these terms in the 1859 Preface involves not only reading that text itself, but also requires one to compare that text with his use of the same, and analogous, terms elsewhere in his work. As a result of course there is much room for different interpretations of what Marx meant in these famous paragraphs.

In this chapter I shall offer one more interpretation of the 1859 Preface, and I shall also address both the first and second questions which arise from it. That is, I shall consider whether Marx was an historical or economic determinist, and I shall also consider whether he does identify any law or laws of historical change. However, since these two questions are very closely interrelated, providing an answer to the first question also provides an answer to the second, so they can be treated together.

MARX, 'LAWS' and HISTORICAL DETERMINISM

Consider these ten quotations:

1. Intrinsically, it is not a question of the higher or lower degree of development of the social antagonisms that result from the natural laws of capitalist production. It is a question of these laws themselves working with iron necessity towards

. . . inevitable results. The country that is more developed industrially only shows, to the less developed, the image of its own future.[4]

2. Even when a society has got upon the right track for the discovery of the natural laws of its movement – and it is the ultimate aim of this work to lay bare the economic law of motion of modern society – it can neither clear by bold leaps, nor remove by legal enactments, the obstacles offered by the successive phases of its normal development. But it can shorten or lessen the birth-pangs.[5]

3. . . . the merit of having discovered either the existence of classes in modern society or the class struggle does not belong to me. Bourgeois historians had presented the historic development of this struggle of the classes, and bourgeois economists the economic anatomy of the same, long before I did. What was new in what I did was 1) to demonstrate that the existence of classes is tied only to *definite historical phases of the development of production* 2) that the class struggle necessarily leads to *the dictatorship of the proletariat* 3) that this dictatorship is only a transition to the *dissolution of all classes* and leads to the formation of a *classless society*.[6]

4. The question is not what this or that proletarian or even the whole of the proletariat at the moment *considers* as its aim. The question is *what the proletariat is*, and what, consequent on that *being* it will be compelled to do. Its aim and historical action are irrevocably and obviously demonstrated in its own life situation as well as in the whole organization of bourgeois society today.[7]

5. The history of all hitherto existing society is the history of class struggle. Freeman and slave, patrician and plebeian, lord and serf, guildmaster and journeyman, in a word, oppressor and oppressed stood in constant opposition to one another, carried on an uninterrupted, now hidden, now open fight that each time ended, either in a revolutionary re-constitution of society at large, or in the common ruin of the contending classes.[8]

6. History is nothing but the succession of the separate generations each of which exploits the materials, the capital funds, the productive forces handed down to it by all preceding

generations, and thus, on the one hand, continues the traditional activity in completely changed circumstances and, on the other, modifies the old circumstances with a completely changed activity. This can be speculatively distorted so that later history is made the goal of earlier history e.g. the goal ascribed to the discovery of America is to further the eruption of the French Revolution. Thereby history receives its own special aims and becomes a 'person ranking with other persons' ... while what is designated with the words 'destiny', 'goal', 'germ', or 'idea' of earlier history is nothing more than an abstraction formed from later history, from the active influence which earlier history exercises on later history.[9]

7. History does *nothing*, it does *not* possess immense riches, it does *not* fight battles. It is *men*, real, living men, who do all this, who possess things and fight battles. It is not 'history' which uses men as a means of achieving – as if it were an individual person – *its* own ends. History is *nothing* but the activity of men in pursuit of their ends.[10]

8. Men make their own history, but they do not make it just as they please, they do not make it under circumstances chosen by themselves, but under circumstances directly encountered, given and transmitted from the past.[11]

9. It is superfluous to add that men are not free to choose their *productive forces* – which are the basis of all their history – for every productive force is an acquired force, the product of former activity. The productive forces are therefore the result of practical human energy; but this energy is itself conditioned by the circumstances in which men find themselves, by the productive forces already acquired, by the social form which exists before they do, which they do not create, which is the product of the preceding generation. Because of this simple fact, that every succeeding generation finds itself in possession of the productive forces acquired by the preceding generation, which serve it as the raw material for new production, a coherence arises in human history, a history of humanity takes shape which is all the more a history of humanity as the productive forces of man (and therefore his social relations) have been more developed. Hence it necessarily follows that the social history of men is never anything

but the history of their individual development, whether they are conscious of it or not. Their material relations are the basis of all their relations. These material relations are only the necessary forms in which their material and individual activity is realised.[12]

10. According to the materialist conception of history, the *ultimately* determining element in history is the production and reproduction of real life. More than that neither Marx nor I has ever asserted. Hence, if somebody twists this into saying that the economic element is the only determining one he transforms the proposition into a meaningless, abstract, senseless phrase. The economic situation is the basis, but the various elements of the superstructure – political forms of the class struggle ... constitutions ... juridical forms and even the reflexes of all these actual struggles in the brains of the participants, political, juristic, philosophical theories, religious views ... also exercise their influence upon the course of the historical struggles and in many cases preponderate in determining their *form*. There is an interaction of all these elements in which, amidst all the endless host of accidents ... the economic movement finally asserts itself as necessary. ...

We make our history ourselves but, in the first place, under very definite assumptions and conditions. Among these the economic ones are ultimately decisive. But the political ones etc ... and even the traditions which haunt human minds also play a part, although not a decisive one.[13]

Perhaps the first comment to make about these quotations – especially when they are laid end to end in this way – is the support they provide to a point which I made in chapter 1 about Marx as a rich but chaotic thinker.

We see in these quotations how he appears to present very different, even contradictory, views of history, so that by focusing on one set of quotations (1 to 4 for example) one can easily find evidence to support the allegation that Marx was an historical determinist, while other quotations (6, 7 and 8) could be brought forward to defend him from this charge. Quotations 5 and 9 occupy a kind of 'mid-way' position and so can perhaps be read either way. Finally, quotation 10 from Engels, seeking to clarify the matter for a later generation of Marxists after Marx's death, only seems to add further confusion, for Engels stresses on the one hand the 'interaction' of economic, political, and ideological factors in influencing the course of history, while on the other hand he insists that the 'economic movement finally asserts itself as necessary'.

However, I suggest that it is possible to bring order into this apparent chaos. Firstly, we should note that these quotations come from very different periods of Marx's life, and are thus abstracted from very different contexts. Once one understands something about these contexts some of these apparent contradictions disappear.

For example, two of the most apparently 'deterministic' quotations (1 and 2) come from Marx's Preface to the first edition of *Capital*. It is clear both from the context there, and from the Preface to the second (1873) edition, that the 'laws' to which Marx refers in these quotations are supposed to operate only *within capitalism*, within this one particular 'mode of production'. So that Marx is here thinking of things such as the 'law of value' and the 'law of the tendency of the rate of profit to fall' which we shall consider in the next two chapters. Thus 'laws' in this context are *not* meant to encompass the long historical transitions between different modes of production. Indeed in the 1873 Preface to *Capital* Marx approvingly quotes a reviewer of the 1867 edition who had stressed that, in Marx's view, 'every historical period has laws of its own'. And Marx goes on to quote the review at length, obviously feeling that it captures his own views well:

> As soon as society has outlived a given period of development, and is passing over from one given stage to another, it begins to be subject to other laws. In a word economic life offers us a phenomenon analogous to the history of evolution in other branches of biology. The old economists misunderstood the nature of economic laws when they likened them to the laws of physics and chemistry. A more thorough analysis of phenomena shows that the social organisms differ among themselves as fundamentally as plants and animals. Nay, one and the same phenomenon falls under quite different laws in consequence of the different structure of these organisms as a whole, ... Marx, for example, denies that the law of population is the same at all times and places. He asserts, on the contrary, that every stage of development has its own law of population.[14]

So Marx seems to be suggesting here, that whereas each individual mode of production is subject to different laws, transitions between modes may not be law-bound. However, it may still be possible that the 1859 *Preface to the Critique of Political Economy* is meant to provide such a 'law of transition' between modes (i.e. 'relations of production' coming to 'fetter' 'forces of production').

However, there are at least two pieces of evidence against such an interpretation of the 1859 Preface. In the first place, the word 'law' never appears in the 1859 text at all. In the second place, as we shall see later in this chapter, when Marx does analyse a number of pre-capitalist modes of production, he is often not concerned with transitions between them (i.e. this is often not the primary focus of the analysis at all), and when he does concern himself with such transitions he frequently identifies factors and mechanisms of transition which have nothing to do with either forces or relations of production however understood.

I therefore think that the 1859 Preface, with which I began this chapter, is intended to have a much narrower historical reference than its highly abstract or universal formulation might suggest. I think that the Preface is meant to refer to (a) the transition from feudalism to capitalism in western Europe and to (b) the predicted transition from capitalism to socialism and communism, also in western Europe.

Indeed, Marx said precisely this in a famous letter of 1877 sent to a group of Russian Marxists who had written to ask him whether his theory of historical change was applicable to Russia, given that Russia had a very different history and social structure to western Europe. Marx replied (making reference to a Russian critic, Mikhailovsky, who had attacked his theory as determinist) that:

> He [Mikhailovsky] feels that he must metamorphose my historical sketch of the genesis of capitalism in Western Europe into a historico-philosophical theory of the general path every people is fated to tread, whatever the historical circumstances in which it finds itself, in order that it may ultimately arrive at the form of economy which ensures, together with the greatest expansion of the productive powers of social labour, the most complete development of man. But I beg his pardon, he is both honouring and shaming me too much.

and after analysing an historical example, Marx concludes:

> Thus events strikingly analogous but taking place in different historical surroundings led to totally different results. By

studying each of these forms of evolution separately and then comparing them one can easily find the clue to this phenomenon, but one will never arrive there by using as one's master key a general historico-philosophical theory, the supreme virtue of which consists in being super-historical.[15]

In short then, both in the case of the most deterministic sounding of our ten quotations and in the case of the 1859 Preface, things are not quite what they seem. Marx is referring in both cases to a much narrower range of historical phenomena than might at first appear. We are therefore not dealing, even in the 1859 Preface, with a universal 'law' of historical development. This conclusion is strengthened by the fact that when Marx *does* talk about transitions between pre-capitalist modes at length, he often does not use the Preface's postulated mechanism to explain them.

However, this conclusion does not imply that all of Marx's problems are solved. Because, even if one does accept his 1877 explanation that his theory is concerned with 'the genesis of capitalism in Western Europe' two major problems still remain. They are:

1. That a lot of Marxist (and other) work on the transition from feudalism to capitalism in western Europe has failed to establish that it *was* the growth of 'forces of production' bursting the fetter of feudal 'relations of production' which brought about the transition to capitalism.[16] Moreover,

2. There has been no 'social revolution' to socialism and communism in western Europe, so it remains an open question whether (a) there will be one or (b) even if there is one whether it will occur in the manner suggested by the 1859 Preface.

Let us now turn to the apparently most 'non-deterministic' of our quotations on history, quotations 6 and 7.

Quotation 6 comes from *The German Ideology* of 1846 and quotation 7 from *The Holy Family* of 1845. In both these works Marx and Engels were, in their own phrase, 'settling accounts' with the philosophies of Hegel and Feuerbach (see chapter 1) which had influenced them so much in the 1830s and early 1840s. Part of this 'settling of accounts' was a rejection – at least in part – of Hegel's 'teleological' conception of history, of the idea that 'history' was an active subject with an end or goal of its own. In Hegel, you will recall, this end or goal of history was mind's coming to a complete understanding of itself and the world. It is not therefore surprising that it is in *this* context – the writings of 1845–6 – that we find Marx's most vehement rejections of this idea and the insistence that 'History is *nothing* but the activity of men in pursuit of their ends.'

But Marx had no sooner formulated this view (in 1845) than he became unhappy with it in this form. So that even a year later, in *The German Ideology*, he is modifying it by referring, not simply to the activity of individual 'men' (human beings) but to that activity as it takes place in the context of *generational* change. And he also insists that this activity always occurs in the context of 'old circumstances' created by 'all preceding generations'.

In my view, this 'generational' conception of history, having been formulated in *The German Ideology* remained central to Marx's whole approach to history until his death. Thus, we find him restating it again in his polemic against Proudhon (*The Poverty of Philosophy* of 1847) and in his letter to Annenkov on the same subject (quotation 9). It is restated once more in *The Eighteenth Brumaire of Louis Bonaparte* of 1869, in its most famous formulation ('Men make their own history but ... under circumstances directly encountered, given and transmitted from the past'). Engels used this phrasing, almost word for word, in both his pamphlet *Ludwig Feuerbach and the End of Classical German Philosophy* of 1888, and in several letters of 1890 when he was endeavouring to restate the essence of 'historical materialism' for a later generation of Marxists (see quotation 10).[17] Indeed in these letters he several times explicitly directs younger Marxists to *The Eighteenth Brumaire* as an 'excellent example' of the 'application' of historical materialism.[18]

MARX'S CONCEPTION OF HISTORY

In short, it is this picture of history – as a process whereby subsequent generations of people both reinforce and modify, through their own individual activity, the 'circumstances' which are however simply the result of the activity of previous generations of individuals – which we must grasp if we are to understand Marx's theory of history. In grasping it, I think, certain of the difficulties about 'determinism' in Marx are resolved, and important connections are established between Marx's philosophy of history and that of Hegel. There are four advantages of this generational picture of history as a theory of history:

1. It allows one to square – at least to some degree – a conception of history as 'nothing but the activity of men' – with a conception which stresses certain structural constraints on what individual human beings or groups of human beings (including social classes) may do at any given point in history. For with this picture we may say that it is human activity, and only human activity, which creates economic, political, and social 'circumstances' (structural constraints) but that individual human beings have a finite life span which is far shorter than human history as a whole. As a result, human beings come and go from the world in generations, and therefore at any given point in time a generation or generations of people will have been born into 'circumstances', inherited from previous generations, which will be, and will be experienced as, real constraints on what they can do.

2. This picture has at its centre the notion of human beings as social creatures, creatures who live in society, and it therefore rejects the kind of notion (perhaps implied in quotation 7) of human beings existing in a kind of 'empty space' in which they can do anything which they individually will or intend. As Marx said in the sixth thesis on Feuerbach, 'Feuerbach dissolves religious nature in human nature. But human nature is not an abstraction dwelling within the single individual. Its reality is the sum-total of human relations.'[19] But at the same time, by stressing the possibilities for social change inherent in the very process of generational change, this conception avoids making human beings simply the products and reproducers of existing social relations. For if they were, 'social revolutions' of any sort would be out of the question.

It should be noted however that this picture of history does not involve a conception of human generations as social actors. It is individuals and social groups, including social classes, all of which are subject to generational change, which are the actors in this conception of the historical process. So, I am not here presenting 'generations' or 'generational change' as some kind of alternative to 'class struggle' in Marx's theory of history. It is rather that classes, like individuals, are subject to generational change, and that 'class struggle', like all other social processes, occurs in this changing context, and may be modified by it.

3. The dialectic of activity and structure centred on generational change allows Marx to incorporate a modified version of Hegelian 'alienation' (see chapter 1) into his philosophy of history.

For such a conception explains how the products of a given generation or generations of human beings – whether these be economic structures, state forms, scientific, moral, or political values and beliefs – are actually *their* products (the products of individuals and social group activity), but at the same time (or rather at a later time!) can appear as 'separate', 'alien' phenomena constraining, even dominating and oppressing, the subsequent generations of individuals and social groups who inherit them.

In fact through the generational conception of history 'alienation' becomes both more mundane and more comprehensible than in its Hegelian form. For in Marx, the human beings who 'produce' these social relations, institutions, values, beliefs, and the human beings who experience them as 'alien' and 'constraining' are often hundreds (or in some cases, thousands) of years apart. By making the human beings who produce and experience alienation concrete historical beings (beings with a chronology and temporality) Marx does, I think, succeed in making alienation both a more mundane but also a more powerfully explanatory concept than it is in Hegel.

4. Perhaps most importantly, the generational conception of human history helps to resolve some puzzles about economic determinism in Marx, puzzles which I considered earlier in this chapter in analysing the 1859 Preface.

For one possible way of interpreting that Preface is as a statement of necessary but insufficient conditions. That is to say, Marx can be construed as saying there not that *when* the forces of production (in western European feudalism or capitalism) 'come in conflict with the existing relations of production' then there *is* or *will be* a 'social revolution'. Rather he is saying that *until* the forces of production do so 'come in conflict' with the relations of production there *cannot* be a 'social revolution'. In other words, the really crucial sentences in the 1859 Preface are not those quoted at the beginning of this chapter, but the ones appearing a few lines later which read:

No social order ever disappears before all the productive forces for which there is room in it have been developed; and new, higher relations of production never appear before the material conditions of their existence have matured in the womb of the old society. Therefore, mankind always sets itself only such problems as it can solve; since, on closer examination it will always be found that the problem itself arises only when the material conditions necessary for its solution already exist or are at least in the process of formation.[20]

The crucial point here is that a '*social* revolution' is supposed to lead to 'new higher relations of production', and it is clear that Marx means by this a new 'higher' form of society which represents an advance in the quality of life for all the people in it compared with its predecessors. Thus Marx is arguing, on my interpretation, that if 'all the productive forces for which there is room' have *not* developed 'in the womb of the old society', then though there may be political revolutions, putsches, *coups d'état*, even violent uprisings of the poor in the 'old society', these will *not* lead to 'new higher relations of production'. Some Marxist scholars have analysed the Russian Revolution of 1917 as being precisely a political revolution but not a social revolution because 'all the productive forces for which there [was] room' had not developed in Russia's 'old society'.[21]

So if this particular interpretation of the 1859 Preface is accepted it can be seen to fit perfectly with Marx's 'generational' conception of history. For we can conclude that if the forces of production do develop to the maximum possible extent 'in the womb of the old society' then this will be the result of the activity of previous generations of human beings. At the point when such a 'complete' development has occurred individuals and social groups existing at that time *may* use the opportunity afforded them by the work of previous generations to make a 'social revolution'. They may or may not do so, and they may or may not succeed, but they only *can* succeed if 'all the productive forces for which there is room' in 'the old society' have been developed, for only *then* will they be 'setting themselves problems' which they can 'solve'.

But this still leaves a problem of criteria. How can either the 'revolutionary' individuals and social groups or the Marxist historian looking back in history *know* whether all the productive forces 'for which there is room' have matured? Marx's answer to this would appear to be that 'they will have matured sufficiently *if* there is a successful social revolution to a new higher form of society', since for Marx such a development of the productive forces is, as I have said, a necessary though insufficient condition for such success.

This seems to me a logically acceptable answer and not

determinist, (since it does not assert that the social revolution *will* succeed). Indeed, as can be seen, in the case of the future (?) transition from capitalism to socialism this criterion leaves a large space for human judgement about whether the productive forces are sufficiently 'matured' (as well as about many other strategic and tactical issues).

MARX AND DETERMINISM: CONCLUSIONS

We are now in a position to answer the first two of the three questions which I posed at the beginning of this chapter. They were: (1) does the 1859 Preface show Marx to be a 'deterministic' thinker? and (2) is the mechanism of change which Marx identifies in that Preface meant to be a universal 'law' of historical development?

The argument of this chapter so far has been that the answer to both questions is No.

1. Marx is *not* a deterministic thinker. It is true that the 1859 Preface can be read in a way which would make him such, and it frequently has been understood in this deterministic manner. It has been seen as providing a universal 'law' of historical development which guarantees that human society will move from an earliest stage of 'primitive communism' (the 'Germanic' and 'Asiatic' modes of production) to a 'final' stage of post-capitalist socialism and communism.[22] I have argued however that it should not be understood in this way, but should be seen as outlining a set of necessary but insufficient conditions of human progress by means of 'social revolutions'.

However, this does not mean that Marx avoided all talk of economic 'laws', and indeed our quotations 1 and 2 showed him writing in exactly this way. However, these 'laws' are meant to operate only *within* particular modes of production, and Marx gave most attention in his work to the economic laws of the capitalist mode of production. I shall suggest in the fourth chapter of this book that much of this talk about 'laws' of capitalism is rather ill-founded, but this is not primarily because it is 'deterministic'.

2. The 1859 Preface does *not* therefore assert a universal law or mechanism of change by which all modes of production succeed each other ('relations of production' becoming fetters on 'forces of production'). At most this is meant to refer to the change from

feudalism to capitalism and from capitalism to socialism and communism in western Europe.

This point becomes very clear when close attention is paid to Marx's writings about pre-capitalist modes of production. When, for example, he analyses the transition from the 'Germanic' (communal) mode of production to the feudal mode in western Europe (in *The German Ideology* and the *Grundrisse*) Marx does not claim that there was much, if any, development of the productive forces in the Germanic mode,[23] while his analysis of the 'Asiatic' mode of production outside of Europe strongly insists that this mode is essentially static or stagnant until it is violently disrupted from the outside (by, for example, British colonialism in India).[24] And the inconsistencies do not end there. Marx analysed a case of the development of capitalism without a feudal predecessor (in North America) and was prepared to consider the possibility of a direct transition from primitive communism to socialism (in Russia).[25]

However, all these inconsistencies are only such if one imagines that Marx had some universal stage theory of history. But, as I have already argued, he had no such theory. In so far as there is even an attempt at a stage theory of history in Marx, it concerned western Europe alone and outlines a Germanic–Feudal–Capitalist sequence of modes linked by some broad evolutionary process. But even then, whatever form this evolutionary process may have taken (and Marx never analysed it at any length) it certainly is not simply a story of forces of production bursting through the fetters of relations of production by means of social revolutions, because he never even claims that this occurred in the case of the Germanic–Feudal transition.

The truth is that what really mattered to Marx, what is at the centre of all his work, was the appearance of the capitalist mode of production in the world, and its (hoped for) disappearance from the world. It is for this reason that Marx paid most attention to – indeed only gave any serious analytical attention to – the transition from feudalism to capitalism. Once however the capitalist mode had appeared in western Europe Marx grasped clearly, and indeed stressed, that it could become dominant elsewhere in the world through economic and military power, and indeed through colonial conquest. As a result it could and would disrupt any 'evolutionary' sequence of modes of production elsewhere in the world, which is precisely why Marx did not imagine that a universal stage theory of history was either possible or desirable.

A FURTHER PROBLEM

However, even if the 1859 Preface is construed in the non-deterministic manner for which I have argued, it is still vulnerable to another sort of attack focused on the meaning of its concepts and the logic of its propositions. To understand the issues involved we need to look again at the second of these crucial paragraphs in the Preface:

> At a certain stage of their development, the material forces of production in society come in conflict with the existing relations of production or – what is but a legal expression for the same thing – with the property relations within the framework of which they have operated hitherto. From forms of the development of the productive forces these relations turn into fetters. Then begins an epoch of social revolution. The changes in the economic foundation lead sooner or later to the transformation of the whole immense superstructure.[26]

Logically, it follows from this that if the 'forces of production' are to 'come in conflict' with the 'relations of production' then these forces *must be clearly distinguishable* from the relations which become their 'fetters'.

There *is* a way to make them clearly distinct, which is to equate 'forces of production' broadly with 'technology'. Thus forces of production would include techniques of production in industry and agriculture, together with the social organization of the people employed in using those techniques. However, even on this technological interpretation the forces of production would have to include the *knowledge* of that technology, both the knowledge of how to create and use it, and of how to develop it.

Given this technological interpretation of the forces, the relations of production would encompass the property relations through which the forces are owned or controlled. These include not only legal rules of ownership, but also substantive relations of control, such as managers or foremen in the capitalist's factory, and the lord of the manor's agents controlling his serfs on the feudal estate.

But even construed in this way there are problems in making Marx's propositions about the forces and relations of production consistent with other propositions in the Preface. Thus, to include scientific and technological knowledge in the forces of production seems to run counter to the picture of capitalist society painted elsewhere in the Preface in which both the forces and relations of production (the 'economic structure of society') are held to be clearly distinct from 'forms of social consciousness' which 'correspond' to them and from the 'intellectual life process' which they 'condition'. Moreover, to include property relations in the relations of production is to include in those relations a *legal* form which Marx clearly says is part of the 'superstructure' of capitalist society.

By far the most rigorous treatment of these issues is that undertaken by Gerald Cohen in the second chapter of his book *Karl Marx's Theory of History: A Defence*, in which he shows, convincingly I think, that these problems at least can be got round. Cohen argues that there is no contradiction in including scientific knowledge in the forces of production, because it is not knowledge but ideology which is 'superstructural' for Marx. This view seems to be borne out by Marx's statement elsewhere in the Preface that:

> a distinction should always be made between the material transformation of the economic conditions of production, which can be determined with the precision of natural science, and the legal, political, religious, aesthetic or philosophic – in short ideological forms – in which men become conscious of this conflict and fight it out.[27]

The clear implication of this passage is that while legal, political, religious, aesthetic, or philosophical ideas can be ideological (which is not of course to say that all of them always are) natural science cannot be ideological. This is not a conception of ideology which I find very useful (I think, for example, that natural science too can be ideological – see chapter 6), but it is none the less what Marx seems to be saying, at least in the 1859 Preface, and to that extent is consistent with Cohen's interpretation.

On the property relations issue Cohen suggests that Marx wished to include in the relations of production only ownership relations which are also relations of effective control over production. Thus the owner/manager of an economic enterprise is to be included in the 'relations of production' of capitalist society, but 'rentiers' (i.e. holders of equity shares in public and private sector enterprises who exercise no managerial control in these enterprises) would not form part of what Cohen calls the '*material* relations of production' in capitalism. Since the owner-managed family enterprise was still the dominant form of capitalist economic enterprise in Britain at the time when Marx wrote *Capital* (the 'joint stock company' was just beginning to emerge), it seems very plausible that Marx is thinking of 'ownership' in this narrower sense. Relations of ownership without managerial control Cohen is therefore quite happy to treat as a purely 'legal' form and to consign to the superstructure with other legal relations.

So far, so good, and there is no doubt in my mind that the forces of production *do* have to be construed in the fairly narrow 'technological' way in which Cohen construes them if they are to be kept conceptually distinct from the relations which are, at some point, to become their 'fetters'. But Cohen runs into problems when he has to give a dynamic account of why the forces of production (= technology of production) should *develop* at all, let alone continuously.

Cohen's problem here is that, to keep his clear distinction between forces and relations of production intact, he has to find a reason purely 'internal' to the forces of production which keeps them developing within feudalism or capitalism until they become 'fettered' by the existing relations. At this point Cohen falls back on the argument that in a world of scarcity 'rational people' – by which he means scientists, technologists, engineers, and managers, or simply the skilled artisans and other workers using the technology of production at any given time – will (a) always seek to increase material productivity and thus (b) will always choose a more productive rather than a less productive technique.

There are a lot of points which could be made about this. Most notably it enshrines a kind of abstract rationalist principle such as is found in both classical and neo-classical economics. In addition it is an almost perfect example of generalizing a practice dominant in capitalist society into a 'trans-historical' tendency in human behaviour. This was precisely the kind of intellectual practice for which Marx explicitly condemned early nineteenth-century classical economists.[28]

But aside from this theoretical objection there is a straightforward historical problem with Cohen's argument here. For there have been long periods of human history, including western European history, when there has been continual and massive scarcity but no great improvements in technologies of production. Moreover, when we ask what factors have brought such periods to an end and initiated periods of more rapid technological development one immediately (and very unfortunately for Cohen's thesis) comes across such factors as changes in the social composition of governments and ruling classes, changes in education systems induced by religious and other influences, the effects of political and military conquest, changes in legal property rules (of land tenure for example), and migrations of skilled artisans and others induced by religious persecution or other reasons.[29]

All of these factors, and varied combinations of them, facilitated more rapid technological progress in this history of Europe (though of course none of these factors *are* technological improvements). Most of them involve changes in the 'social relations of production' (including 'superstructural' legal and political relations), changes which then 'reacted back' – to use Engels' phrase[30] – positively on production. So at this crucial point – in explaining how the 'forces of production' could have developed to the point where the 'relations of production' became their 'fetters' – Cohen's defence of the concepts and propositions of the 1859 Preface breaks down. Is there any other defence to be made?

I think there is, and once again it involves making use of the dynamic 'generational' perspective on history which I outlined earlier in the chapter. Now however this perspective has to be applied to thought itself, as well as to what is thought about (i.e. as well as to economic, social, or political trends or phenomena in history). From the perspective which I shall outline, the problem with nearly all interpretations of the 1859 Preface is that they treat its concepts as if they themselves had no history, and they also treat them as though they were applicable to all history.

Thus Cohen is at one with most other commentators on the Preface in trying to produce a conceptual distinction between forces and relations of production which is absolutely clear and unambiguous and which can be 'applied' to the analysis of *all* societies, capitalist or pre-capitalist.

I would argue however that the distinction between 'forces'

and 'relations' of production only becomes thinkable at a given moment in history. Broadly speaking this was the moment in history when (a) the technology of production had developed to a point at which it could deliver an historically unprecedented volume of products or commodities, and (b) when the development of technology had acquired an impulsion of its own derived from a specialist division of labour which made the development of that technology itself a specialized task – through scientific and technological research etc.

In *that* context, at *that* moment; in a society in which 'modern industry never looks upon ... the existing form of a process as final' and in which 'the technical basis of that industry is therefore revolutionary, while all earlier modes of production were essentially conservative',[31] *then*, and only *then*, is a separate concept of the 'forces of production' (and therefore the distinction between 'forces' and 'relations') either thinkable or useful.

Marx himself makes an essentially analogous point in the *Grundrisse*, with reference to the abstract concept 'labour' developed by Adam Smith. Commenting on Smith's intellectual achievement here, Marx says:

> it might seem that all that had been achieved thereby was to discover the abstract expression for the simplest and most ancient relation in which human beings – in whatever form of society – play the role of producers. This is correct in one respect. Not in another. Indifference towards any specific kind of labour presupposes a very developed totality of real kinds of labour, of which no single one is any longer predominant. As a result, the most general abstractions arise only in the midst of the richest possible concrete development, where one thing appears as common to many, to all. *Then it ceases to be thinkable in a particular form alone.*[32]

Marx is here asking, in regard to the categories used by the classical political economists (see chapters 3 and 4) *when* in history certain things become 'thinkable' and other things cease to be 'thinkable'. I am arguing here that the same historical perspective must be applied to Marx's own categories, in this case to the categories of the 1859 Preface. A separate concept of the 'forces of production' only becomes thinkable, I am arguing, at a particular point in the development of material production and of the social division of labour. Moreover, at the time when it becomes thinkable it is also descriptively and analytically useful. In this context we should reflect again on another passage from the Preface, already quoted:

> Therefore mankind always sets itself only such problems as it can solve; since, on closer examination it will always be found that the problem itself arises only when the material conditions necessary for its solution already exist or are at least in the process of formation.[33]

This passage is frequently quoted, but it is seldom noted that a 'problem' is a category of *thought*. That something is a 'problem' is not, as it were, a characteristic of *it*. It is a characterization of it in thought. Hence Marx is saying here that it is only possible to think of certain things as 'problems' at a given moment in history. For example, malnutrition and starvation are now categorizable as 'social problems' because it is known that the material conditions exist for their solution. Malnutrition and starvation existed in 1350 and they were human tragedies at that time too, but they were not social 'problems' since they were not 'soluble'. The same point could be made with reference to such 'problems' as disease, squalor, unwanted pregnancies, polluted water supplies, infertile men and women.[34] *When* in history do these 'problems' appear? Or, to put it another way, *when* are these things thinkable as 'problems'? Marx's answer is the right one – only *when* they are at least potentially soluble.

To return however to the 1859 Preface. If it is true that the distinction between 'forces' and 'relations' of production only becomes thinkable and useful at a given point in history, then two further points follow from this:

1. That the distinction will be that the *more* useful, the *more* human societies 'hive off' technological development as a separate task of a socially separate group of scientists, engineers, and industrial managers whose profession it is to maintain or accelerate the rate of technological change and the increase of productivity.[35] It follows that the distinction will be more analytically useful in say, the USA or USSR of 1987, than it was in the Britain of 1887. I think that this is broadly correct. The analytical distinction becomes truer as it were.

2. Conversely, the distinction is very likely to be useless, even misleading, if applied to pre-industrial or pre-capitalist societies. In particular, it is not likely to be very helpful in explaining the generally much slower pace of technological change in pre-capitalist societies. It is much more likely that in these societies

(we may take feudal Europe as the case most relevant to the 1859 Preface) the development of the forces of production takes place – in so far as it takes place at all – through a complex interactive process involving, as I have already said, factors which in the Preface would be categorized as 'superstructural' as well as those which it categorizes as part of the 'economic structure'. In other words, these distinctions are not helpful or useful ones for the analysis of technological change in pre-capitalist Europe.

In this respect however, both Marx and Engels were less intellectually self-aware than they might have been. For they both did tend to 'read back' these categorical distinctions of the 1859 Preface on to pre-capitalist modes of production in precisely the way Smith and the other classical economists had 'read back' *their* categories on to previous history and which Marx had criticized them so roundly for doing. In particular, they did so while attempting to explain technological changes within feudalism.

The net result of all this was that years later Engels had to try to 'back off' this position, and did so in a very confused way. He tried at one and the same time to maintain the 'base/ superstructure' distinctions of the Preface as universally applicable distinctions while *denying* or *qualifying* them. We see this clearly in his letter to Bloch of 1890 (quotation 10), and also in his letter to Schmidt of the same year.[36] But in both these cases Engels treats the distinctions between what he terms, 'the economic element' or 'the economic situation' and 'the various elements of the superstructure' as though they were timeless distinctions existing in some pure epistemological void. It is not surprising therefore if later Marxists have made the same mistake.

There is a further point about this. It should be stressed that the argument above denies the validity or usefulness of the distinction between 'forces' and 'relations' of production in any attempt to explain technological change in pre-capitalist societies, or, more generally, in any attempt to explain the transition between pre-capitalist modes or between feudalism and capitalism in terms of 'relations' 'fettering' 'forces'.

I have argued that these concepts cannot do the explanatory work required of them when put into propositions of this type. This does not mean of course that one could not use these terms in describing, for example, the economy of a feudal manor, or the life of the Visigoths. But it does mean that in such sentences and propositions these concepts *would not be doing the same kind of work* as they are doing in the 1859 Preface. They would not have the same kind of role, the same kind of function in those propositions. One almost wants to say that *they would not be the same concepts* if they were doing different descriptive or explanatory work in other sentences and propositions.

This is important, because of course it is perfectly possible for someone to reply to the argument above by pointing to the large amount of Marxist historical writing on (say) feudal Europe which does make use of the *words* 'forces' and 'relations' of production.

On the basis of the argument constructed above, one would say that some part of this literature may be perfectly 'all right' provided that these concepts are not being used in the '1859 Preface' manner. (If, for example, they were being used to explain why the distinction was not very useful in explaining technological change in feudal Europe!)

This in turn leads us to a more general point which will be developed at length later in this book. This is that the elucidation of Marxism – as of nearly any other body of thought – is best attained by paying attention to its *propositions* rather than its '*concepts*'. For many purposes concepts are in fact best regarded as tools or instruments which are only put to use, only given a specific meaning, in the context of sentences and propositions.

So, on this account a question like 'The distinction between forces and relations of production might not be of much use in explaining technological change under feudalism, but has the distinction in general got any validity?' would have to be regarded as very confused. I would hold it to be a confusing and confused question on the grounds that the concept of 'the distinction in general' has no meaning. *What* the distinction *is* in any specific case is shown by the explanatory or descriptive propositions in which it is being developed and it has no other meaning than that.

Indeed, if we look back to the 1859 Preface we see that 'the distinction' is developed there in the very same sentence in which it is being put to explanatory use. ('At a certain stage in their development, the material productive forces come in conflict with the existing relations of production – or what is but a legal expression . . .' etc.) So what is denied in the argument above is the general trans-historical validity of the distinction *as it is being put to use in those sentences of the Preface*. I am not of course denying the validity of *all* uses of this distinction or of this terminology. Indeed this would be, quite literally, a meaningless thing to do.

But even if this 'historical' interpretation of the concepts of the 1859 Preface is accepted, what sense does it make of the Preface's central prediction, that the transition from capitalism to socialism and communism will be possible only when the 'forces of production' become 'fettered' by capitalist 'relations of production', having developed as far as they can within those relations? I think that the only plausible sense which can be made of it is that:

(a) Socialism and communism require, as prerequisites, a certain level of material abundance. However, this, as I have said, is a statement of necessary conditions. It does not follow that if capitalism produces such abundance there will be a 'social revolution' to socialism and communism.[37]

(b) In a capitalist society, where technological development is a socially separate and specialist task within the division of labour, and such development is also fuelled by the need of enterprises to stay ahead in market competition, one is much more likely – than in pre-capitalist periods – to have a situation in which society has to adjust to technological change which is, as it were, thrust upon it.

In other words capitalist society is not one in which society (through state policy for example) controls technological change in the name of social goals. The rapid and wide-ranging social and occupational change currently being initiated within capitalism by the 'micro-electronic revolution' would be a perfect case in point.[38] Whether the 'adjustments' which capitalist society has to make in order to accommodate such change are so dramatic, so wide-ranging, and so conflictual as to constitute 'an epoch of social revolution' is a necessarily open question which perhaps only historians can answer with the benefit of hindsight.

CONCLUSION

I have suggested in this chapter that Marx's theory of history is certainly an 'evolutionary' theory, but only so far as a particular period of western European history – say the twelfth to the twentieth century – is concerned. It is not however a 'deterministic' theory, and it is not meant as a universal 'stage' theory of history. It is capable of accommodating a role for conscious intentional human activity and a role for a notion of structure or structures which constrain that activity. It can only do this however if it is understood in a 'dynamic' temporal or chronological way which focuses on social activity within a generational context, and the results ('circumstances') of that activity. When so understood, I have argued, it is an exciting and immensely sophisticated approach *both* to the history of society and to the history of thought.

However, it takes a great deal of reading, thought, and work to clarify Marx's theory of history and to present it in a way which brings out its greatest strengths. And while I believe that this account *does* represent the 'materialist theory of history' as Marx and Engels understood it, it must be said that both of them bear responsibility for having frequently presented the theory in ways which positively invite allegations of 'determinism' and 'teleology'.[39] This is mainly because both of them were heirs to, and users of, a great many eighteenth- and nineteenth-century metaphors about natural science and about human society which served them very ill in explaining their theory, but which they never transcended.

One of the worst of such metaphors is at the heart of the 1859 Preface. This is the metaphor, drawn from the world of physical construction, which likens society to a building with a 'base' or 'foundation' at the 'bottom' and a 'superstructure' at the 'top'. As a metaphor for society this has a great many limitations, limitations which are discussed at length in the seventh and final chapter of this book. However, one in particular stands out and can be mentioned briefly here.

There is nothing more static, more unmoving than a building, and the better it is built the more immobile it is. However, it is of the essence of human society and of human thought that they *move*. Social institutions, social groups, even whole societies, merge and mingle with each other through time. It is of the essence of the categories of human thought too that they are open, that they too merge, mingle, interpenetrate with each other, and are subject to continual reformulation and change. For this reason alone Marx's choice of the building metaphor for what has been regarded as his most authoritative methodological statement was very unfortunate. The positively mesmeric effect that this ponderously static metaphor continued to exert on the whole Marxist tradition after the death of its founders, was not only unfortunate, it was a disaster. For it has acted as a positive barrier to the comprehension and enjoyment of a theory whose aspiration at least was to be a continual celebration of movement.

CHAPTER 3

MARX'S ECONOMICS: A PRESENTATION

This chapter is concerned with Marx's economic theory as set out in his great book *Capital*, or to give it its full title in English, *Capital: A Critical Analysis of Capitalist Production*, which he himself regarded as his major scientific work, and on which he laboured for nearly twenty years between the late 1840s and the mid-1860s. Most of the concepts and propositions dealt with in this chapter derive from volume 1 of that three-volume work, the only one to be published in Marx's own lifetime (in 1867), and the only one to be published in the finished form which he intended. We shall however also consider some issues dealt with in volume 3 of *Capital*, notably the 'law of the tendency of the rate of profit to fall' which is developed in that volume.

As I noted in the previous chapter, Marx regarded *Capital* as a 'scientific' work designed to 'lay bare the economic law of motion of modern society', and indeed it was his intention to dedicate volume 2 of the book to Charles Darwin, but the latter (perhaps understandably given the notoriety of his own work!) cordially refused the honour.[1] Precisely because both Marx and Engels regarded *Capital* as a work of 'science', it is necessary, before coming to the content of the book itself, to say a little more about their conceptions of science and of the role of the scientist in society.

MARX AS SCIENTIST

In his Preface to the first edition of *Capital*, Marx claimed that he regarded 'the evolution of the economic formation of society'[2] as 'a process of natural history', and as we can see from his attempt to dedicate part of his book to Darwin, Marx did see clear parallels between his work and the theory of biological evolution set out in *On the Origin of Species* (1859). Engels, in his speech at Marx's funeral made the comparison explicit:

> Just as Darwin discovered the law of development of organic nature, so Marx discovered the law of development of human history: the simple fact, hitherto concealed by an overgrowth of ideology, that mankind must first of all eat, drink, have shelter and clothing, before it can pursue politics, science, art, religion etc.; that therefore the production of the immediate material means of subsistence and consequently the degree of economic development attained by a given people or during a given epoch, form the foundation upon which the state institutions, the legal conceptions, the ideas on art, and even on religion, of the people concerned have been evolved, and in the light of which they must, therefore, be explained, instead of *vice versa* as had hitherto been the case.

> But that is not all. Marx also discovered the special law of motion governing the present day capitalist mode of production and the bourgeois society that this mode of production has created. The discovery of surplus value suddenly threw light on the problem, in trying to solve which all previous investigations ... had been groping in the dark.[3]

None of this means that Marx (or Engels for that matter) was a 'social Darwinist'. Neither of them belonged to that large class of nineteenth-century thinkers who, after the appearance of Darwin's work, attempted to apply his ideas of 'the struggle for existence' and 'the survival of the fittest' to human individuals, societies or even races.[4] On the contrary, their view seems to have been that Darwin's theory was – to quote Engels – 'simply a transference from society to living nature of Hobbes' doctrine of "a war of each against all" and of the bourgeois economic doctrine of competition together with Malthus' theory of population.'[5]

In other words they thought that Darwin had taken dominant 'bourgeois' ideas about the nature of human society (particularly Malthus' doctrine of population)[6] and then applied them to animal and plant life. Since for Marx and Engels even the best 'bourgeois' economic and social theory was true – in so far as it was true at all – only of 'bourgeois' (i.e. capitalist) society, and was thus an historical product which would disappear with the society which it theorized, they were of course very dismissive of attempts to apply Darwin's theory *back again* to human society as some kind of universal truth, applicable to all human societies in all times and places.

In so far then as Marx did see any parallels between his own work and that of Darwin they were of a far looser and more general sort, and are perhaps best captured in the Preface to the 1873 edition of *Capital* (see pp. 41–2). Here Marx quotes with approval the idea that 'social organisms differ among themselves as fundamentally as plants and animals' and that 'economic life offers us a phenomenon analogous to the history of evolution in other branches of biology' (I, 18).

In other words Marx saw societies succeeding one another in history in a broadly evolutionary way, as did species of plants and animals in Darwin. He also thought that there was something common to *all* such human societies – what he called 'the mode of production of material life', that is the necessity for human beings to work with and upon nature to secure their basic subsistence and that the particular 'mode' (form or manner) in which this was done was an important influence on the type of society which emerged at each given point of human evolution.

But, as Engels also noted, precisely because human beings '*produce*' as a conscious process while 'animals at most *collect*' it is impossible simply to transfer laws of animal societies to human societies.[7] Thus the 1873 Preface notes that the 'laws' which govern human societies are not only quite different from those which govern animal life (i.e. have nothing to do with 'the struggle for existence' or 'the survival of the fittest' etc.), they are also different from one human society to another. This was so precisely because, for Marx and Engels, a primary way of distinguishing such societies is through the different forms of production which are dominant within them.

Marx also manifested a distinct liking for the use of biological analogies and metaphors in describing and analysing human societies (see page 46) and an analysis of such analogies and metaphors, their strengths and limitations, would be a fascinating exercise in itself.[8] But this tendency was commonplace among nineteenth-century writers of many ideological and theoretical persuasions, and it is unclear how far it reflects the influence of Darwin specifically.

However, what does emerge from all this, is that neither Marx nor Engels made any strong or qualitative distinction between their own enterprise and that of natural science. On the contrary, for them, 'political economy' at least *was* a science on a par with any other natural science. This is shown in their very willingness to compare it with such sciences – and especially with biology – even if that comparison was meant to bring out differences as well as similarities.

Thus, neither Marx nor Engels would have belonged to that school of thought which wishes to make a *qualitative* distinction between the methods and subject of 'social science' and those of 'natural science'. For them, the study of human society, or at least of the economic 'laws' of human society, was a part of natural science,[9] though one having its own methods, theories, and tools of analysis.

This means of course, as I have already noted, that Marx would have held the 'results' of this 'scientific investigation' of capitalist society carried out in *Capital* to be true, 'absolutely' or 'scientifically' true, true whoever believed them, and indeed true if nobody believed them. Marx would have been insulted if it had been suggested to him that *Capital* was true from a working-class point of view or from the standpoint of the proletariat, but not from the standpoint of the bourgeoisie – just as insulted as Darwin would have been if told that his theory of evolution was true from the point of view of biology but not from the point of view of religion.

So Marx's view of science was *not* a relativistic one in this sense. He believed that there were criteria to establish the truth or falsehood of any scientific theory (such criteria as conceptual rigour and exactitude, logical coherence of propositions, and empirical verification or falsification) and that his theory should be judged true or false by such scientific criteria.

This does not mean however (as I suggested in chapter 1) that he thought such formal criteria were enough to determine a theory's significance. A scientific theory was only significant if its being true or false made some difference to something outside itself (i.e. if it had implications for other human practices or activities) and this view derived from Marx's 'philosophy of praxis' as we have seen. But it does mean that for Marx the claim to be a scientist was a proud claim and *not* a claim that conflicted in any way with his claim to be a revolutionary. Again Engels made the point explicit at Marx's graveside:

Science was for Marx a historically dynamic revolutionary force. However great the joy with which he welcomed a new discovery in some theoretical science whose practical application perhaps ... was as yet quite impossible to envisage, he experienced quite another kind of joy when the discovery involved immediate revolutionary changes in industry, and in historical development in general. ...

For Marx was before all else a revolutionary. His real mission in life was to contribute, in one way or another, to the overthrow of capitalist society and of the state institutions which it had brought into being, to contribute to the liberation of the modern proletariat, which he was the first to make conscious of its own position and its needs, conscious of the conditions of its emancipation.[10]

I shall consider how it was possible for Engels to equate these two, apparently quite different, notions of 'revolutionary' change – 'scientific' or 'technological' revolutions and 'social' revolutions – when I come to discuss Marx's conception of revolution in chapter 5. But here I want simply to note that both Marx and Engels could and did link 'science' and 'revolution' so closely and unselfconsciously in their view of the world because they shared another view, a view which a twentieth-century reader may well find problematic.

For neither Marx nor Engels had the slightest doubt that *natural science was a 'progressive', a 'liberating', a 'life-improving' force for humankind*. They were certain that science had made human life better and that it would go on making human life better, and in this of course they were quintessentially men of their time. They were nineteenth-century men, Victorian men, with a Victorian faith in the 'progressive' nature of science, and of industry and industrial production. Furthermore, seeing themselves as 'scientists' calling for further revolutionary changes in society, changes which were to be based on Marx's scientific 'discoveries' in political economy, they also saw themselves as contributing to the progress, the enhancement, of the human condition.

If one were to try and sum up their point of view in a sentence, it would be that developments in natural science and the application of such developments to industrial and agricultural production had created, for the first time in the world's history, the *potential* for an end to material want and suffering among human beings (i.e. for an end to suffering deriving from hunger, cold, disease, etc.).

But Marx and Engels also thought that the 'social relations' of capitalist society – the highly unequal form of society in which those scientific inventions were currently being applied to production – guaranteed that this potentiality of science for general liberation would never be realized. Their task and role as 'scientists' therefore was to point this out, explain why it was so (why potentiality would never become actuality under capitalism) and to engage in a revolutionary political practice in order to bring about the overthrow or fundamental restructuring of capitalist society.

Now where a modern late twentieth-century reader may find this conception very problematic is in its uncritical acceptance of the 'liberating', 'life-enhancing' nature of natural science. We, unlike Marx and Engels, live in the shadow of nuclear warfare, of bacteriological warfare, of 'star wars' and Sellafield leaks, and consequently we are much less sure of the 'positive' 'liberating' nature of natural science. For Marx and Engels, natural science was a positive force but capitalist society prevented the full realization of that positive potential. A modern reader may well think that this is an inadequate view, that *in itself* natural science is neither a positive nor a negative force, but that it may be either, depending upon the use to which it is put, and that *that* (the use made of natural scientific theories and their applications) is socially and politically determined.

But at any rate, Marx considered himself a scientist, on a par with other natural scientists of his day. He believed that the economic theories – of exploitation and capital accumulation – put forward in *Capital* were scientifically true, that there were non-relativistic criteria which could be applied to determine this, and that the application of such criteria (of logical coherence, conceptual exactitude, empirical validity) would verify that truth. In the rest of this chapter, and more particularly in the next chapter, I shall take him at his word.

MARX'S ECONOMIC THEORY

There are two preliminary points to be made as an introduction to Marx's economic theory.
1. Marx's theory is heavily influenced by the tradition of classical political economy developed in Britain in the late eighteenth and early nineteenth centuries, and especially by the ideas of David

Ricardo. This is true even though Marx's theory was also meant as a critique of that tradition.

2. Marx's theory is a 'macro-economic theory' to use the modern terminology, that is, it is a theory which deals in an abstract way with a whole economy, not with the constituent units of it. *Capital* itself can sometimes be a bit misleading in this respect, in that sometimes Marx talks about 'the capitalist' and 'the worker' as 'abstract' or 'average' individuals who are meant to typify or represent 'the capitalist class' as a whole and 'the working class' as a whole.

Similarly, Marx's concept of 'constant capital' refers to the whole stock of fixed capital (plant, machinery, raw materials) of an entire capitalist economy, and his concepts of 'variable capital' and of 'surplus value' refer to the total of wages and the total of profits in an entire capitalist economy. Or at least this is true of volume 1 of *Capital*, the volume with which I shall mainly be concerned in this chapter.

Thus, in reading this chapter and the next one, readers should try and concentrate on a picture of a capitalist economy and society *conceived as a whole*, rather than thinking of a single firm or a single group of workers. If thinking of real world analogies helps you to grasp what follows, it is probably best, in the late twentieth century, to think of Marx as analysing the economies of North America, western Europe and Japan conceived as a single unit, as *one* capitalist economy ('Ameujap' perhaps!), not as separate entities.

The labour theory of value

The main reason why Marx must be seen as an economic theorist deeply influenced by the tradition of classical political economy is that he accepts, and indeed his whole economic theory is founded on, the so-called 'labour theory of value' which was, in itself, one of the central ideas of early nineteenth-century political economy from Adam Smith's *Wealth of Nations* of 1776 to John Stuart Mill's *Principles of Political Economy* of 1848.

In fact historians of economic thought usually distinguish classical political economy from its 'neo-classical' or 'marginalist' successor (or modern non-Marxist economics) by stating that classical economics accepted the labour theory of value, while neo-classical economics abandoned or overthrew it.[11]

The origins of the labour theory of value are much disputed.

Some historians of economic thought trace it back to the seventeenth century, some even to the medieval period.[12] But it is generally agreed that the first serious attempt to systematize the idea and to make it the foundation of a modern economic theory was made in Adam Smith's great book *Wealth of Nations* of 1776. It was then further systematized, with some of Smith's logical inconsistencies removed, by the economic theorist David Ricardo in his *Principles of Political Economy and Taxation* of 1817.[13] It was Ricardo's version of the labour theory of value which Marx essentially adopted lock, stock, and barrel, although he made one development of it (the theory of 'surplus value') which Marx believed to be very important, and which Engels hailed, as we have seen, as Marx's 'great discovery' in political economy.

The major economic postulates of Marx's *Capital*

There appears below a list of nine 'economic postulates', as I have called them, of which the economic theory set out in *Capital* is composed.

I The amount of *socially necessary abstract labour* time (SNAL) embodied in a commodity determines the *magnitude* of the value of that commodity.

II All commodities exchange, on average, at their values.

III Labour power is a commodity.

IV The magnitude of the value of the commodity labour power is determined in the same way as that of any other commodity.

V However, labour power is the *only* commodity capable of producing a value greater than itself. This extra value is called *surplus value*.

VI Profit is therefore only the monetary form of excess or unpaid labour time. Profit is the monetary form of surplus value.

VII Surplus value takes two forms, '*Absolute*' surplus value produced by lengthening the working day and '*Relative*' surplus value produced by increasing the productivity of each hour of living labour by improved machinery.

VIII Accumulation through relative surplus value tends to lower the *value* of all commodities while increasing the *mass* of commodities.

IX Increase of relative surplus value can only occur continually by increasing the mass of constant capital ('C') faster than the mass of variable capital and surplus value ('V' + 'S'). Therefore the *value rate of profit* tends to decline as capitalism advances technologically.

In other words in *Capital*, volumes I and III, Marx offers these nine analytical propositions about a capitalist economy. For propositions I and II he takes no credit, as they come directly from Ricardo.[14] Propositions III to IX are his own, and III to VI in particular constitute his 'discovery' in political economy, the 'theory of surplus value'. This, Marx claims, explains how profit is generated in an economy in which all commodities exchange at their values.

I will now take each of these nine postulates in turn and try to clarify what Marx meant by each one. The truth or falsity of each one will be considered in chapter 4.

Postulate I
'The amount of socially necessary abstract labour time – or "SNAL" for short – embodied in a commodity determines the magnitude of its value'.

We should note here that:
1. The amount of SNAL in a commodity determines the *magnitude* of a commodity's value. So in Marx's terminology we should say that the value of a table is so many hours' SNAL, of a house so many months' SNAL, of a space shuttle so many years' SNAL, etc. In other words, the more SNAL is embodied in a commodity the greater its 'value' (in Marx's sense) and the less SNAL is embodied in it the less its 'value' in this sense.

However, although the amount of SNAL which it takes to make a commodity determines the magnitude of a commodity's value – i.e. determines how much value it has – this is not what makes it valuable. For Marx, 'commodities' (which are products of human labour which are made *in order to be sold or exchanged*) are valuable to human beings for two reasons.

Firstly, and most importantly, they are valuable because they are useful. Bread is useful because it stops me being hungry and milk is useful because it stops me being thirsty. Tables are useful to eat off and write on. Space shuttles are useful for spying on other countries, conducting scientific experiments, and monitoring the weather, etc. Marx calls this the *use value* of commodities (I, 36–41).

Commodities are also valuable to human beings however because they can be exchanged for other commodities. This is the *exchange value* of commodities, in Marx's terminology, and is particularly important in a market economy with a highly developed division of labour. For in such societies people themselves produce only a small part of the products, or 'use values' (food, clothing, shelter, etc.), which they need in order to live. Rather what they do is to produce one product, or even a small part of one product (e.g. a worker in a car factory) and then, by means of money, they exchange what they produce for the other commodities which they need.

So then for Marx, a commodity, any commodity, can be looked at or thought about in two ways. Firstly, it is a useful product, it has a use for human beings, fulfils a human need. This is its *use value*. Secondly, it can be exchanged for other products because it is useful to people other than the people who make it. This is its *exchange value*.

But the *magnitude* of this exchange value (i.e. the *amount* of any other commodity which can be obtained in exchange for it) is determined by the amount of SNAL embodied in the commodity. Marx refers to this – the *magnitude* of the exchange value of any commodity – as simply its *'value'* (I, 35–83). So that, for example, a table with six hours of SNAL embodied in it, will, in Marx's model, exchange for one lamp with six hours' SNAL similarly embodied, or for two video cassettes with three hours each embodied, or for six cups with one hour each embodied etc. And the 'value' of the table is six hours' SNAL, the 'value' of each video cassette is three hours' SNAL, and the 'value' of each cup is one hour's SNAL, etc.

It is especially important in what follows that the reader thinks about 'value' only in Marx's sense ('value' as so many hours, days, weeks, etc. of SNAL, i.e. value as a unit of *time*). Today, when we talk of 'value', even in economic terms, we usually mean *price*, money price. 'Last year Japan exported video recorders to the value of £500 million' or 'Is that diamond ring valuable? Yes, it is insured for £25,000' etc. This is not what Marx means, and it is not what is meant by 'value' in the 'labour theory of value' in general. In that theory value and price are very clearly distinguished from one another. So, to understand what follows the reader must try and keep that distinction clear and not let 'value as price' enter his or her head at all. To understand all of what follows you must understand 'value' as a unit of time, of labour time.

2. Marx's first postulate says however not that 'the amount of labour time embodied in a commodity determines its value' but that 'the amount of *socially necessary, abstract* labour time' so embodied determines that value. By 'socially necessary' Marx means here the amount of labour time, *of average productivity* in the economy as a whole (I, 39).

Thus, for example, imagine an economy in which there are twenty firms producing ball-bearings. Seventeen of these firms use machines which can produce 2,000 or more ball-bearings every hour. In three of the firms, however, ball-bearings are made by hand, and only two are made every hour. They are beautiful however, each one lovingly crafted by really skilled artisans and each one made in slightly different metal alloys, so that they all have a slightly different texture and colour. The only problem is that while the ball-bearings from the other seventeen factories cost anything from 6p to 9p each, these hand-made ball-bearings cost £10 each, and they do not wear any better. For Marx, the labour time expended by these loving craftsmen, though wonderfully skilled, *is not part of the 'socially necessary' labour time* in the ball-bearing sector. Why? Because these ball-bearings do not sell. They are not, as it were, viable *commodities* as ball-bearings, and so, in a sense, the labour time expended upon them is wasted. And the way in which this wasted, below average productivity, 'socially unnecessary' labour time will take its toll of course, is that these three firms will go out of business if they do not modernize rather quickly, which means, if they do not ensure that their workers are equipped with machines of average productivity or above.

By 'abstract' labour (in socially necessary abstract labour) Marx means labour time of an average type and of an 'average' level of skill and intensity. In other words, for the purpose of using labour time as a measure of value, Marx is making abstraction from the 'real world' facts about labour, i.e. that there are millions of different types of labour (weaving, boring, cutting, digging, polishing, painting, etc.) and different *levels of skill and intensity* with which any particular type of labour is undertaken. There are skilled and less skilled carpenters, skilled and less skilled computer programmers, strong miners and less strong miners, lazy fitters and zealous fitters, etc. Marx is 'abstracting' from these differences by assuming 'average' levels of skill and intensity of labour for the economy as a whole, and also by 'abstracting' from different types of labour, and treating all labour time as of one 'average' type (I, 44).

Doing this – 'abstracting' labour time in this way – gives rise to a number of problems with Marx's economic theory which we shall examine in the next chapter. But for the moment, the reader is merely required to be clear about what 'socially necessary abstract labour' means.

Postulate II
'All commodities exchange, on average, at their values.'

In principle, the meaning of this postulate is simple enough. In the capitalist economy as a whole (as Marx conceives it in volume 1 of *Capital*) exchange is so arranged that all commodities exchange, *on average*, at their values. Thus, as we noted before, a commodity with 4 hours' SNAL embodied in it will, on average, exchange for another commodity with 4 hours' SNAL (or for 2 commodities with 2 hours' SNAL, or for 8 commodities with a half hour's SNAL etc.). And if, in this economy, exchange of commodities occurs by means of money – which is what Marx assumes – then the *prices* of the commodities will be such that the price of the '4 hours' SNAL' commodity will be £4 (or 40p or 4p) and the price of the '2 hours' SNAL' commodity will be £2 (or 20p or 2p). In other words, *the relative prices of commodities will reflect their values* (in SNAL).

Now Marx does not ignore the effects of 'supply and demand' on relative prices. He readily admits that if the demand for a commodity rises sharply for some reason, or if its supply suddenly falls, then its price may rise 'above its value'. Conversely, if demand for it suddenly falls, or the supply of it increases sharply, then its price may fall 'below its value'.

But Marx argues, none the less, that for all commodities taken together and looked at over the long run, these fluctuations of prices produced by supply and demand will be seen to be fluctuations around an 'average' or 'mean' price and *the long-run movement of these mean or average prices will be determined by the movement of values*. In other words, if, in the long run, the amount of SNAL embodied in a commodity falls, then its long-run average price will fall. Conversely, if, in the long run, the amount of SNAL embodied in a commodity rises, then its long-run average price will rise (I, 94–103, 158–66; III, 173–99). Marx in fact argued that there were factors at work in a capitalist economy which meant that the amount of SNAL embodied in all commodities tended to fall over time. This implies of course that the prices of all commodities would fall as well.

It may not be very clear to you what it means to say that the prices of all commodities would fall (as against the relative price of one commodity falling *vis-à-vis* another, or the price of some commodities falling *vis-à-vis* some others), and we will discuss this later in this chapter. For the moment figure 3.1 attempts to summarize Marx's argument on the relationship between long-run average prices and values.

Figure 3.1 Long-run average prices and values of two commodities

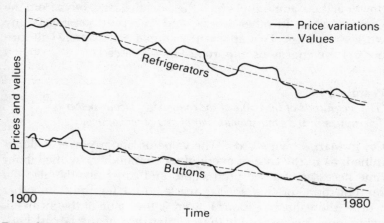

Postulate III

'Labour power is a commodity.'

Marx makes great play of the distinction between 'labour' and 'labour power' in his theory. According to volume 1 of *Capital* when 'free' wage workers (i.e. workers who are legally 'free' people, not slaves or serfs, and who have been 'freed' from means of production of their own, i.e. they own no land, no machines, or raw materials of their own, by which they may provide their own subsistence) contract with a capitalist or a capitalist firm, they contract to sell their labour *power*, not their labour. If the worker sold his or her labour, then he or she would, according to Marx, be a slave (I, 167–76). They would be selling themselves.

In a capitalist economy however, this does not happen. Rather, workers sell their *abilities*, their strength, their skill, their intelligence, for a set period of time – so many hours in the day or days in the week, etc. For the rest of the time – during their leisure time – these abilities 'return' to the worker, as it were. He or she may use them in whatever way they wish in the time when they are *not* the property of the capitalist employer. In fact Marx defines labour power as: 'the aggregate of those mental and physical capabilities existing in a human being which he [*sic*] exercises whenever he produces a use value of any description' (I, 167). The point, therefore, for Marx, is that *labour power becomes a commodity under capitalism*. Labour power is the only property which the free wage worker possesses. It is all that he or she has to sell in order to obtain a subsistence. And labour power is the commodity which the capitalist class buys from the working class. In other words, and to repeat, capitalists buy workers' *abilities*. This apparently simple observation will turn out to have enormous importance as we proceed.

Postulate IV
'The magnitude of the value of the commodity labour power is determined in the same way as that of any other commodity.'

Or, in Marx's own words: 'The value of labour power is determined, as in the case of every other commodity, by the labour time necessary for the production, and consequently, also the reproduction, of this special article.' And he adds: 'In other words, the value of Labour Power, is the value of the means of subsistence necessary for the maintenance of the labourer' (I. 170–1). Now, if we add to this postulate, the postulate that all commodities exchange, on average, at their values, then the commodity labour power must also exchange, or be bought, at its value.

In other words, assume that it takes twenty hours' SNAL to produce, at an average level of productivity, the subsistence goods required to maintain an average worker for a week. It would then follow that the week's wages of that worker, paid in money, must allow him/her to purchase subsistence or wage goods to the value of twenty hours' SNAL. To put it another way, however much SNAL it takes to produce, and reproduce, the labour power of the working class, as a whole, for one year, the capitalist class as a whole, in order to purchase that labour power at its value, must pay a total of money wages in that year which will allow the product of that amount of SNAL to be purchased. Or to put it in yet another form of words, money wages must, on average, equal 'the value of labour power'. And Marx is very insistent upon this. In his theory the capitalist class *does not cheat* the working class. It pays the working class the full 'value' (in Marx's sense) of the commodity – labour power – which it purchases from the working class (I, 185–98).

But for Marx, this only produces a puzzle. It was a puzzle which he believed was found in Ricardo's work, but which Ricardo never solved. If the amount of SNAL embodied determines the value of *all* commodities, and *all* commodities exchange at their values, including labour, then how can there be any profit for the capitalist class to appropriate?[15] Marx resolves this puzzle (a) by insisting that the capitalist class buys labour *power* not labour, and (b) by bringing in his fifth postulate.

Postulate V

'Labour Power is the only *commodity capable of producing a value greater than itself. This extra value is called* surplus value'.

In other words, when the capitalist class pays the working class a money weekly wage equal to the value of the working class's labour power for that week, there is no cheating. The working class's only commodity is bought at its value. But whereas the 'average' capitalist (representing the whole class) has bought the 'average' worker's labour power, worth twenty hours' SNAL, at its full value, he or she can then *use* that labour power, set it to work, for a period much longer than twenty hours per week. The capitalist can set the worker, can use his/her labour power, for forty or fifty hours per week. And provided that that labour time is of average level of productivity or above, then *all* that additional labour time will produce an additional value – a 'surplus value' in Marx's terms – which is the source of the profit of the capitalist class. (I, 193–8).[16]

Or to put it another way – in the 'macro' way in which Marx intended – the capitalist class as a whole, obtains from the working class as a whole, in any given period of time (one year, ten years, a hundred years) a product in excess of the product required by that working class for its subsistence. The amount and type of that subsistence product varies through time. At one time it barely included adequate clothing or shelter, now it includes fitted carpets, colour televisions, saloon cars, and Spanish holidays. But at any given time it is what it is, and for it to be 'worthwhile' for the capitalist class to employ the working class, the working class *must* produce a physical mass of products in excess of the 'subsistence' product. When this excess physical product (the product of excess or surplus labour is sold, the capitalist class acquires its monetary profit, a profit which it uses to reinvest in plant, equipment, and raw materials, and to raise its own standard of living (through dividends, salary rises etc.). This then brings Marx to his sixth postulate, his 'revolutionary' conclusion from the previous five.

Postulate VI
'Profit is therefore only the monetary form of excess or unpaid labour time. Profit is the monetary form of surplus value.'

This then, is the so-called 'theory of surplus value' which both Marx and Engels believed to have been Marx's great 'discovery' in political economy. It was a great discovery, they believed, not only because it solved the puzzle which Ricardo had failed to solve (how can there be profit in an economy in which all commodities, including labour, exchange at their labour values?) but also because it appeared to demonstrate scientifically that, in a capitalist economy, *capital accumulation – accumulation of profit and reinvestment by the capitalist class – could only occur through the exploitation of the working class* (where 'exploitation' is defined as 'the appropriation of surplus value, expropriated from the working class').

However, to complete his theory, Marx had to link his theory of surplus value to a theory of capital accumulation, and this he does by means of postulates VII, VIII, and IX.

Postulate VII
'Surplus value takes two forms, "Absolute" surplus value produced by lengthening the working day, and "Relative" surplus value produced by increasing the productivity of each hour of living labour by improved machinery.'

To understand postulate VII however, we need to master Marx's basic macro-economic concepts, i.e. the concepts by which he describes an entire capitalist economy. These are:

1. *'Constant capital'*, or 'C' in Marx's notation. This is defined by Marx as 'that part of capital which . . . does not, in the process of production, undergo any quantitative alteration of value', that is, 'means of production, raw auxiliary material and the instruments of labour' (I, 209).

2. *'Variable capital'*, or 'V' in Marx's notation. This is defined by Marx as:

> that part of capital, represented by labour power [which] . . . does, in the process of production, undergo an alteration of value. It both represents the equivalent of its own value, and also produces an excess, a surplus value which . . . may be more or less according to circumstances. This part of capital is continually being transformed from a constant into a variable magnitude. I therefore call it . . . *variable capital* (I, 209).

3. *'Surplus value'*, or 'S' in Marx's notation. This is defined by Marx as 'the difference between the value of the product and the value . . . of the means of production and . . . labour power' (I, 208). It will be noted from Marx's definition of variable capital that, as postulate five states, surplus value is produced *entirely* by, or from, V *and not from* C.

Putting all this in other words; C is the value – measured in SNAL – of the total of 'means of production' (plant, machinery, raw materials) in an economy at any one time. V is the value – measured in SNAL – of the total of labour power (i.e. the labour power of the entire working class) in an economy at the same period of time. S is the value of the unpaid or excess labour of that class, also measured in hours, days or weeks of SNAL. Thus, in Marx's notation, the total production or output in a capitalist economy at any one time can be represented by the formula:

$$C + V + S$$

From this general macro-economic formula Marx derives two others. These are:

(i) $$\frac{S}{V}$$

This is the *'rate of surplus value'* or the 'rate of exploitation' of the working class as a whole. In other words

$\frac{S}{V}$ is the amount of surplus value being produced by the entire working class expressed as a proportion of the value of its total labour power.

(ii) $$\frac{S}{C+V}$$

This is the *rate of profit* in the entire economy in value terms. In other words, $\frac{S}{C+V}$ is the amount of surplus value being produced by the entire working class expressed as a proportion of the total value of constant and variable capital – or total capital – in the economy at any one period of time (I, 210–20).

But what is important for Marx is not these static macro-economic relationships as such, but the *dynamic* way in which they interrelate through time to allow for the accumulation of capital and the expansion of the capitalist system. Broadly speaking, the idea is that the capitalist class makes profit by appropriating surplus value – excess or unpaid labour time – from the working class. This surplus labour time is embodied in a mass of commodities which the capitalist class sells for money and this money constitutes its profit.

With its profits the capitalist class can do three things:
1. It can replace the existing stock of constant capital – or C – by replacing worn-out plant and machinery and buying in raw materials for a new round of production 'next year'; and/or
2. it can raise its own standard of living (through paying dividends to shareholders etc.); and/or
3. It can invest in *additional* constant capital and raw materials, and hire *additional* labour power to expand production 'next year'.

If the capitalist class only does (1), or (1) and (2), with its profits, then the system does not expand. It will simply be the same size, will produce the same amount of commodities 'next year' as it did 'this year'. But if the capitalist class does (1) and (3) or (1), (2) and (3) with its profits then the system will be bigger next year than it is this year. There will be 'expanded reproduction' of the system in Marx's terms (I, 566–78 and 579–88).

We can now examine how absolute and relative surplus value fits into all this.

ABSOLUTE AND RELATIVE SURPLUS VALUE

To best understand these concepts, it will be helpful to take two simple numerical examples.

Absolute surplus value

Suppose that on an average working day in 1840, the situation was as follows:

$$C \qquad + \qquad V \qquad + \qquad S$$

(5 hours' SNAL producing 100 commodities)   (5 hours' SNAL producing 100 commodities)   (2 hours' SNAL producing 40 commodities)

In other words there is a twelve–hour working day throughout the year. This being so then:

$$\frac{S}{V} = \frac{2}{5} = 40\% \text{ (the 'rate of surplus value' = 40\%)}$$

and

$$\frac{S}{C+V} = \frac{2}{5+5} = \frac{2}{10} = 20\% \text{ (the 'value rate of profit' = 20\%)}$$

Total daily production, or total daily output in this economy is 240 commodities produced by 12 hours' SNAL, which means that 20 commodities are produced every hour. Thus there is, on average, 3 minutes of SNAL embodied in each commodity, i.e. in 1840 the *value* of the average commodity is 3 minutes' SNAL.

Imagine now that a year later, in 1841, the working day is increased to fourteen hours. Then the situation would be

$$C \qquad + \qquad V \qquad + \qquad S$$

(5 hours' SNAL producing 100 commodities)   (5 hours' SNAL producing 100 commodities)   (2 hours' SNAL producing 40 commodities)

$$\frac{S}{V} \text{ is now } \frac{4}{5} = 80\% \text{ (the 'rate of surplus value' is now 80\%)}$$

and

$$\frac{S}{C+V} \text{ is now } \frac{4}{5+5} = \frac{4}{10} = 40\% \text{ (the 'value rate of profit' is now 40\%)}$$

Since the same number of commodities are produced every hour as in 1840 (20), with the addition of two hours to the working day, total daily output rises from 240 commodities to 280 commodities. But because the same number of commodities (100) are required to replace constant capital and the same number of commodities (100) are required to replace the value of labour power (variable capital), all of the additional 40 commodities accrue to the capitalist class as surplus value. Thus, both the rate of surplus value and the rate of profit measured in value terms rise. In fact both are doubled.

This is the process which Marx called raising absolute surplus value, that is raising the mass and rate of surplus value *by lengthening the working day* and keeping both the amount of capital investment and the wage level unchanged. This was a common way of raising profits in the early nineteenth-century British economy (I, 406–10 and 508–30).

But Marx noted that as capitalism developed, this absolute method of raising surplus value tended to be replaced by another – the relative – method. I will illustrate this method by a second example.

Relative surplus value

We will now move forward in time. It is now 1920. At that date, as a result of both trade union pressure and government legislation the working day has been reduced to ten hours. Now if productivity had remained the same as in 1840, the situation would be:

$$C \quad + \quad V \quad + \quad S$$

C	V	S
(5 hours' SNAL producing 100 commodities)	(5 hours' SNAL producing 100 commodities)	(0 hours' SNAL producing 0 commodities)

It is hardly necessary to work out $\frac{S}{V}$ or $\frac{S}{C+V}$ in these circumstances! They would both equal zero, that is there would be no surplus value and there would be no profits in value terms. However, Marx noted that when the working day was reduced, this was not what happened. Rather, capitalists typically reacted to such a reduction by *equipping their workers with more productive machinery* (I, 412–27). Suppose that this has occurred over the whole economy, so that on average, using these improved machines, each worker can produce twice as many commodities in each hour in 1920 than in 1840. Then the situation would be as follows:

$$C \qquad + \qquad V \qquad + \qquad S$$

| (4 hours' SNAL producing 160 commodities) | (4 hours' SNAL producing 160 commodities) | (2 hours' SNAL producing 80 commodities) |

In other words, because productivity has doubled and 1 hour of SNAL = 40 commodities, not 20 commodities as in 1840, then in the average 10-hour working day 400 commodities can be produced – as against the 240 commodities in 1840 or the 280 commodities in 1841. This is despite a reduction of 4 hours in the working day from the 1841 level and of 2 hours from the 1840 level.

However, since there is more constant capital – more plant and machinery – more commodities (160 as against 100) are required to replace worn out C. And since both the labour force and wages have increased, more commodities (160 as against 100) are required to replace the value of labour power or V. Thus 8 out of the 10 hours worked are required to replace C + V. But this still leaves 2 hours of SNAL – or 80 commodities – As S or surplus value.

$$\frac{S}{V} \text{ is now } \frac{2}{4} = \frac{1}{2} \text{ (i.e. the rate of surplus value is 50\%)}$$

and

$$\frac{S}{C+V} \text{ is now } \frac{2}{4+4} = \frac{2}{8} = \frac{1}{4} \text{ (i.e. the value rate of profit is 25\%)}$$

Thus, by increasing the productivity of labour power with improved machinery, the capitalist class has actually managed to increase the rate of surplus value from its 1840 level (50 per cent as against 40 per cent). It is true that the capitalists are not doing so well as in the 'super–exploitative' days of 1841, but they are doing better than in 1840 despite a two–hour fall in the working day from the 1840 level.

This is what Marx calls raising or maintaining the mass and rate of surplus value by the *relative* method. And as I have already noted, Marx believed that *as capitalism developed, relative surplus value tended to replace absolute surplus value as the primary mechanism by which the capitalist class appropriated surplus value from the working class* (I, 409–27). And of course if the working day falls continually in the real world – it has of course fallen well below ten hours since 1920 – then this would have to be the case. For otherwise either the capitalist class would make no profit at all, or both capital investment and wages would fall as the working day was reduced. And we know that in the real world – or in 'Ameujap' at any rate – neither of these things has happened.

However, increasing surplus value by the relative method – by increasing the productivity of each hour (or day or week) of SNAL through improved machinery – has further consequences. These consequences bring us to Marx's next postulate.

Postulate VIII
'*Accumulation through relative surplus value tends to lower the* value *of all commodities while increasing the* mass *of commodities*'.

The second part of this postulate should be clear enough. Indeed we have already covered it in the examples above. With the doubling of labour productivity between 1840 and 1920, 400 commodities are produced daily in our economy, as against just 240 in 1840. If one multiplies these figures by the number of working days in the year (say 300 or so) then we see that the mass of commodities has increased greatly.

The first part of postulate VIII may not be so obvious however. We have already seen that in 1840, when 240 commodities were produced in an average 12-hour working day, there were 3 minutes' SNAL embodied in each commodity. In other words, the *value* of the average commodity in 1840 was 3 minutes' SNAL. (Check back to postulate I if you have forgotten how Marx measures the value of commodities.) But in 1920, 400 commodities are produced in 10 hours, or 40 per hour. Thus there are just 1.5 minutes of SNAL embodied in the average commodity in 1920. As a result, in Marx's sense, *between 1840 and 1920 the value of all the commodities in our economy has been halved*. Moreover, since the 160 commodities daily required for the subsistence of the working class in 1920 embodies 1 hour's *less* SNAL than did the 100 commodities required daily in 1840, then *the value of labour power* (the value of V) *has fallen too*.

Now note what all this talk of 'falling commodity values' does *not* mean.

1. It does *not* mean that there are fewer commodities. On the contrary there are many more.

2. It does *not* mean that the money *prices* of these commodities have fallen. Indeed in simple money terms their prices may have risen (see below).

3. It does *not* mean that either the money *wages* or the real *wages* of the working class hav fallen. Indeed, though the 'value of labour power' has halved between 1840 and 1920, there are *more* commodities required every day (160 as against 100) for V, for the subsistence of the working class. Thus, if the size of the working class has not increased very much, real wages per head may well have risen.

However, Marx did state that if the value of all commodities in any economy – measured in SNAL – had fallen, then the *'real'* prices, as against the *'money'* prices, of all commodities would have fallen too. It is therefore necessary to explain now what he means by 'all real prices falling'. What he means is that in any economy where the value of all commodities has fallen, *everybody will have to work less time to acquire the money to buy the commodities being produced in that economy.*

In other words, if a loaf cost 1p in 1840, and 6p in 1920, but in order to earn the money to buy that loaf the 'average' worker in 1840 had to work 20 minutes (i.e. wages were such that 20 minutes = 1p) but only had to work 10 minutes in 1920 (i.e. wages were such that 10 minutes = 6p), then the price of a loaf of bread has fallen in *real* terms even though its *money* price is six times higher. If this happens for all commodities, then the real price of *all* commodities can fall, even if their nominal money prices have risen.

If the reader thinks about it, this 'general fall of real prices' is just another effect which can be produced by rapidly rising labour productivity, precisely the same factor which causes 'values' to fall when values are measured in labour time.[17]

The effects of relative surplus value – or the rising productivity of labour time – on the physical productivity of an economy and on the 'value' and 'real price' of commodities are absolutely central ideas in understanding Marx's model of capitalist accumulation. They are also absolutely central in understanding 'the law of the tendency of the rate of profit to fall' to which Marx gave such importance, and which is our postulate IX to be examined next.

It is therefore absolutely essential that the reader understands what is meant by 'relative surplus value' and that he or she understands all its implications. So if you have not understood the last four pages please go over them again until you do so. Very little of what is said in the rest of this chapter, or of what is said in the next chapter, will make very much sense to you unless you do understand relative surplus value. In many ways this is the key concept for the understanding of all of Marx's economics.

Postulate IX

'*Increase of relative surplus value can only occur continually by increasing the mass of constant capital ('C') faster than the mass of variable capital and surplus value ('V' + 'S'). Therefore the* value rate of profit *tends to decline as capitalism advances technologically*'.[18]

This postulate simply follows logically from the relationship between the macro-economic concepts which we outlined on pages 76–8. For if the value rate of profit is $\frac{S}{C+V}$ and if, in order to raise relative surplus value C *must* rise faster than S + V, then at time t_2 $\frac{S}{C+V}$ will always be less than at time t_1.

In order to make this clearer I have devised a simple numerical example which appears below. It will be seen that, for consistency's sake, I have kept to the same dates (1840 and 1920) as in our previous examples, but that I have altered the magnitudes of SNAL to make them slightly more realistic for an economy as a whole. They are perhaps best thought of as the amounts of SNAL expended in one year in a small economy. I have also tried to devise an example which would be moderately realistic from Marx's point of view, that is, which will illuminate well the trends or patterns which he thought actually occurred in a real capitalist economy as it developed. Let us now see what is happening in this example.

In the period between 1840 and 1920 the capitalist class in our economy has been raising relative rather than absolute surplus value. As a result of this they have kept the mass of surplus value –1 million hours' SNAL – at the same level throughout, but by raising the productivity of each hour of SNAL considerably, they have actually managed to *reduce* the amount of SNAL required to reproduce the labour power of the working class – from 5 million hours' to 4 million hours' SNAL. Thus the value of labour power has fallen.

Figure 3.2

'The law of the tendency of the rate of profit to fall'
Worked Example:

Time — t_1 (1840)

$$\frac{S}{V} = \frac{\text{1 million hours' SNAL}}{\text{5 million hours' SNAL}}$$

Therefore $\dfrac{S}{V} = \dfrac{1}{5}$ or 20%

$$C = \text{10 million hours' SNAL}$$

Therefore $\dfrac{S}{C+V} = \dfrac{1}{10+5} = \dfrac{1}{15} = 6.66\%$

- -

Time — t_2 (1920)

$$\frac{S}{V} = \frac{\text{1 million hours' SNAL}}{\text{4 million hours' SNAL}}$$

Therefore $\dfrac{S}{V} = \dfrac{1}{4}$ or 25%

But C now = 16 million hours' SNAL

Therefore $\dfrac{S}{C+V} = \dfrac{1}{16+4} = \dfrac{1}{20}$ or 5%

This of course could be perfectly compatible with the real wages of the working class having risen considerably in this period. (If you do not understand why this is so, you have *not* understood relative surplus value. You should really return to page 80 and start again.)

Moreover, because each hour of SNAL is now more productive, the 1 million hours' SNAL making up the capitalist class's surplus value would be the equivalent of many *more* commodities than in 1840, and these would presumably realize much more monetary profit when they are sold.

But in order to do all this the capitalist class has had to build much more advanced industrial plant, and to install much more highly productive machinery. In Marx's notation, this is constant capital – or C – when measured in value terms. Thus to raise surplus value in this way – presumably in response to a shortening of the working day and year – the capitalist class has had to raise C from 10 to 16 million hours' SNAL. Thus, in 1920, 16 million hours' SNAL had to be worked by the working class just to replace the worn-out or 'depreciated' part of the much increased mass of C.

Thus, although between 1840 and 1920 $\frac{S}{V}$ the rate of surplus value (or the 'rate of exploitation' of the working class), has risen by 5 per cent (from 20 to 25 per cent), because of the large increase in C the value rate of profit $\frac{S}{C+V}$ has actually fallen from 6.66 to 5 per cent.

Now the reason why a large increase of C always reduces the value rate of profit is that in Marx's theory it is *only* living labour power, *only* the 'present' living working class, which produces surplus value. In Marx's notation, only V produces S[19] (to check this see pages 77–8). Thus C does not produce any S, that is constant capital does not produce any surplus value.

However, in the course of the development of capitalism, C tends constantly to increase relative to V. Marx sometimes expressed this by saying that capitalist development tends to lead to the replacement of 'living labour' by 'dead labour'. He calls machinery 'dead labour' because it embodies living labour power of the past, labour no longer living. Thus, in Marx's theory, the sole source of surplus value (V) tends to be reduced proportionately to C all the time. The reason for this is that in order to increase the rate of surplus value by the 'relative' method, C *has* to increase proportionately to V (I, 621–8; III, 211–3).

Thus Marx thought that this relative method, used by the capitalist class to offset the effects of the gradual loss of absolute surplus value, might be successful in the short term, but in the longer term would be self-defeating for capitalism. Because as people are replaced by machines, the *only* source of surplus value, 'living labour power', is gradually expelled from the production process and thus the value rate of profit falls even as the rate of surplus value rises.

It may seem odd to you that Marx's theory treats living labour power as the *only* source of surplus value, that is that he denies that machines can produce surplus value (and thus denies that machines can be a source of capitalist profits). In the next chapter I shall argue that from a strictly economic point of view this *is* odd. Indeed I shall argue that it is an unsustainable idea which Marx arrives at by playing an accounting trick on himself. But none the less it is what Marx's theory says, and it is why, in his theory, if C increases relative to V this always produces a fall in the rate of profit, even if it raises the rate of surplus value.

This then is Marx's 'law of the tendency of the rate of profit to fall', one of the economic laws of capitalism which he believed worked 'with iron necessity toward inevitable results'. In this case the 'inevitable result' was supposed to be the gradual approach of the rate of profit to zero or near zero, making it impossible for the capitalist class further to expand the system on the basis of private profit. Thus, a total revolutionary transformation of the system – in a socialist direction – was supposed to be required if the 'forces of production' were to be further expanded. Of course it was the working class which was supposed to make such a revolution (see chapter 5).

CONCLUSIONS

I have now completed my outline of the fundamentals of Marx's economic theory. I wish now to draw the reader's attention to two broader points about that theory, points which relate back to philosophical issues discussed earlier.

Firstly, note how well this theory of the capitalist economy fits with Marx's Hegel-derived theory of history. Labour values of commodities are determined by the amount of SNAL, the amount of socially necessary abstract labour time *'embodied'* in them. The ease with which such an economic notion fits into a philosophical idea of the world as 'objectified' and 'alienated' human activity should be fairly obvious.[20]

Secondly, and perhaps less obviously, note how Marx's economics, just like his philosophy, is a dynamic economics, an economics of movement. After the complex discussion of the ramifications of relative surplus value in the last few pages, the reader can hardly be in any doubt about that. The labour values of commodities falling while their money prices rise but their real prices fall. The value of labour power falling but real and money wages rising. The value of all commodities falling while the mass of them increases. The value rate of profit falling as the rate of surplus value rises. The reader may feel that he or she has been on an intellectual roller coaster. Perhaps you are even experiencing a little cognitive giddiness!

Moreover, all this rising and falling is going on *through time*, as the capitalist economy expands and develops, as more capital is accumulated, more workers employed, more surplus value produced and appropriated, more commodities, and new types of commodities, manufactured. Labour values themselves are of course measures of *time*, or rather they are measures of the amount of 'living labour power' expended by the working class in a given period of time to produce a given amount of commodities.

And what matters to Marx throughout his analysis is not the value of commodities as such, but what is happening to the value of commodities, that is whether they *are* rising or falling. For, as we have seen, *if* labour values fall then the mass of commodities increases and their real price falls, but *if* labour values rise then the mass of commodities falls (that is, it takes more of the stock of living labour power to produce any one commodity and thus fewer commodities can be produced in any given period of time) and their real prices rise. In this sense too then, Marx's economics is of a piece with his philosophy and with his history. All is movement, all is flux, both in the world itself and in thinking about (conceiving) the world.

To complete this chapter, I will list six points in Marx's economic theory which have to be justified if it is to be regarded as true. I will deal with each of these points in turn in the next chapter. Thus, if Marx's theory is to be true, it has to be the case that:

1. All commodities *do* on average, in the long run, exchange at their values.

2. Labour power *does* exchange at its value.

3. Labour power *is* the only commodity capable of producing a value greater than itself, and in particular that

4. *Only* living labour power (only V) and not 'dead' or 'embodied' labour power (C) produces profit.

Moreover, in order for the 'law of the tendency of the rate of profit to fall' to hold, it has to be the case that

5. There *is* a tendency for capitalism to replace 'absolute' by 'relative' surplus value as it develops technologically, and that

6. Raising the rate of relative surplus value *does* require the increase of C always to be greater than the increase of V+S, so that $\frac{S}{C+V}$ always falls.

Perhaps it may keep readers interested if I inform them that in the next chapter I shall argue that points 1 and 2 are unprovable, 3 and 4 are false, and that 5 is, in a sense, true, but its being true strongly suggests that 6 is false.

CHAPTER 4

MARX'S ECONOMICS: A CRITIQUE

We may turn immediately to the six points with which I ended the last chapter; the six points which had to be justified if Marx's theory as a whole was to be justified. We will take them in order.

Points 1 and 2 (That commodities exchange on average at their values, and that labour power also exchanges at its value.)

There is one overwhelming difficulty with justifying either one of these propositions. This is quite simply that *in the real world it is impossible to measure 'values' in Marx's sense*. The reason for this is partly that in real economies (in 'Ameujap' for example) there are millions of commodities being produced every year, so that the practical task of measuring their values would be beyond the largest most sophisticated computer.

But more importantly, in the real world measuring labour values is an impossibility because of the way Marx defines them. Remember that the value of any commodity is determined by the amount of 'socially necessary *abstract* labour time' (SNAL) embodied in it. But the problem here is that in practice it is impossible to find a non-arbitrary method of 'abstracting' or making equivalent different types of labour, or different levels of skill and intensity in the performance of labour. It is possible, for example, to take the training time of a skilled worker (say seven years) and then divide that time into the number of commodities he or she produces in a lifetime. In that way it is possible to say that, for example, an hour of a skilled worker's labour time is worth – say – 1½ hours of an unskilled worker's labour time, because of the additional 'training time' embodied.

But the problem is to find a non-arbitrary way of accounting the additional time required to impart the skill. For example,

I picked 'seven years' above, because that was the typical duration of apprenticeships in a number of skilled trades in Britain, but of course the actual training time is only part of that seven years in fact – say six hours a day – and perhaps a given worker was only concentrating for three hours of that![1] Moreover, it would be equally plausible to argue that some amount of the time taken for general schooling and some of the time taken to learn skills 'on the job' should be added to the apprenticeship years to get an accurate 'time' measure of skill.

The problems posed by different types and intensities of labour are even greater, and all suggested methods of finding labour time equivalents for them are even more arbitrary. In *Capital*, vol. 1, Marx constructs a model of the capitalist economy in which market exchange takes care of this problem. For in that model a commodity with a greater level of skill and intensity of labour embodied always exchanges for one with less skill and intensity of labour embodied at a price which exactly reflects this differential. But though this is a convenient simplifying assumption for Marx's theory it clearly does not reflect reality. For in the real world the price mechanism does not seem to be that sensitive to labour differences, at least for the vast majority of commodities. And even if it were, these market differentials would still be *price* differentials, and therefore would not help the Marxist economist who was seeking a direct measure of labour values.

It is sometimes pointed out that, in principle at least, one could measure the amount of *labour time* embodied in commodities. Thus, if one takes a Ford Granada car for example, one could measure the amount of labour time required to mine the iron ore, the amount of labour time required to smelt the iron ore into steel, the amount of labour time required to get the steel to the car plant, the amount of labour time embodied in the machines in the car factory and in all the other factories which make components for the Granada, then the amount of labour time required to manufacture the car itself and to transport it to wholesalers and retailers. But imagine trying to do this for 100,000 or 1 million Granadas, and all other cars, and all other commodities produced in 'Ameujap' last year! And because all of these measures would still not be measures of 'abstract' labour time (they would be measures of different types of labour, of different skills, etc.) they would still not be measures of 'values' in Marx's sense.[2]

There is considerable disagreement however, even among Marxist economists, about how much this practical problem of measurement actually matters in the assessment of Marx's theory. Some theorists have pointed out that the problem of measurement is not uncommon in science. Thus, atomic physicists tell us that 'in principle' the earth and its atmosphere is composed of atoms and sub-atomic particles. The scientific status of this proposition is never challenged because we cannot, in practice, *count* the number of atoms and particles involved.

So it can be argued that Marx's problem is not unique in science, and that what matters is that in theory, in principle, production *could* be measured in labour values, even if in practice, in the real world, this is impossible. What is important, it is said, is that if production could be measured in values, the long-run average real prices of commodities would be found to rise and fall with values, so that it would make sense to say that values 'determined' prices.[3]

Other more sceptical economists reply that there are other difficulties, even 'in theory' with value measurement,[4] and that in any case the practical problems with value measurement in the real world are so severe as to amount to a difficulty in principle. For if, in the real world, we can never in fact *know* what the values of commodities are, what exactly does it mean (does it mean anything?) to assert that 'values determine prices'? For all we can ever know (in the sense of measure) in real capitalist economies is the *prices* of commodities, not their values.[5]

It should be noted however, that one aspect of Marx's value theory – one important use which he makes of it – is a commonplace in economics. Marx's insistence that 'supply and demand' alone cannot explain the pattern or trend of *long-run* relative prices is just a particular variant of what is called 'cost of production' economics. In the cost of production approach it is simply pointed out that all commodities have, at any point in time, a certain minimum cost of production. Moreover, these minimum costs vary enormously between commodities, being greatest for the most complex and large commodities and least for the simplest and small commodities. Thus, for example, however high the demand for pins rises, or however low the demand for Polaris submarines falls, Polaris submarines will always cost much more than pins.

It is of course true that falls in demand or increases in supply can push prices of commodities below their minimum costs of production for a while, but if this goes on for very long, at least in a competitive market economy, the less efficient firms making such commodities will go out of business. This will of course reduce the supply of the commodity in question and push prices up again above 'average' costs of production. In other words, costs of production tend to place broad 'ceilings' and 'floors' in the variations of commodity prices which can be induced by supply and demand alone. Figure 3.1 on p.73 illustrates Marx's version of the principle involved.[6]

It should also be noted that, to a degree, it is possible to find 'surrogate' price measurements for value magnitudes which can be used in the real world. Thus, calculating the amount of wages (measured in money) and the amount of profit (also measured in money) and then expressing the latter as a proportion of the former, is, with some qualifications, a fairly good approximation to the 'rate of surplus value'. Similarly the amount of profits in an economy expressed as a proportion of total production or output, is a rough approximation to the 'rate of profit' in value terms.[7]

Moreover, calculating what I have called the 'real price' of commodities in Marx's sense (i.e. the *time* which an average worker has to work to obtain the money to buy a particular good or selection or 'basket' of goods) is widely regarded by many economists as the best comparative measure of material standards of living in different economies. Certainly it is a far more accurate measure than measures using money prices alone. For example, comparing material living standards in the USA and the USSR using this measure has produced some surprising results (although the result obtained does depend a lot on the selection of goods chosen).[8]

It has also been confirmed that as industrial economies advance technologically this 'real price' of commodities (measured by their labour time cost) *does* tend to fall. This is hardly a very surprising finding, given that technological improvement normally takes the form of saving time in production, that is, producing more commodities more quickly by 'streamlining' the production process in one way or another. But none the less it is empirically verified as a long-run trend, and as such has been responsible for much of the rise in material standards of living that has occurred in the world. To that degree Marx's formulation

– that as capitalism advances the value of commodities falls as their mass increases – can be seen to embody an important insight about the process of capitalist development and indeed about industrial development in general.[9]

Finally, it should be noted that there is another tradition of economic theorizing, also descended from Ricardo, which measures production theoretically in non-monetary ways. This is the so-called 'neo-Ricardian' school, which uses not labour values, but actual *physical quantities* of commodities, and expresses the 'real prices' of commodities in terms of the physical quantity of one good which can be obtained by a given physical quantity of another good.[10]

Once again, this is an approach to economics which has no application in the real world, where millions of different physical commodities produced cannot be directly bartered in this way and can only be priced relative to on another by using their only common economic measure – money. But this impossibility of direct practical application does not prevent neo-Ricardian economic theory from being extremely fruitful and illuminating in some ways, and indeed later in this chapter I shall use it in an attempt to help Marx out of some theoretical difficulties.

Overall then, I feel that the impossibility of measuring labour values in the real world, although a severe problem in *applying* Marx's economics (especially to the planning of production in actual socialist economies) is not an insuperable objection to values as a theoretical tool. Marx, like the classical economists, wanted to measure or enumerate production of goods and services in a particular way – by the amount of labour time embodied in them. No doubt he, like Ricardo and others, knew that, in practice, this was an impossibly cumbersome way. But he did not choose the 'labour values' method of enumerating production on the assumption that it would be used in socialist planning, or because he thought that it could replace calculation in money prices in the real world. Marx chose labour values as a theoretical instrument of his *purposes*, and the most that can perhaps be said is that, given the 'technical' difficulties which they pose, and given the posssibility of finding surrogate price measures for values, then as *economic accounting measures* at least, labour values may be redundant instruments for Marx's purposes. Labour values pose more economic problems for Marx than they are worth, because there are other measures which will serve his purposes almost equally well, and which do not have the same technical problems attached to them.

However, this leaves open the question of what Marx's purposes were in this regard, of what purposes 'values' were meant to serve for Marx. We have already said something about this in earlier chapters; values were a means by which Marx hoped to found a 'scientific' theory of exploitation of the working class. To consider how far values could and did serve Marx's purposes in this regard we must proceed to an analysis of the next crucial points in his argument.

Points 3 and 4 (That labour power is the only commodity capable of producing a value greater than itself, so that only V and not C produces S.)

Unfortunately it is precisely here, I will argue, in Marx's theory of surplus value or exploitation and his closely related theory of capital accumulation, that the really insuperable theoretical difficulties are encountered. It is here in fact that values 'let Marx down', as it were, that they prove incapable of demonstrating what he wants them to demonstrate. Or, more exactly, when Marx deploys values, uses values, in a number of interlinked theoretical *propositions*, those *propositions* prove incapable of demonstrating what Marx wishes them to demonstrate.

To begin this analysis of the crucially flawed core of Marx's economic theory let us recapitulate briefly. Marx's theory, we should remember, purports to 'prove' that all profit derives from, or is just the monetary form of, excess or unpaid labour time. In other words, his theory purports to prove that 'Capital', or the capitalist class as a whole, can *only* obtain a surplus product for reinvestment and expansion of the system by exploiting the living labour power of the working class. Marx's theory purports, as we have said, to be a 'scientific' proof of capitalist exploitation. In fact it aims to turn exploitation into a scientific rather than a purely moral or political term. But how does Marx do this? Basically by presenting a two-stage representation of the capitalist production process. I have attempted to capture this representation diagrammatically in the two following figures.

We can take both of these figures together as Marx's picture or representation of capitalist production. Thus, in *Capital* Marx asks us to picture or conceive capitalist production in two ways.

Figure 4.1 Marx's representation of capitalist production as a physical process

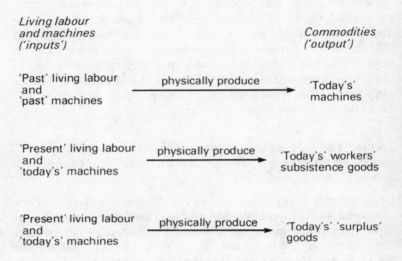

He asks us, firstly, to conceive of it as a physical process, a process by which physical goods and services are produced. But secondly, he asks us to conceive of it or picture it as an economic process, as a process in which those physical goods and services *and* the factors of production themselves (machines, raw materials, workers) are *valued* one against another. In the physical representation of the production process we have to picture physical commodities being produced by a physical process. In the economic representation of the production process, physical production is taken as completed, as it were, and the question is how to measure or evaluate what has been produced.

I have tried to reproduce these two pictures or representations of the capitalist production process in figures 4.1 and 4.2, but it should be noted that the figures are not equivalent in one respect. In figure 4.1 the arrows represent a physical production process, with living labour of the past and present *together with* machines producing (1) 'present-day' machines, (2) workers' subsistence goods and (3) surplus (or 'profit') goods. Thus, when describing capitalist production as a physical process, Marx happily admits that machines play a part in the physical production of all his three types of commodities.

In figure 4.2 however, no production process is involved.

Figure 4.2 Marx's two enumerations of commodities

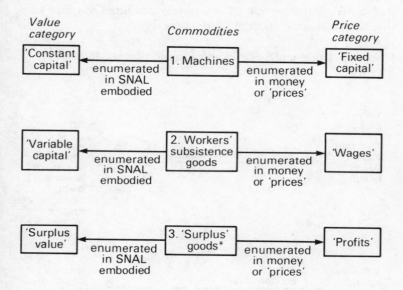

Note: * Another way of representing these relationships would be to see each physical commodity as being composed of a 'constant capital' part, a 'variable capital' part and a 'surplus value' part with each of these parts being 'realized' and put to their different uses, after the commodity has been sold for money (this sum of money, unlike the physical commodity being actually, rather than just theoretically, divisible). This slightly complicates things but does not alter the essential logic of Marx's theory.

Here the arrows simply represent two different ways in which Marx measures or enumerates commodities produced. He enumerates them as embodiments of SNAL (as 'values') and as given amounts of money (as 'prices'). So the stock of machines existing at any one time has a value representation ('constant capital') and a price representation ('fixed capital'), and so do workers' subsistence goods ('variable capital' and 'wages') and the economy's surplus goods ('surplus value' and 'profits').

Now the question which immediately arises is this. If, as figure 4.1 suggests, machines play a part in the *physical* production of all commodities, including the surplus or 'profit' commodities, and if the surplus commodities can be enumerated in money terms (as 'profit') as well as in value terms (as 'surplus value'), then why do machines make *no* contribution to surplus value or to capitalist money profits? Marx denies that they do, because, as we have seen, Marx denies that constant capital (the SNAL enumeration of machines) produces surplus value (the SNAL enumeration of surplus goods).

Figure 4.3 'Value' and 'price' relations in capitalist production

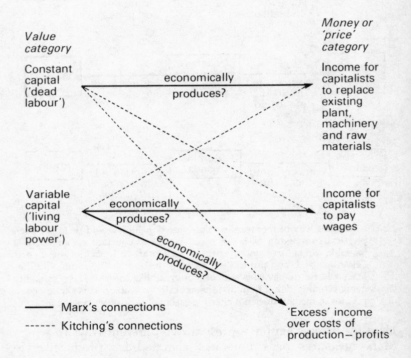

In short, the theory of exploitation of *Capital*, vol. 1, rests on the curious logic illustrated in figure 4.3. Here I have marked the arrows as representing 'economic production', but I am really somewhat uncertain of this, because it is in fact unclear what precise relationship Marx has in mind here. Sometimes, for example, he talks about the way machines 'transfer' value to commodities as if the 'transference' of such values by machines, and the 'creation' of 'additional' or surplus value by the working class, were economic *events* which somehow occurred alongside the physical production process.

Consider this quotation for example:

We have seen that the means of production transfer value to the new product, so far as during the labour process they lose value in the shape of their old use value. The maximum loss of value that they can suffer in the process is plainly limited by the amount of the original value with which they came into the process, or in other words by the labour time necessary for their production. *Therefore the means of production can never add more value to the product than they themselves possess* independently of the process which they assist. However useful a given kind of raw material, or a machine, or other means of production may be, though it cost £150, or say, 500 days' labour, yet it cannot, under any circumstances, add to the value of the product more than £150.

(I, 205 – emphasis added)

Now the first sentence of this quotation makes it sound as if means of production 'transferring value' to new products was some kind of economic *event*, which happens during the labour process, that is during the physical process of production. The last two sentences of the quotation, however, refer not to the production process at all but to an *accounting procedure*.

A machine which has a value of 500 days' SNAL 'cannot', we are told, add to the value of the products it produces more than that 500 days' SNAL. But all that Marx does is to create an accounting procedure to ensure that this 'cannot' happen. Suppose this machine, worth 500 days' SNAL, produces 500,000 commodities from the day of its installation until, as Marx says, 'the day of its banishment to the lumber room' (I, 203). Then, according to Marx's calculations, it will simply 'transfer' one-thousandth of a day's SNAL to each commodity (i.e. approximately 1.24 minutes of value to each product). And thus one can conclude from this, as Marx does, that the said machine adds no 'additional' value to the commodities it produces. A machine only 'transfers' the value already embodied in it to those commodities. Only living labour power, says Marx, can 'add' value to commodities. The quotation below sums up this view, which is also represented in figure 4.3.

It is otherwise with the subjective factor of the labour process, with labour power in action. While the labourer preserves and transfers to the product the value of the means of production, he at the same time, by the mere act of working *creates each instant an additional or new value*. Suppose the process of production to be stopped just when the workman has produced an equivalent for the value of his own labour power, when, for example, by six hours' labour he has added a value of three shillings. This value is the surplus, of the total value of the product, over the portion of its value that is due to the means of production. It is the only bit of value performed during this process, the only portion of the value of the product created by this process. Of course we do not forget that this new value only replaced the money advanced by the capitalist in the purchase of the labour power, and spent by the labourer on the necessaries of life. With regard to the money spent, the new value is merely a reproduction; but nonetheless it is an actual, and not as in the case of the value of the means of production, only an apparent reproduction. The substitution of one value for another, is here affected by the creation of new value.

We know however ... that the labour process may continue beyond the time necessary to reproduce and incorporate in the product a mere equivalent for the value of labour power. Instead of the six hours that are sufficient for the latter purpose, the process may continue for twelve hours. *The action of labour power, therefore, not only reproduces its own value, but produces value over and above it. This surplus value is the difference between the value of the product and the value* of the elements consumed in the formation of the product, in other words *of the means of production and the labour power.*

(I, 208 – emphasis added)

But Marx only sustains this assertion because he does not apply his 'constant capital' accounting procedure to living labour. If he did so, then he could just as easily derive the result that living labour too 'adds no value'.

Suppose, for example, that the 'value of labour power' of a given labourer is 500 days' SNAL. Now if, during his/her working life that labourer produces 500,000 commodities, then one can derive precisely the same result as in the machine example above. The labourer simply 'transfers' 1.24 minutes of the value of his labour power to each commodity and 'adds no value'.

Marx's reply to this objection is to say that living labour power, unlike 'dead labour', unlike machines, can work for a period of time in excess of the SNAL required for its production (see paragraph two of the last quotation). But this reply is no reply at all, *because it is not true*. Machines can do this too. Indeed, if a capitalist could *not* run machines productively (i.e. at average or above average levels of productivity) for a time well exceeding the labour time embodied in them, it is doubtful whether he or she would want to install such machines at all.

In other words, if Marx accounts the value of labour power in the same way in which he accounts the value of machines (and there is no obvious reason for him not to do so) then he is left with the paradoxical result that neither machines nor people 'add value' to commodities, which makes the existence of surplus value quite mysterious. If he accounts machines in the same way in which he accounts living labour power then he has to admit that machines *do* 'add value' to commodities and thus *do* contribute to surplus value, along with living labour power. If he applies one accounting procedure to machines and another to living labour power (which is what in fact he does) then he is simply being inconsistent in a way which is very convenient to his argument, but has no other economic justification.

The obvious way out of this dilemma would appear to be for Marx to adopt the second of these alternatives and 'allow' machines to add value to commodities (and thus contribute, along with living labour, to surplus value and profits). Since this also fits with his physical representation of capitalist production (figure 4.1) and is perfectly consistent with both value and price enumeration of commodities (figure 4.2), it also seems, from the point of view of his economic theory, to be the correct solution, and is represented by the dotted lines which I have added to figure 4.3.

Why then does Marx not adopt it? Why does he insist that only living labour power can produce surplus value? I will suggest shortly that the answer to this question is that Marx is committed to a particular *philosophical* position which he attempts to 'build in' to his economic theory. The philosophical position has its merits, but it does not fit nearly so neatly into his economic theory as he thinks it does, and in fact it seriously undermines Marx's economics while gaining no greater philosophical strength in the process. But this is to anticipate. For the moment, I wish to complete this critique of Marx's economic theory of labour exploitation and capital accumulation.

Points 5 and 6 (That in gradually replacing absolute by relative surplus value the process of capitalist development always increases C faster than V+S so that the value rate of profit falls.)

We saw in the previous chapter that Marx links his theory of exploitation to a theory of capital accumulation through 'relative surplus value'. The concept of relative surplus value (or of the rising productivity of labour time) led in its turn to Marx's 'law of the tendency of the rate of profit to fall', since, according to Marx, in order for the rate of relative surplus value to rise continually, C had to rise faster than V+S, and therefore the value rate of profit must fall, even though the rate of surplus value rises.

Since the central premise of this 'law' is that C produces no S, that is that constant capital produces no surplus value, and we have already rejected this premise on the grounds that it relies on an inconsistent accounting procedure, it might seem that there is no more to say. But in fact the 'law' has other weaknesses as well as this fundamental one, most notably that it is constructed by Marx in partial disregard of some of the implications of his own concept of 'relative surplus value'. Indeed the concept of relative surplus value can be deployed, and is below, to construct another powerful critique of the 'law'. In reading this critique the reader might wish to reflect upon points made in the first chapter of this book about the merits of inconsistency and about the capacity of truly great thinkers to provide the tools by which their own thought may be criticized.

Let us review Marx's argument again. According to him, faced with a reducing working day, and driven on by competition, capitalists raise relative surplus value by equipping workers with more productive machines so that they can produce more commodities in any given period of time. In Marx's words improved machines lower the 'socially necessary labour time' required to produce a given commodity or group of commodities. But, says Marx, capitalists can only do this by raising the *mass* of C rapidly, that is by continually raising the *mass of value* embodied in machines, plant and equipment, raw materials, etc. – 'means of production' in short – and thus lowering $\frac{S}{C+V}$. But why does this *have* to happen? Why cannot the capitalist firms who are producing plant, equipment, firms who are producing plant, equipment, machines, raw materials, etc. – firms in the constant capital sectors – not *themselves* be raising relative surplus value, that is equipping their workers with more productive machines to make machines, plant, raw materials for other industries? If they are doing this, and they are doing it continuously (so that 'technical change' in the 'capital goods industries' is continuous, to use the conventional economic terminology) *then the value of constant capital may be stable or even falling, even as its physical mass is rising*. And since what Marx is measuring in $\frac{S}{C+V}$ is the value (in SNAL) of C and not its physical mass, then rapid and continuous technical change in the constant capital sectors could completely subvert his law of the falling rate of profit, even if it *were* true – which it is not – that only V produces S.

Oddly enough, Marx does consider this possibility in volume III of *Capital* when he is considering five 'counteracting influences' which may slow down the fall in the value rate of profit. One of these counteracting influences, he notes, is the 'cheapening of elements of constant capital', and this is what he says about it:

> For instance, the quantity of cotton worked up by a single European spinner in a modern fantory has grown tremendously compared to the quantity formerly worked up by a European spinner with a spinning wheel. Yet the value of the worked-up cotton has not grown in the same proportion as its mass. The same applies to machinery and to other fixed capital. *In short, the same development which increases the mass of constant capital in relation to the variable reduces the value of its elements as a result of the increasing productivity of labour*, and therefore prevents the value of constant capital, although it continually increases, from increasing at the same rate as its material volume ... *In isolated cases, the mass of the elements of constant capital may even increase, while its value remains the same, or falls.*
>
> (III, 236 – emphasis added)

The question which arises here is how does Marx *know* that it is only in 'isolated cases' that 'the mass of ... constant capital may ... increase, while its value remains the same, or falls'? Why cannot technical change in the constant capital sectors not be a continuous and widespread process which *continually* frustrates the operation of his 'law'? Marx himself gives no reason, either here or anywhere else in *Capital* for thinking that such rapid technical change only occurs in 'isolated cases'.

However, this issue was taken up again in the 1970s in the course of a lively debate in the Conference of Socialist Economists (CSE). Broadly speaking, one side argued that since capitalist firms do not calculate in values, there is no mechanism in capitalism to ensure that technical change in the constant capital sectors (or in any other sectors for that matter) will continually produce machines embodying less SNAL than their predecessors. The other side argued that capitalists may not calculate in values, but that they are continuously on the look-out for technical improvements which save on *all* factors of production (that is, which save labour, save raw materials, save on depreciation costs of machines, etc.). This would, it was argued, be equivalent to lowering or stabilizing the value of constant capital even as its physical mass was increased.[11]

About the safest summary of this debate, I think, is to say that it was indeterminate. There are plausible arguments on both sides, and it is in fact an empirical question – a question to be investigated factually – or at least it would be if values could be directly measured! But that it is an empirical question means that, at the very least, Marx cannot assume, as he does, that this 'counteracting influence' to his law would only act in 'isolated cases' and would thus only modify but not negate the law. No such theoretical assumption can be made.

Finally, when attention is turned to the real world, and attempts are made to measure trends in capitalist rates of profit over long time periods (and here of course one has to measure 'money' or 'price' rates of profit, not 'value' rates) the results are similarly indeterminate. Data which have been available since the 1850s suggest that on an international scale (say on an 'Ameujap' scale) such rates go up for long periods and down for long periods, with no clear overall trend.[12] Perhaps then the safest conclusion is that if one has to wait for the rate of profit in the world capitalist system to reach zero or near zero before revolution is attempted one may be waiting a very, very long time indeed.

But the reader may well be thinking that all this additional argument against the 'law of the tendency of the rate of profit to fall' is really unnecessary. The law, like Marx's theory of labour exploitation, rests on the proposition that only V produces S, that only living labour power produces surplus value – and thus profit – and this proposition has already been rejected. Perhaps the reader is in fact more puzzled as to how Marx could ever have believed this. After all, capitalist firms continually install new machines, continually try to find new and cheaper raw materials, continually try to save on wage costs for 'living labour power'. Surely they would hardly be doing all this if its only effect was to reduce profits, given that the whole aim of the capitalist system is to maximize profitability.

However, it should be noted that Marx does have an answer to this point. He agrees of course that capitalist firms do continuously introduce new and more productive machinery (and indeed both in *Capital* and the *Grundrisse* he has some interesting comments and speculations about the automation of production), and he says in fact that they are driven to do this by competition. Moreover, he acknowledges that by raising its rate of relative surplus value, a given firm or number of firms will gain a higher rate of profit for a while through technical innovation. But he says that:

(a) this advantage will soon be wiped out by other firms adopting the same innovation and so lowering the rate of profit in the innovator firm back down to the 'average' rate; and, more importantly

(b) the net result of all this 'competitive innovation' induced by the pursuit of additional profit *is to raise the value mass of constant capital*, both in individual sectors and across the economy as a whole. The increase of C, relative to V and S, is what lowers the rate of profit overall, that is for *all* firms in the economy.[13]

In other words, Marx is arguing that capitalists are driven, by competition, to do what is genuinely in their individual – or individual firm's – interest for a while, but which is destructive of the overall interest of 'capital-in-general' over the longer term. However, they cannot stop being collectively self-destructive in this way. Competition, and the short-term, myopic perspective which it generates, drives them always to put individual interests before class interests.

But again, this is only true *if* the value of C is necessarily increased in this way, and *if*, more particularly, C does not produce any S, and we have already rejected these propositions.

So there is no way out. We are returned again and again to the same question. How, why, could Marx have believed that *only* living labour power (only V) produces S? This proposition is central to his whole theory, is set out in volume 1 of *Capital*, and is not altered by any of the 'complexifications' of his model which Marx introduces in volumes II and III. Yet it rests, as a piece of economic theory, on a fairly obvious 'double accounting' procedure which appears to have no defensible basis. It is also manifestly inconsistent with what Marx says about the physical or material production process, where he is quite happy to acknowledge that machines, and other means of production, are essential, along with living labour, to the production of all commodities, including the ones which he enumerates as 'surplus value'. Moreover, if Marx could conceive – as he does in the *Grundrisse* – of a future in which capitalist production was ever more automated (in which there was ever more C in proportion to V), could he really have imagined that capitalism would increasingly dispense with that factor (living labour power) which, if his theory was correct, was its only source of profits?

THE PHILOSOPHY OF PRAXIS AND CLASSICAL ECONOMICS: A RAREFIED MUDDLE

I will now suggest that Marx was committed to this extraordinary view, not on the basis of his economic theory at all, but on the basis of his philosophy of praxis. He then mixed up this philosophical position with his economic theory in a manner which he thought assisted both, but which, I shall argue, actually detracted from both.

Consider these two quotations, both from volume 1 of *Capital*:

The labourer adds fresh value to the subject of his labour by expending upon it a given amount of additional labour, no matter what the specific character and utility of that labour may be. On the other hand, the values of the means of production are preserved, and present themselves afresh as constituent parts of the value of the product; the values of the cotton and the spindle, for instance, re-appear again in the value of the yarn. The value of the means of production is therefore preserved by being transferred to the product. This transfer takes place during the conversion of those means into a product, or in other words, during the labour process. It is brought about by labour; but how?

The labourer does not perform two operations at once, one

in order to add value to the cotton, the other in order to preserve the value of the means of production ... [Rather] ... by the very act of adding new value he preserves their former values. Since, however, the addition of new value to the subject of his labour, and the preservation of its former value, are two entirely distinct results, produced simultaneously by the labourer during one operation, it is plain that this two-fold nature of the result can be explained only by the two-fold nature of his labour. At one and the same time, it must in one character create value, and in another character preserve or transfer value.

Now, in what manner does every labourer add new labour and consequently create new value? Evidently, only by labouring productively in a particular way; the spinner by spinning, the weaver by weaving, the smith by forging. ... In so far then as labour is such specific productive activity, in so far as it is spinning, weaving or forging, it raises by mere contact, the means of production from the dead, makes them living factors of the labour process, and combines with them to form the new products.   (I, 199–200)

A machine which does not serve the purposes of labour is useless. In addition, it falls a prey to the destructive influence of natural forces. Iron rusts and wood rots. Yarn which we neither weave not knit, is cotton wasted. Living labour must seize upon these things and raise them from their death sleep, change them from mere possible use values into real and effective ones. Bathed in the fire of labour, appropriated as part and parcel of labour's organism, and, as it were, made alive for the performance of their functions in the process, they are in truth consumed, but consumed with a purpose, as elementary constituents of new use values, of new products, ever ready as means of subsistence for individual consumption, or as means of production for some new labour process.
                                                            (I, 183)

To understand clearly what Marx is saying in the first quotation, it is perhaps best to picture in one's mind, a labourer – man or woman – standing beside a weaving loom and producing cotton cloth. If we stand and watch him or her, we see cloth appearing from the loom as the weaver works with it. We see cloth being produced from the cotton thread (or 'yarn') by the weaver working with the weaving loom. But Marx suggests that at the same time, and in the same process by which this is happening, something else is happening. The 'value' of the yarn, and part of the 'value' of the weaving loom is being 'transferred' to the cotton cloth as it is produced. In addition, the labour power of the weaver is 'adding' new value, or 'creating' new value and 'adding' it to the cloth as it is being produced.

Well now, how do I perceive this process – this 'transferring' and 'adding' of value? I do not have any difficulty perceiving the physical process of cloth production. I can see it happening, hear it happening (looms are very noisy things), even smell it happening. But how do I perceive the 'value' process which is supposed to be going on 'at the same time'? Could I perceive it if I went right close up to the weaver and her machine, peered at the process closely, even smelt the cloth as it appeared? Would I then perceive values 'transferring' from machine to cloth, or being 'added' to the cloth by the weaver's labour power?

No, none of this is going to help me to perceive this value process. Why? *Because it is not a physical or material process at all*, which can be perceived through the senses. What 'it' is (if 'it' is anything) is a process going on *in Marx's mind*. In other words, what we have here is a particular way of conceiving or thinking about the production process. What we have here is a mental or cognitive phenomenon which *can* be perceived, by reading Marx's mind (by reading *Capital* in fact) but which cannot be perceived in a cotton factory, or indeed in any other kind of factory.

It is true that Marx does not write in a way which makes it easy to grasp this. He writes about values being 'preserved', 'transferred', 'created', and 'added', as if these *were* processes occurring in factories as part of the physical production process, and he should clearly be held culpable for writing in that very misleading way. It is not clear to me whether he was in fact misleading himself as well as others here (that is whether he himself thought he was describing an aspect or characteristic of the physical production process). On balance I am inclined to think him too good a philosopher to have misled himself in this way and I think that the quotation from *Capital* on page 24 supports this view, which is why I drew attention to it at the time.

But whether he did or did not mislead himself, the fact is that he has misled generation upon generation of readers of *Capital* who have concluded that because value preservation, or value transfer or value addition are not phenomena which can be perceived sensibly (through the senses) then they are 'imaginary' or 'metaphysical' phenomena, 'unreal' phenomena, which have no place in economic theory. And when one adds to the fact that values cannot be sensibly perceived 'transferring' or 'adding' etc., the fact that in the real world they cannot even be measured, it is unsurprising that many economists have dismissed them as tools of economic theory.[14]

And I agree with this view. 'Value analysis' as a form of economic theory leads to unnecessary complexity, generates magnitudes which cannot be measured, and, as used by Marx, leads to one conclusion (that machines and other means of production do not contribute to profits) which is economically untenable and indefensible except via blatantly inconsistent accounting procedures. But it does not follow from all of this that values have no *philosophical* worth or use as a means of conceptualizing production.

So what philosophical use are labour values to Marx? What is the philosophical point of them? What purpose do they serve? I think the answer to these questions is found in the second of the quotations above. 'Living labour', says Marx, must 'seize upon' physical means of production and 'raise them from their death sleep'. Iron, wood, yarn, etc. must be 'bathed in the fire of labour'. They must be 'appropriated as part and parcel of labour's organism', for only this way will they be 'made alive for the performance of their functions in the [production] process'.

This powerful, and in some ways very beautiful paragraph, is a perfect example – perhaps the best single example in *Capital* – of what Kolakowski calls Marx's 'Promethean' conception of human beings.[15] Prometheus was a hero of ancient Greek legend who stole fire from the gods in heaven, and brought it down to earth to be put to work for human purposes. For his pains he was bound on a rock in the middle of the sea by Zeus, the leading Greek god. But as we can see, the image of Prometheus, wreathed in fire, is very appropriate to the quotation above. Inanimate nature (iron, wood, yarn) only *comes alive* when 'bathed' in the Promethean 'fire of human labour', and even machines, standing quiet in the darkness of an unoccupied factory, are 'dead' things until animated – 'made alive' – by the workers who use them, who put them to work.

So what we have here is a conception of human beings as the only 'animating spark' in the world, the only self-propelling, self-motivating creative entities in the world. Human 'labour power' is, for Marx, the *only* creative force which, as it were, puts itself into action, which does not have to *be put* into use by something else, as does even the most sophisticated machine. Indeed at the centre of this philosophical conception of human beings as Promethean creators is the concept of labour power as self-generating activity. Remember that Marx defines labour power as 'the aggregate of those mental and physical capabilities existing in a human being which he [*sic*] exercises whenever he produces a use value of any description' (see p.74). What makes human beings self-activating, self-motivating is their 'capabilities', and Marx means by this their physical skills, but above all their intelligence, their imagination, their reason. It is *this* which the capitalist class buys when it buys 'labour power'.[16] And it is this transaction which really sickens Marx about capitalism. It is this transaction to which he really objects philosophically. He hates capitalism because it is a form of society in which *human creativity itself* (and not just the products of that creativity) is bought and sold. Since for Marx that creativity is the source of all change, and the source of a great deal of beauty, then its degradation to the status of a commodity simultaneously degrades both those who sell it and those who buy it.

If we understand labour power as a *philosophical* concept, as a concept – perhaps *the* concept – which links *Capital* to Marx's philosophy of praxis,[17] then we also have a clue to the resolution of a puzzle which has long concerned serious students of Marx's economics. For Marx (and Engels) made a great fuss about his 'discovery' of 'labour power', and Marx also vigorously insisted that the resolution to problems generated in Ricardo's economics was to understand that, under capitalism, workers sell 'labour power' not 'labour'. Yet to many students of Marx's economics this has seemed a tendentious, not to say hair-splitting, distinction. After all, why *cannot* one say, with Ricardo, that workers sell their 'labour' to capitalists for a finite number of hours in the day, days in the week, etc.? It is not obvious, for example, that saying that workers sell their labour rather than their labour power does commit one to a confusion between wage labour and slavery (as is sometimes claimed). As a tool of economic theory, the distinction between labour and labour power seems redundant, or certainly fairly unilluminating.[18]

But of course if 'labour power' is a philosophical rather than a strictly economic concept, then the whole issue is recast. Since for Marx the essence of human beings (their 'species being') is their capacity for creative activity, then in selling this, in reducing this to a commodity, they quite literally 'sell their soul'. A positively Faustian bargain is struck between the capitalist and the worker. The full force of Marx's philosophical objection to capitalism becomes clear.

And this also gives us a clue to how Marx would reply to my point about his 'accounting trick' made earlier in this chapter (see pages 99–101). You will remember that I said there that Marx accounts the value of machines so that they 'cannot' add value to commodities (essentially by simply dividing the value of the machine into the number of commodities it produces before it is depreciated), but he does not account living labour power in this way. Rather he 'proves' that only living labour power adds value to commodities, by accounting the *time* for which the working class works in excess of the value of its labour power. But this, I said, was no proof at all. Because, I said, 'machines can do this too', that is machines can also work, or produce at average or above-average levels of productivity, for a time well in excess of the SNAL taken to produce them.

I think that Marx's reply to this point would be philosophical, not economic. He would say, 'Ah, but machines do not *do* anything. Rather they *are made* to do things by human beings. They are made to work for a period in excess of their own value both by the capitalist's managerial decision and by the workers who operate them. Thus, any additional commodities which they produce in that 'excess' time can still be conceived as simply the products of living labour power.'

And I would find this reply quite acceptable as a *philosophical* reply, but I would not find it at all acceptable as an *economic* reply. And this is the point really. It is perfectly acceptable, philosophically, to say something like 'no commodities could exist at all without human creativity, so in that sense *all* commodities are the products of that creativity', just as it is perfectly acceptable, philosophically, to say something like 'machines, no matter how complex, are simply embodiments of human skill and intelligence, and require human beings to design and use them'. But it is not at all acceptable, economically, to say things like 'machines and other means of production make no contribution to profits' or 'living labour power is the *only* source of capitalist profits'.

But what allows Marx to move from the acceptable philosophical propositions to the unacceptable economic ones (or what he *thought* allowed him to do so) was a particular use of the concept of 'value'. Marx seems to have thought that a proposition like 'only living labour power *adds value* to commodities' either logically followed from, or was just another form of words for, a proposition like 'machines only run for as long as human beings *want* them to run'. But of course this is not so. The first proposition is neither simply another form of words for the second proposition, nor does it follow logically from the second proposition. On the contrary, the 'value' proposition is a proposition *in economic theory* which commits one to all sorts of other propositions which the 'philosophical' proposition does not.[19] Moreover, most of the other economic propositions to which this 'value' proposition committed Marx were false! In other words, and to use a rather trendy term, Marx has two intellectual *discourses* hopelessly muddled and mixed up here, and he muddled himself in muddling the discourses.

That he did muddle himself is shown by one simple fact; that Marx does seriously seem to have thought that if capital-in-general did not employ *people* it would make no profits. In other words, by dint of his economic theory Marx derived from his philosophical premise – that only living human beings are self-activating creators – the economic conclusion that capitalism could not be profitable without them as direct producers.

But of course this conclusion does not follow at all from this premise, and some reflections on an automated economy will make that clear. Suppose that we imagine a world in which the vast bulk of commodities are produced by self-regulating machines. These machines have cybernetic 'feedback' circuits by which they can monitor their own performance, and the level of output which they produce is controlled by another machine – a computer. In addition all these machines are designed with the help of computers and are repaired by computerized robots. Let us say that, as a result of these developments, the working class in manufacturing in the whole of 'Ameujap' has been reduced to 250,000 people, most of whom are computer designers and programmers.

Now even in such a world, it would still be possible, philosophically, to regard the output of this automated economy as simply 'the product of human creativity'. For all these machines may still be regarded as mere embodiments of human intelligence, and as obedient to human will and purposes. But equally it would make even less sense in this kind of world than it does now to say of this economy that 'surplus value is only the product of living labour power' or 'all these machines do not "add value", you know, they make no contribution to surplus value and profits'. In other words, Marx's philosophy would still hold in such a world, but his economics would look even more ridiculous than it does now.

Very interestingly, there is one fascinating passage in the *Grundrisse* where Marx comes close to a recognition of this problem and of its implications for value analysis. In Notebook VII he says:

The exchange of living labour for objectified labour ... is the ultimate development of the *value relation* and of production resting on value. Its presupposition is – and remains – the mass of direct labour time, the quantity of labour employed, as the determinate factor in the production of wealth. *But to the degree that large industry develops the creation of real wealth comes to depend less on labour time* and on the amount of labour employed *than on the power of the agencies set in motion during labour time, whose 'powerful effectiveness' is ... out of all proportion to the direct labour time spent on their production*, but depends on the general state of science and on the progress of technology, or the application of this science to production. ...

Real wealth manifests itself, rather ... in the monstrous disproportion between the labour time applied and its product as well as in the qualitative imbalance between labour, reduced to a pure abstraction, and the power of the production process it superintends. Labour no longer appears so much to be included within the production process; rather the human being comes to relate more as a watchman and regulator to the production process itself. ... He steps to the side of the process instead of being its chief actor. In this transformation, *it is neither the direct human labour he himself performs, nor the time during which he works, but rather the appropriation of his own general productive power, his understanding of nature and his mastery over it by virtue of his presence as a social body – it is, in a word, the development of the social individual which appears as the great foundation stone of production and of wealth.*[20]

And Marx goes on directly from this passage, to draw the conclusion that 'As soon as labour in the direct form has ceased to
be the well-spring of wealth, *labour time ceases and must cease to be
its measure.*'[21]

The puzzle however is how Marx could have thought that this
stage could possibly be reached under capitalism, since, according to his own theory, long before it was reached, the capitalist
class would find its profits disappearing (and would therefore
presumably have been forced to cease the process of automation?).

Interestingly too, whereas Marx included, in *Capital*, a number
of passages about the development of 'an automated system of
machinery' in 'modern industry', he dropped all the *Grundrisse*
speculations about the ultimate implications of this in making
value analysis redundant.[22] The reason for this is presumably
that in Marx's own time the prospects for an even predom-
inately automated industrial structure were so remote as to be
discountable.[23] However, they are not nearly so remote for us in
the late twentieth century,[24] and therefore for us the logical gap
which automation makes obvious between Marx's philosophy
of praxis and his economic theory becomes a practical as well as
a theoretical issue.

But despite this, this passage from the *Grundrisse* prompts yet
another reflection on the merits of inconsistency, and is also a
perfect example of a marked intellectual characteristic of Marx.
For so often it is when he leaves behind the narrowing demands
of strict theoretical consistency and lets his speculative genius
take wing that he is at his brilliant best.

And as he himself suggests – brilliantly and with astonish-
ing historical prescience – in a highly automated production
structure it is *knowledge*, socially developed and applied *knowledge*,
which human beings contribute (primarily) to the productive
process. In our world the human 'creative spark' still counts. It
is at work in every university and in every 'R & D' department of
every public and private corporation. Indeed, in some ways the
spark counts more than ever *in* production, but no longer requires direct human labour for its physical transmission *to* production. To that degree the 'labour theory of value' and the
theory of exploitation which Marx derives from it, become
manifestly flawed in our world. Reality disconfirms a logically
weak economic theory but validates an inspired philsophy.

In short then, all the really basic problems in Marx's economics derive from his having mixed up his philosophy of praxis,

and his related philosophy of history – see chapters 1 and 2 – with classical political economy, and especially with the labour theory of value.

In fact it is clear that when Marx discovered classical political economy for the first time (in the mid-1840s), what he *thought* he had discovered was the perfect completion, in the realm of 'science', of the philosophical system which he had already elaborated. In particular, he thought that an economics which treated all commodities as embodiments of varied quantities of human *labour*, was the perfect complement to a theory of history which treated both the world and thought as 'objectifications' of human activity or *practice*.

But I believe, and have argued, that Marx was simply wrong here. Classical political economy was *not* the perfect completion of his philosophy of praxis. On the contrary, it narrowed that philosophy in a damaging way (essentially by encouraging Marx to concentrate on economic activity to the exclusion of many other human activities). It also made use of concepts which looked very similar to, but whose implications were very different from, Marx's philosophical concepts.

Let me offer one final example to illustrate this. Classical economics treated machines as 'dead' (meaning 'embodied') labour, that is as living labour of the past embodied in machines.[25] And Marx often uses the concept 'dead labour' in this way.[26] But he also uses the concept 'dead labour' to mean something like 'nature without life of its own' or 'nature unanimated by the human spark', 'nature unappropriated by human beings'. So for example, machines are not merely 'dead' because they embody the living labour power of the past, they are dead *whenever* they lie unused, *whenever* they are switched off. Marx thought that these two meanings of 'dead labour' went together. They do not. They lead one in very different directions.

SALVAGING MARX'S ECONOMICS

In the final section of this chapter, I want to consider what can be salvaged from this mess (for there is no doubt that it is a mess) produced by Marx's failure genuinely to integrate his philosophy and his economic theory. Since, as may be clear, I have a lot more time for his philosophy of praxis than I have for his economics, I propose to follow the former in dealing with this problem.

If the philosophy of praxis is sound, it would suggest that we should first ask of Marx's economic theory 'what purpose is it meant to serve?' or 'what is the *point* of this theory, what does Marx want to do with it?' Below I have set out four propositions which Marx wished to justify by means of his theory. In each case I have presented the proposition and then assessed its truth or falsehood and its degree of dependence upon the labour theory of value. As I hope to show, some, though not all, of the propositions which Marx wished to justify using the labour theory of value can be justified without it. This is particularly so of course for the propositions which rest on his more general philosophy of history and not on his economic theory.

Propositions to which Marx is committed

1. 'Living labour is historically prior to machines and other means of production. There can be, and there were, people without machines, but there can be no machines without people. It is people who make, develop and above all, *use* machines.'

Comment Perfectly true. But showing this to be true does *not* require one to measure the value of commodities in labour time, or to deny that machines and other means of production contribute to producing a physical surplus product and therefore – in a capitalist system – to profit.

2. 'At the macro-economic level, profit cannot be explained as simply the excess of the monetary price of output over monetary costs of production. Individual firms and even individual capitalist economies, can obtain a profit on this way, but the world capitalist system as a whole must produce *a constantly increasing physical product per head* if overall profitability is to be maintained, and real accumulation of wealth and rising material living standards are to occur.'

Comment True and very important, and the basic proposition of much contemporary 'neo-Ricardian' economics (indeed this was the central insight provided by Ricardo's own economic theory).[27] But while net profit in the system as a whole *does* require an increasing physical product per head, there is no reason, either in economic logic or in empirical evidence, to treat this surplus product as simply the product of living labour. It is the joint product of living labour and means of production – especially machines.

3. 'Capitalists have no right to profit.'

Comment The problem here is that Marx thought that in order to deny that capitalists, as a class, had a right to accumulate *private wealth* in the form of profit, he had to deny that capital *as plant, machinery, raw materials* was productive of surplus. But this is to take a very large theoretical sledge hammer to smash a much smaller political nut. One can perfectly well agree that physical capital is productive, but deny that capitalists have right to it as private property.[28] Partly in the present stage of capitalism where corporate and financial capital is highly developed and legal ownership of assets is often totally divorced from control and management of them, that case is, if anything, rather easier to make than it was in Marx's day (when the family firm with an owner-manager was the dominant form of enterprise).

Indeed one of Marx's other insights in *Capital* – that 'Capital' is a massive social force, requiring the interacting activities of thousands or even millions of people, but that this social force is in private hands – is even truer today than it was in the nineteenth century. The case for the 'socialization' of capital on these grounds is therefore stronger than ever.[29]

4. 'The social and political power of Capital is a perfect example of a human product – the product of past and present human activity – becoming an alien force dominating and oppressing those people, the working class, who continually produce and reproduce it.'[30]

Comment An important and, I think, broadly true proposition but again one does not need the labour theory of value to justify it. The more general propositions of historical materialism will suffice for such a justification, and are, significantly, the only ones employed in the famous section 4 of volume 1 of *Capital* ('The Fetishism of Commodities and the Secret thereof') where this case is made (I, 71–83).

In short, I think a great deal of what Marx wished to validate or justify with the economic theory of *Capital* can be validated or justified without it. This is especially so of proposition 3 ('Capitalists have no right to profit') which was politically dear to his heart.

But it must also be said that another proposition even more dear to him ('profit comes *only* from the exploitation of the working class') cannot be justified either by Marx's theory or, in my view, by any other economic theory, *for the simple reason that it is false*.[31]

Marx may well have found such a conclusion alarming, and there are many contemporary Marxists who would find it equally alarming. But, once again, the philosophy of praxis would suggest that how alarming it is depends upon what we think can be done with such a proposition, upon what would follow for other human practices if it were true, and what follows if it is false. Marx believed that if it was true this was an additional reason, perhaps even the major reason, for the working class to make a revolution against capitalism. If the proposition is false however, then of course this reason has to be given up. But the question still arises whether there are other reasons why the working class, or anybody else, might still want to do this or need to do it. These questions are taken up in the sixth chapter of this book.

One final point. On page 110, I said that what sickened Marx about capitalism, one of the things which most revolted him about it as a form of society, was that in it human creativity itself becomes a commodity, is bought and sold. The reader might wish to reflect on how far he or she agrees with Marx's value judgement here. For my own part I have to say that I partially concur with it and partially do not.

For example, I enjoy fine art. I very much enjoy looking at beautiful paintings and sculpture, but I also find my enjoyment diminished to a degree by the reflection that they often become enormously costly *commodities*. They are, moreover, often the private property of a few rich individuals, and are so valuable not because of their beauty but simply because of their scarcity or rarity. Or again, I have often stood in a stately home looking out at beautifully designed formal gardens or parkland or looking inward at fine furniture, carpets, tableware, etc., and reflected that there is something ultimately obscene about such humanly created *beauty* being itself the private property of, or for the enjoyment of, one family. Or yet again, I find it hard to view television or magazine advertising without reflecting that in both media fine creativity, in the taking and printing of photographs, in the designing of sets, in the blending of colours or forms, in the cutting and editing of film and video, is being used to sell clothing, or cosmetics, or cars, or chocolate. Surely it could be put to better use with better social arrangements?

On the other hand, however it does not seem to me that there is much human creativity involved in mining coal, or packing cakes into boxes, or assembling transistor radios from standard components. Would one not much rather that machines did all these repetitive, boring, dangerous, or dirty tasks? Why have 'living labour power' involved in them at all?

But these are personal reflections, designed to stimulate agreement or disagreement, not to convince. Quite why one feels these things, if one does feel them (or not, if one does not), quite why Marx felt them, seems to me to be very mysterious. Perhaps the reader would like to reflect on that question as well.

CHAPTER 5

MARX ON REVOLUTION AND COMMUNISM

I shall treat these two topics in order, dealing first with Marx's ideas about revolution and then with his ideas on communism. However, even taken together these two topics do not exhaust Marx's political concerns. As I will hope to show, many of Marx's other political ideas – especially those concerned with classes and with the state – can best be understood within the context of his commitment to revolution and communism. But none the less this context does not embrace all the other dimensions of his political thought.

In the next chapter, therefore, I shall consider Marx's views on class and class struggle, on the state, and on ideology more explicitly, suggesting as I do so, that rather more importance has been attached to all three of these concepts than perhaps they deserve or than Marx intended. Or rather, I will suggest that the way in which Marx's writings on class, on the state, and on ideology have been understood and appropriated by subsequent generations of Marxists has perhaps been somewhat misleading, mainly because, once again, they have treated as static and general that which is best understood as dynamic and specific.

MARX ON REVOLUTION

We have already seen in previous chapters, how broadly and variously both Marx and Engels used the term 'revolution', but it is certainly worth bringing out that variety here by a more systematic – though by no means exhaustive – listing.
1. In the 1859 Preface (chapter 2, p.36) we saw Marx suggesting the possibility of a 'social revolution' when the forces of production become fettered by the relations of production.

2. And yet in an article on 'The British Rule in India' published in *The New York Daily Tribune* for 25 June 1853 we find Marx saying that only the colonial conquest of India by Britain could have 'dissolved' the 'small semi-barbarian, semi-civilized communities' of the Indian village and have produced thereby what Marx describes as 'to speak the truth, *the only social revolution ever heard of in Asia*'.

3. We have already noted how Engels, in his speech at Marx's graveside, ran together effortlessly, even thoughtlessly, revolution as *technological* revolution (that is revolutionary changes in science, in the forces of production, and, therefore, in the technical division of labour) and revolution as *social* revolution (i.e. the replacement of one form of society by a new and better form).

4. In addition, however, in the *Communist Manifesto*, the *Eighteenth Brumaire*, and *The Civil War in France* we find Marx and Engels using the term 'revolution' in the way which is perhaps most closely associated with Marxism, that is to mean an assault upon state power, and the taking over of that power by a new social class or group.[1]

So just as in chapter 2 with Marx's ideas on history, we seem to be faced here with both a great deal of imprecision and a great deal of inconsistency in Marx's use of the term 'revolution'. However, just as in chapter 2, I wish to argue that a great deal of this imprecision is merely apparent, and is indeed fairly easily accounted for if we understand the historical context in which both Marx and Engels were living and writing. Indeed, if I had to sum that context up in a phrase it would be precisely to say that Marx and Engels lived in and through a 'revolutionary' period of human history.[2]

This can easily enough be seen if we take the period of Marx's own life alone, the period 1818 to 1883. Let us outline some of the most revolutionary features of that period.

First, Marx was born only three years after the final defeat of Napoleon, in 1815, and indeed he was born in a part of Europe – the Rhineland – which had been conquered by the armies of revolutionary France in 1793 and then administered as a part of revolutionary and Napoleonic France for twenty-two years. As a result Marx's home city, Trier, and other parts of the Rhineland had been profoundly affected by social, political, and legal changes brought about by Napoleon, changes which reflected, at least to a certain degree, the liberal and radical ideas of the great French Revolution of 1789 to which the Napoleonic Empire claimed to be heir.[3]

Secondly, Marx grew to adulthood as the industrial revolution in Britain was reaching its high point of international economic dominance. He moved permanently to Britain in 1849 to live in the country which just two years later styled itself 'the workshop of the world' and held the first Great Exhibition of manufactured goods.[4] He lived in the home of the first industrial revolution for the rest of his life.

Thirdly, in 1830 there was a major change of political regime in France. This was just fifteen years after the more conservative governments of Europe had thought the spirit of the French Revolution finally dead, with Napoleon militarily defeated and the old monarchy of France restored. This was followed in 1848 by further attempts at revolutionary political change not only in France, but in Germany, Austria, and Italy, while in Britain the Chartist movement of workers and artisans seemed also to challenge state power.[5] Then, after a period of quiescence in the 1850s and 1860s, there was yet another revolutionary upheaval in France (in 1871) giving rise, briefly, to the Paris Commune, an institution which was profoundly to influence Marx's later views about socialism and communism (see pages 145–7).

Fourthly, throughout Marx's life, and indeed after his death, the industrialization and urbanization of society which had begun in Britain, spread slowly west to east across Europe. In virtually every country to which it spread, mass socialist movements arose, movements which from the 1850s onwards were often influenced by Marx's own ideas.[6]

Fifthly, Marx lived out his life in a period which witnessed major ('revolutionary') advances in natural science, and especially in chemistry, physics, and biology. Perhaps the most remarkable of all these advances was marked by the publication of Charles Darwin's On the Origin of Species in 1859, a work which Marx considered 'revolutionary' in every sense, not only in its scientific content but in its social, political, and religious implications. Moreover, in Marx's lifetime these scientific advances began to be applied, to industrial and agricultural production, to health and medicine, to housing and sanitation, and to human nutrition. Generally speaking it can be said that by the end of Marx's life – in 1883 – a significant proportion of the population of Europe lived longer, were healthier, and were better fed, clothed, and housed than they had been at the time of his birth in 1818. Also, of course, a far larger proportion of that population lived in cities, and especially industrial cities, than at the time of Marx's birth.[7]

I do not know how one could characterize such a period other than as a period – a century – of revolution, a 'revolutionary period' in every respect. So if Marx's concept of revolution is shifting and multi-layered that is because the process it is trying to grasp was endlessly shifting and multi-layered.

The question, however, was what the relationship was between these different aspects or types of revolutionary change. More particularly – and what obsessed Marx and Engels throughout their lives – was the question of the relationship, the connection between the revolution in science and industry and that in society and politics. Marx and Engels were convinced that there was, that there must be, some connection between these two forms of revolution. For them it was not, it could not be, a simple coincidence that the century of the industrial revolution was also a century which saw more political revolutions and attempted revolutions in Europe than had been seen in all previous periods of the continent's history combined.

Chapter 2 of this book has already outlined the answer which they gave to this question. But it bears repeating here. It was the view of Marx and Engels that in earlier centuries of feudal Europe there had been a slow growth of the 'forces of production' within the 'relations of production' of feudalism. This process had been, at the same time, a process by which a new social class ('the bourgeoisie') had slowly gained economic power at the expense of the old landed aristocracies.

However this economic power was not at first matched by increased political power, for this still tended to be monopolized by the old landowners. Thus from the seventeenth century onwards, the bourgeoisies of different European countries had begun to make 'bourgeois revolutions' against the old ruling classes. Sometimes that process was gradual and – mainly – peaceful, as in Britain where it had begun (for the bourgeoisie had first developed and grown powerful there). Sometimes however it had been sudden and violent, as in France in 1789. In all cases however the aim was the same, to overthrow or sharply reduce the power of the old landed ruling classes and to change the form of state through which that power was exercised.

Marx saw this process of bourgeois revolution as still continuing in his own lifetime, and he hoped and expected that its result would be the replacement of 'absolute monarchies' by what he termed 'bourgeois democratic' forms of state.[8] In other words, he hoped that in his own lifetime he would see throughout Europe an end to states in which, in theory, hereditary kings, queens, and princes ruled 'absolutely' by the will of God (by 'divine right' it was called) and in which either there was no tradition of popular elections of governments at all, or such elections were effectively restricted to the landed class alone (as in eighteenth-century England). Marx hoped and expected that through the process of 'bourgeois revolution' these types of states would be replaced by 'bourgeois democracies' in which there was rule by governments elected on a wide or universal franchise of the people and responsible to some form of popular assembly. Such states would also possess other 'bourgeois' freedoms such as equality before the law, freedom of the press, freedom of speech and assembly, etc.

In his youth, and up to about 1848, Marx was quite optimistic that such bourgeois revolutions would come to pass in Europe quickly and easily, and in his *Critique of Hegel's Philosophy of Right* of 1844 he writes quite optimistically about the degree of democratization of European states which would follow simply from the attainment of a universal franchise of their peoples. Moreover, throughout this early period, Marx's ideas about the bourgeois revolution were heavily influenced by the French Revolution of 1789.[9] In other words he tended to envisage it as a sudden and violent upheaval.

However, from 1848 onwards Marx became more and more uncertain, about both the prospects of such bourgeois revolutions in Europe and their desirability. For the general failure of most of the 1848 revolutions in Europe to dislodge 'absolutist' rulers, and especially the total failure of such attempts in Germany, revealed a problem to Marx and Engels.

This problem derived from the very same historical process which had given Marx such hopes for bourgeois revolution. For the rise of a bourgeoisie in pre-industrial Europe was just a part of a complex historical process which had another class dimension – the creation of an industrial proletariat or working class.

In his more optimistic moments (for example, in the *Communist Manifesto*) Marx saw the implications of this historical process as quite straightforward. The bourgeoisie would first make its revolution against the landed classes and their 'absolutist' states. This process might be gradual or sudden, peaceful or violent, but in order for it to occur the bourgeoisie would require the aid of the working class, because on its own it was not powerful enough to carry through the revolution against the old ruling classes. Marx anticipated that the bourgeoisie would win this working-class support through the promise of universal suffrage. In this way bourgeois democracies would be created throughout Europe, and would be distinguished, as we have already noted, by popularly elected governments and a range of civic freedoms.

Bourgeois democracy would however represent only a first stage in the revolutionary process. For, once enfranchised and given freedom to organize itself politically, the working class – becoming conscious of its shared material situation and shared exploitation – would use the civic freedoms provided by bourgeois democracy to make its own revolution against the bourgeoisie and for a transition to socialism and communism.

However the experiences of 1848 revealed to Marx and Engels that there was a considerable 'catch' with this neat two-stage vision of revolution. For the experience of 1848, in Germany in particular, but (in slightly different ways) in France and Italy as well, seemed to reveal that the bourgeoisies of Europe were very alive to the dangers of a subsequent 'proletarian revolution', and indeed were more afraid of the rising power of the working classes than they were of the old landed ruling classes (or of the 'absolutist' states which they dominated).

In other words, Marx and Engels read the 1848 experiences in western Europe as showing that, in general, the bourgeoisies of Europe were actually prepared to accept a subordinate political position to the old ruling classes in return for being protected (by the absolutist states) from the demands of the working class. To put it another way, if the full realization of the political and civic freedoms of 'bourgeois democracy' was only going to create the perfect conditions for the working classes of Europe to organize politically against them, then the bourgeoisies of Europe would rather not have a full-blown bourgeois democracy at all.[10] They would rather seek an accommodation with the old pre-industrial ruling classes in some hybrid form of non-democratic state.

But this turned out not to be the only problem with Marx's early optimistic vision of the future. For as Marx (and Engels) grew to maturity and then into old age in Britain, they saw a society in which the 'forces of production' *had* been developed to a higher point than anywhere else in the world (that is, where the necessary conditions for a social revolution specified in the 1859 Preface seemed to have been fulfilled). For here the bourgeoisie was securely in power, there was a 'bourgeois democracy' which was more developed than in most other countries in the world and the industrial working class was larger and more politically organized than in most other parts of Europe.

Yet the British working class did not seem to be interested in making a further 'proletarian revolution' at all. Marx and Engels expressed continual disappointment about this, and adduced many different explanations of it, from the role played by British colonialism in Ireland and by prejudice against immigrant Irish workers in keeping the working class politically divided, to the rise of a 'labour aristocracy' (to use Engels' phrase) of skilled workers who were relatively privileged and provided a very conservative leadership to that class.[11]

At any rate, all these complexities and developments were important in restructuring Marx's early and optimistically simple projections for the revolutionary process in Europe. Notably:

1. The 'faint-heartedness' of the bourgeoisies of Europe in 1848 led Marx and Engels increasingly to the view (expressed from the 1850s onwards) that over most of Europe the working classes themselves might have to make the 'bourgeois revolution' (that is the revolution against absolutism and for a democratic form of state) before 'pushing on', as it were, to the subsequent revolution to socialism and communism.

2. The accommodation of the bourgeoisies of Europe to absolutism, and then the subsequent demonstration (in France, Germany, and Italy) that universal suffrage could be granted while keeping power in the hands of the old monarchies and aristocracies, led Marx and Engels to believe that the *form* of state was in itself an important issue. If the working classes of Europe were truly to gain power, they could not be content, Marx argued (in *The Civil War in France* of 1871), simply to take over the existing form of state. The revolutionary working classes would have to 'smash' and then restructure the institutions of the state themselves.[12] This conclusion was heavily influenced by the experience of the Paris Commune of 1871, and I shall consider that experience shortly in discussing Marx's views on socialism and communism.

But before leaving the subject of revolution, two further points need to be dealt with. The first concerns the role of violence. What part was violence to play in the 'social revolution' envisaged by Marx? The answer to this question is, in principle at least, very simple. *Marx and Engels were totally pragmatic about the use of violence.* Basically, where either (a) there was no 'bourgeois' state, that is, no political or civic freedom for the working class to organize politically in an open or constitutional way or (b) where such freedoms formally existed but any attempts at such organization were in fact violently suppressed, then clandestine organizations of workers and violent means of revolution were necessary and justified. Marx and Engels were themselves founders and members of several such clandestine organizations of German workers.[13]

However, if, in any particular case, there was a well established bourgeois state with genuine traditions of political and civic freedom, then the working class could and should use those traditions and institutions to make the 'social revolution' peacefully and constitutionally. This of course is not incompatible, at least in theory, with using such constitutional methods to 'smash' and restructure state institutions in a fundamental way.

Marx himself put it perfectly simply and straightforwardly in a speech which he made in Amsterdam in September 1872. In it he said:

> We know of the allowances we must make for the institutions, customs and traditions of the various countries; and we do not deny that there *are* countries such as America, England, and I would add Holland if I knew your institutions better, where the working class may achieve their goal by peaceful means. If *that* is true, we must also recognize that in most of the continental countries it is force that will have to be the lever of our revolutions.[14]

So for Marx and Engels it was the end which mattered, the creation of a 'social revolution' to a new and better form of society – socialism and communism; the means were a subsidiary issue. However, in their later years certainly, they both seem to have preferred peaceful means to violent ones where there was, in their judgement, a real possibility of such means succeeding.[15]

However, both during and since the days of Marx and Engels, human history has repeatedly raised another issue concerning the use of violence, an issue which may well be troubling the reader. For if violence is resorted to, even in situations where there is no constitutional alternative, what guarantee is there that such means will not merely lead to widespread suffering and death *without* the achievement of any of the goals which were aimed at?

Again, I think the answer of Marx and Engels to such a question would have been quite straightforward. For they both knew, from the experience of the French Revolution of 1789 alone, that there was no such 'guarantee'. Indeed in the *Communist Manifesto* Marx noted that all previous class struggles had ended 'either in a revolutionary reconstitution of society, or in the common ruin of the contending classes'.[16] Whether, in any particular situation, it was worth taking the risk of such 'common ruin' was a matter for human judgement. It depended upon an assessment, an assessment of the risks involved, of the relative strength of the contending social forces, of the social and human cost of accepting the status quo, and so on. These are terribly serious judgements to make, and they necessarily involve taking responsibility for decisions with very onerous moral and political implications. But Marx and Engels thought that such moral and political responsibilities were unavoidable for anybody who purported to be a serious revolutionary.

There is a second and final point which arises from this discussion of Marx's views on revolution. For if all that Marx meant by 'bourgeois democracy' and by the 'bourgeois revolution' was a revolution to a society rather like the ones which exist in North America and western Europe now, to a democratic form of society, why did he not simply say this? Why call them *bourgeois* democracies? Why not simply 'democracies'? Is this not simply an unnecessary piece of name-calling? Well, it can certainly degenerate into that (and has done so repeatedly in the subsequent history of Marxism), but that was not the point of the term as Marx originally used it. Marx called 'our' type of society a 'bourgeois' democracy for two reasons.

Firstly, he thought that, historically, it was the revolutionary actions of the bourgeoisie against absolutism which had initially created such societies in the world, in Britain first, and then in France and Holland. But moreover, and secondly, he thought that the political and civic institutions of bourgeois democracy benefited the social class of the bourgeoisie more than any other class. Note that '*more* than any other class'. He did not argue that such institutions are of *no* benefit to other classes, but that they benefit the bourgeoisie disproportionately.

Thus, if there is equality before the law but the rich can afford the best lawyers and the poor are utterly unrepresented, such 'equality' may not mean very much. Thus, if there is freedom of the press but only a tiny rich minority of very similar views can afford to set up newspapers, then such 'freedom' may not mean very much. If the capitalist is a legally free person and so is the worker, but the worker cannot survive unless employed by the capitalist, then the legal equality and freedom of both parties can coexist perfectly easily with great power on the one side and almost total powerlessness on the other.

In other words Marx and Engels thought the freedoms of bourgeois democracy *were real but limited*, because legal, political, and civic equality was not matched by social and economic equality. Hence one primary aim of socialism and communism would be to create the economic and social equality which would make democratic freedoms equally meaningful for everybody in society. This of course implies that such freedoms were to be maintained, but deepened and strengthened by a change in the economic and social structure of society. Democratic freedoms were *not* to be abandoned or attenuated under socialism and communism.[17]

MARX ON COMMUNISM

Bourgeois revolutions had been total 'social revolutions' creating a new and better form of society. This new form of society was 'capitalist' society distinguished by an industrial mode of economic production and (where the bourgeois revolution had been completed) by a democratic form of politics. The proletarian revolution of the future was also to be a total 'social revolution' creating a new and higher mode of industrial production and an even more democratic form of politics. In accord with this view, therefore, in his rather few writings about 'socialism' and 'communism' Marx uses both these terms to refer to the form of society of the future *as a whole* (that is to both its mode of economic production and its political structure). So then, the 64,000 dollar question is, where was this next total 'social revolution' to lead? What did Marx think that a communist society would be like?

Especially in his later life, Marx was continually cautious about drawing such 'blueprints' of the future society. For such blueprints smacked, for him, of the so-called 'utopian socialism' of early nineteenth-century Britain and France which he had criticized in his polemic against the French thinker Proudhon (Marx's *The Poverty of Philosophy* of 1847) and in the *Communist Manifesto* and elsewhere.

In a letter to F. Domela-Nieuwenhuis in The Hague, written two years before his death, Marx said:

> The doctrinaire and necessarily fantastic anticipation of the programme of action for a revolution of the future only diverts one from the struggle of the present. The dream that the end of the world was near inspired the early Christians in their struggle with the Roman Empire and gave them confidence in victory. Scientific insight into the inevitable disintegration of the dominant order of society continually proceeding before our eyes, and the ever growing fury into which the masses are lashed by the old ghostly governments, while at the same time the positive development of the means of production advances with gigantic strides – all this is sufficient guarantee that the moment a real proletarian revolution breaks out the conditions of its immediately next *modus operandi* will be in existence.

And he goes on;

> I regard all workers' congresses and socialist congresses, in so far as they are not directly related to the conditions existing in this or that particular nation, as not merely useless but actually harmful. They will always fade away in innumerable stale, general banalities.[18]

None the less, Marx was not always quite so guarded or dismissive about envisaging the future communist society. For, firstly, in his early philosophical writings we find generalized descriptions of it as the form of society in which all human alienation is to be abolished. And secondly, in his later life Marx was occasionally forced to speculate about various aspects of socialism and communism; about, for example, the division of labour, the principles of economic distribution, or the form of state under socialism.

He was forced to do this simply because, as his ideas became more influential and political parties and movements which claimed to embody his ideas came into being all over Europe, so he came under insistent pressure to be somewhat more precise about socialism and communism. For after all the 'working class' throughout Europe and the world (or at least the politic-ally aware sections of it) was supposed to be bending all its revolutionary energies to achieving a goal about which Marx was reluctant to say anything! Two texts in particular are im-portant for Marx's later views of socialism and communism. They are *The Civil War in France* of 1871 and the *Critique of the Gotha Programme* of 1875.

We shall analyse both these texts in some detail later in this chapter. For the moment however let us consider three much earlier texts in which the younger Marx speculates, in a mainly philosophical manner, about communism.

Supposing that we had produced in a human manner; in his production each of us would have doubly affirmed himself and his fellow men. (1) I would have objectified in my pro-duction my individuality and its peculiarity, and would thus have enjoyed in my activity an individual expression of my life and would have also had – in looking at the object – the individual pleasure of realizing that my personality was ob-jective, visible to the senses and therefore a power raised beyond all doubt; (2) in your enjoyment or use of my product I would have had the direct enjoyment of realizing that by my work I had both satisfied a human need and also objecti-fied the human essence and therefore fashioned for another human being the object that had met his need. (3) I would have been for you the mediator between you and the species and thus been felt by you and acknowledged as a completion of your own essence and a necessary part of yourself, and I would thereby have realized that I was confirmed both in your thought and in your love; (4) in my expression of my life I would have fashioned your expression of your life, and thus in my own activity have realized my own essence, my human communal essence. In such a situation our products would be like so many mirrors, each one reflecting our essence. Thus, in this relationship what occurred on my side would also occur on yours. My work would be a free expression of my life, and therefore a free enjoyment of my life. In work the peculiarity of my individuality would have been affirmed since it is my individual life. Work would thus be genuine active property. Presupposing private property, my individuality is so far externalised that I hate my activity: it is a torment to me and only the appearance of an activity and thus also merely a forced activity that is laid upon me through an external arbitrary need – not an inner and necessary one.[19]

Communism is the positive abolition of private property, of human self-alienation, and thus the real appropriation of human nature through and for man. It is therefore the return of man himself as a *social*, i.e. really human, being, a complete and conscious return which assimilates all the wealth of previous development. Communism as a fully developed naturalism is humanism and as a fully developed humanism is naturalism. It is the definitive resolution of the antagonism between man and nature, and between man and man. It is the true solution of the conflict between existence and essence, between objectification and self-affirmation, between freedom and necessity, between individual and species. It is the solution to the riddle of history and knows itself to be the solution.

   ... the supersession of private property is, therefore, the complete *emancipation* of all human qualities and senses. It is such an emancipation because these qualities and senses have become *human*, from the subjective as well as the objective point of view. The eye has become a *human* eye when its object has become a *human* social object, created by man and destined for him. The senses have, therefore, become directly theoreticians in practice. They relate themselves to the thing for the sake of the thing, but the thing itself is an *objective human* relation to itself and to man and vice versa. Need and enjoyment have thus lost their egoistic character and nature has lost its mere *utility* by the fact that its utilisation has become *human utilisation*.[20]

In communist society, where nobody has one exclusive sphere of activity but each can become accomplished in any branch he wishes, society regulates the general production and thus makes it possible for me to do one thing today and another tomorrow, to hunt in the morning, fish in the afternoon, rear cattle in the evening, criticise after dinner, just as I have a mind, without ever becoming hunter, fisherman, shepherd or critic. This fixation of social activity, this consolidation of what we ourselves produce into an objective power above us, growing out of our control, thwarting our expectations, bringing to naught our calculations, is one of the chief factors in historical development up till now.[21]

The first two of these quotations are, in a sense, simply logical extensions of Marx's views on 'alienation', and in particular on 'alienated labour' which we reviewed in chapter one (pp. 19–21). In accord with his view that the human essence (which for him, we remember, is creative or productive *activity*) is denied in a society in which such activity has to take the form of coerced *labour*, Marx, in these early texts, sees communism as a form of society in which 'the conflict between existence and essence' is resolved. It is resolved by making all labour a free uncoerced activity, a free expression of human creativity.

Concretely, this appears to mean that things will be so organized that:

(a) individuals will produce directly for each other's needs, that is there will be no commodity production. Production and consumption will not be mediated by money;

(b) all labour will be undertaken 'for its own sake', that is for the satisfaction and pleasure it brings as an expression of human creativity and not as a means of existence. Thus, Marx conceives communist society as a form of society in which *people live in order to work* (but productively and creatively and for the needs of others), rather than, as under capitalism, a society in which people *have to work in order to live*; and

(c) in communist society there will be no technical division of labour. That is to say, there may be specialized tasks, but these will not be undertaken by task specialists, that is by people who do one thing and only one thing throughout their working lives. Rather people will undertake different tasks both at any one time and through their lives so as to express different aspects of themselves and also so as to create different aspects of themselves (since Marx believes that human activity shapes human nature, we *are* what we *do*, to a large extent). This last point is made explicit in the third quotation, from *The German Ideology*, in what is perhaps the most famous 'shorthand' sketch of communist society found in Marx's early writings.

The abolition of the division of labour, outlined in the *The German Ideology* quotation, is of such importance for Marx because he sees it as the principal cause of the 'antagonism . . .

between man and man'. Since, as we have seen, Marx believes human beings to be the only consciously *acting* creatures in the world, and since for him human consciousness is formed by and through activity, then different activities breed different attitudes, values, outlooks on the world. Thus, by abolishing a division of labour as a division among individuals, and substituting a society of multi-functional generalists familiar with manual labour, mental labour, artistic activity, and scientific activity, etc., Marx believed that the active foundations of a far greater human understanding and social solidarity would be laid. At the same time a greater 'all-round' individuality would be created by such varied activities and hence 'the free development of each' would no longer be in conflict with 'the free development of all'.[22] Thus the alienated antagonism between the individual and society is resolved. Under communism human beings become *social* beings. What people want to do for themselves is at the same time what society needs them to do. That from which they get most happiness and fulfilment (creative work) is also that which fulfils the needs of others as well as of themselves.

Now it hardly needs to be said that this vision, however attractive, or otherwise, it may seem to the reader, begs a very large number of questions. To enumerate just a few:

1. How, in practice, and in a complex industrial society, is it *possible* to organize production and consumption without the use of some form of money or market exchange (without commodity production in short)? We shall return to this question by a rather different route later in this chapter.

2. As I mentioned earlier in passing, it is possible to imagine some forms of labour in society being undertaken as quite literally 'labours of love' (see quotation 1, p. 131) or 'for their own sakes'. One thinks possibly of artistic, intellectual, and scientific activity, highly skilled artisan activity, many sporting and recreational activities. But is, for example, coal-mining, or road-sweeping, or production-line work in a factory, or routine office work, or sewer maintenance or road gritting *ever* 'an expression of human creativity'? And if such tasks are not expressions of any form of creativity, if they do not constitute forms of self-expression of any type *and yet they are socially necessary*, then who is to do them?

Interestingly there are only two possible answers to this question. One is, 'we all do them'. That is, with the abolition of the division of labour 'everybody' has to 'take a turn' at the dangerous, dirty, or just plain boring jobs, as well as at the more creative or self–fulfilling activities. This is what might be termed the 'Maoist' answer to the question.[23]

The other answer is *machines do them*. That is, one solves the problem by conceiving communist society as a highly *automated* form of society and economy in which all the 'dirty work', all the repetitive, dangerous, or generally unrewarding tasks are undertaken by automata (robots, automatic machines, etc.) leaving human beings ('living labour power') free to be invested only in creative, self-expressive activity.

There is some evidence to suggest that in the course of his life Marx's position on communism moved from answer one to answer two. In the 1840s his stress on the abolition of the division of labour seems to imply (though he himself never explicitly stated this) a 'Maoist' answer to the question about who will undertake the unfulfilling tasks in society. In later life however – and once again taking his cue from developments in capitalism – Marx seems to have moved toward a picture of communist society as a highly automated society with human creativity being released from all forms of drudgery by machines.

Thus in the *Grundrisse* he says:

As soon as labour in the direct form has ceased to be the great well spring of wealth, labour time ceases and must cease to be its measure, and hence exchange value [must cease to be the measure] of use value. The *surplus labour of the mass* has ceased to be a condition for the development of general wealth, just as the *non-labour of the few* [has ceased to be the condition] of the general powers of the human head. With that, production based on exchange value breaks down, and the direct material production process is stripped of the form of penury and antithesis. *The free development of individualities*, and hence not the reduction of necessary labour so as to posit surplus labour, but rather *the general reduction of the necessary labour of society to a minimum, which then corresponds to the artistic, scientific etc. development of the individuals in the time set free, and with the means created, for all of them.*[24]

But even if one opts for the 'machine' solution (and obviously in some societies in the world – in 'Ameujap' for example – such a solution through automation is somewhat nearer realization now than in Marx's day) there is still a major problem. For,

3. Who is to say what *is* 'creative', 'fulfilling', 'self-expressive' activity and what is not? In other words, what are we to make (and, more pertinently, what would Marx have made?) of people who insist that they *do* find packing cakes in boxes, or mining coal, or typing accounts, or gritting roads 'creative', 'fulfilling' activities? Is Marx not guilty here of imposing a particular view of what *is* creative, fulfilling, essentially human activity on others?

Indeed we could turn Marx's own insight against him here. We could say that if it is not 'social consciousness that determines social being' but 'social being that determines social consciousness' then are not his own ideas about 'essentially human', 'self-creative' activities precisely the sort of ideas which one might expect a highly educated, professional, even 'bourgeois' *intellectual* like Marx to have? Given Marx's social role, his 'social being', *he* might not have found sewer-cleaning, or box-packing or account-typing very fulfilling. But is he not guilty, on the basis of this, of making the élitist assumption that nobody would? And is he not also assuming equality of ability, or at least equality of potential among human beings, as well as what one might call a 'uniformity of interests'?

Actually Marx was once explicitly challenged on just this issue and in replying he denied that he was assuming equality of ability or potential among human individuals. He said rather that communist society would be a form of society in which people were genuinely free to discover what *they* found fulfilling and non-fulfilling, rather than having such a choice precluded by being forced into, or being born into, a particular place in the occupational structure.[25]

In discussing this issue with some of my students during seminars, we amused ourselves with speculations about 'Community Activity Centres' set up in an automated communist society, and including specially installed production or assembly lines, or typing pools, or specially installed (and continually dirtied) sewers, walls, etc., for those who still found these 'redundant' activities fulfilling, despite their being performed by machines in the outside world. It is not clear what Marx would have made of such speculations. Most probably he would have found them irritating rather than amusing.

And finally, even if we assume that Marx himself was not making *any* assumptions about what all human beings living in a communist society would experience as 'creative', 'fulfilling' activity, there is still a further problem.

4. For what is one to make of Marx's assumption that all such 'free', 'individual' activity would always be *socially desirable* activity, would *only* be such activity as society would need and want of individuals?

In Marx's communist society the question confronting every young person would not be 'what shall I do for a living?' for one's 'living' (in the sense of one's material needs) would already be guaranteed by automated production. The question would rather be 'what shall I do with my life?' In other words, the issue facing every individual would be to decide on the most creative, self-fulfilling activity or group of activities to engage in during his or her life.

Now suppose that after having given due consideration to this question a person, or group of people, decided that what they really wanted was to be murderers, rapists, thieves, or drug pushers, and they insisted that these *would* be 'self-fulfilling' activities for them and they could not be dissuaded from this decision. There are two possible replies to this troublesome conjecture.

(a) It could not happen. In other words, Marx could have a view of what it is to be truly human, or a view of the causality of anti-social behaviour such that this behaviour is *precluded by assumption* once capitalism has been abolished and 'true human potential' released.

(b) Or Marx could reply that this is a possibility. In which case, if he accepts that such behaviour is 'anti-social', then there would be no total resolution of the antagonism between the individual and society under communism. Hence it would follow that a communist society would still require some kind of *coercive* mechanism either to prevent such choices from being effected, or to punish them if they were acted upon.

I must confess that it has never been very clear to me which of these alternatives Marx would have chosen. Some scholars have argued that Marx does possess an 'essentialist' view of human nature which would result in his taking position (a) above. Others have denied this, or have argued that Marx's conception of the 'creative' or 'productive' essence of human beings does not imply that what human beings produce is always, or even predominantly, morally *good*.[26]

Personally I hold to this latter view – that Marx's concepts of human 'creativity' or 'productivity' are morally neutral, that they embrace the possibility of gas chambers as well as chamber orchestras, nuclear wars as well as wars on want.

But in this context I do not think that it matters very much. For if Marx held that 'true' human nature was such that once people were released from the constraints of capitalism (from poverty, inequality, and competitive materialism) *all* anti-social behaviour would be totally eradicated, then I simply want to say that he was wrong. Such behaviour might be reduced in incidence or change its form, but that is another matter. If he did not hold this view, then his vision of communist society as the society in which the antagonism between individual wants and needs and social wants and needs has been finally eliminated cannot be sustained. Either way there is a problem.

So far however, we have only considered Marx's early or earlier writings on communism. Let us now consider the most important of Marx's later or mature writings on this topic – the *Critique of the Gotha Programme* of 1875.

Critique of the Gotha Programme

What we have to deal with here is a communist society, not as it has *developed* on its own foundations, but, on the contrary, just as it *merges* from capitalist society; which is thus in every respect, economically, morally and intellectually, still stamped with the birth marks of the old society from whose womb it emerges. Accordingly, the individual producer receives back from society – after the deductions have been made – exactly what he gives to it. What he has given to it is his individual quantum of labour. For example, the social working day consists of the sum of the individual hours of work; the individual labour time of the individual producer is the part of the social working day contributed by him, his share in it. He receives a certificate from society that he has furnished such and such an amount of labour (after deducting his labour for the common funds), and with this certificate he draws from the social stock of means of consumption as much as costs the same amount of labour. The same amount of labour which he has given to society in one form he receives back in another.

Here obviously the same principle prevails as that which regulates the exchange of commodities, as far as this is exchange of equal values. Content and form are changed, because under the altered circumstances no one can give anything except his labour, and because, on the other hand, nothing can pass to the ownership of individuals except individual means of consumption. But, as far as the distribution of the latter among the individual producers is concerned, the same principle prevails as in the exchange of commodity equivalents: a given amount of labour in one form is exchanged for an equal amount of labour in another form.

Hence, *equal right* here is still in principle *bourgeois right*, although principle and practice are no longer at loggerheads, while the exchange of equivalents in commodity exchange only exists *on the average* and not in the individual case.

In spite of this advance, the *equal right* is still constantly stigmatised by a bourgeois limitation. The right of the producers is *proportional* to the labour they supply; the equality consists in the fact that measurement is made with an *equal standard*, labour.

But one man is superior to another physically or mentally and so supplies more labour in the same time, or can labour for a longer time; and labour, to serve as a measure, must be defined by its duration or intensity, otherwise it ceases to be a standard of measurement. This *equal* right is an unequal right for unequal labour. It recognises no class differences, because everyone is only a worker like everyone else; but it tacitly recognises unequal individual endowment and thus [unequal] productive capacity as natural privileges. *It is, therefore, a right of inequality, in its content, like every right*. Right by its very nature can consist only in the application of an equal standard; but unequal individuals (and they would not be individuals if they were not unequal) are measurable by an equal standard in so far as they are brought under an equal point of view, are taken from one *definite* side only, for instance, in the present case, are regarded *only* as *workers* and nothing more is seen in them, everything else being ignored. Further, one worker is married, another not; one has more children than another, and so on and so forth. Thus, with an equal performance of labour, and hence an equal share in the social consumption fund, one will in fact receive more than another, one will be richer than another, and so on. To avoid all these defects, rights instead of being equal would have to be unequal.

But these defects are inevitable in the first phase of communist society as it is when it has just emerged after prolonged birth pangs from capitalist society. Right can never be higher than the economic structure of society and its cultural development conditioned thereby.

In a higher phase of communist society, after the enslaving subordination of the individual to the division of labour, and therewith also the antithesis between mental and physical labour, has vanished; after labour has become not only a means of life, but life's prime want; after the productive forces have also increased with the all-round development of the individual, and all the springs of co-operative wealth flow more abundantly – only then can the narrow horizon of bourgeois right be crossed in its entirety and society inscribe on its banners: From each according to his ability to each according to his needs![27]

The reader will note a distinct change of tone in this quotation, which was written thirty years or more after Marx's earlier philosophical pronouncements on communism. Marx's long study of political economy in the intervening period has clearly left its mark, and indeed it is the language of political economy – rather than that of Hegelian philosophy – which predominates. This is shown particularly in the much more realistic discussion of the principles of economic distribution which will prevail in the first stage of communist society, the stage which Marx calls 'socialism'. In this first phase, Marx tells us, distribution of society's economic product will not be on the basis of need, but on the basis of labour performed, and given unequal abilities between workers (which Marx explicitly assumes as we see) then such a principle of distribution will mean a degree of economic *inequality* between workers in this first, socialist, stage.

The reason for this inequality is given by Marx in the first sentence of this quotation. 'What we have to deal with ... is a communist society, not as it has developed on its own foundations, but, on the contrary, just as it emerges from capitalist society.' This implies, according to Marx, that such a society will be stamped 'economically, morally and intellectually ... with the birth marks of the old society'. In other words, Marx is anticipating that people – including the working class – born and brought up in a capitalist society, will still possess many of its values and attitudes, even as they are trying to make the transition to communism.

This is also the reason why a principle of distribution according to labour performed would have to predominate in the first phase of communism. It will have to be adopted, Marx anticipates, because it is the principle which, in this transitional situation, the majority of people will regard as 'fair' or 'just'. Indeed, in the struggle against capitalism it will have been necessary to stress the justice of economic distribution according to work precisely because this is *not* the principle which predominates under capitalism (rather, under capitalism, distribution of income is according to wealth or private property owned). Thus, in this first stage of communism (which might last for a very long time) the majority of people will not be ready to go beyond the principle of economic distribution according to labour performed, and will indeed consider this right and just (given natural inequality of abilities) even if it leads to some economic inequality.

However, in the second, 'higher' phase of communism this principle is to be abandoned and society will, apparently, 'inscribe on its banners: From each according to his ability to each according to his needs.' In other words, in this higher phase (what might be termed communism proper) *only* the material and social needs of individuals will be taken into account in the distribution of goods and services. The aim will be to ensure that those needs are met equally, for all individuals irrespective of the type or quality of their labour performed. So, even if one worker is 'superior to another physically or mentally' so that 'his' labour is more productive than another, none the less what 'he' – the superior worker – receives will be determined by 'his' needs (and those of 'his' family etc.) as will what the inferior worker receives.

The implication here is that the satisfaction which the superior worker gets in a communist society will be (a) the performance of the creative, productive labour itself, as an activity and (b) the knowledge that his or her superior abilities have contributed to fulfilling the needs of others. In particular it implies that he or she will have no need of superior *material* remuneration to mark or reward the superiority of his or her labour.

This conception of course takes us right back to the ideas of 1844 (quotations 1 and 2 on pp. 131–2) in which:

> in your enjoyment or use of my product I would have had the direct enjoyment of realizing that by my work I had both satisfied a human need and also objectified the human essence

and therefore fashioned for another human being the object that had met his need.

And in which:

> Need and enjoyment have ... lost their *egoistic* character and nature has lost its mere *utility* by the fact that its utilisation [in production] has become human utilisation.

Indeed the underlying continuity of Marx's conception of communism over these thirty years, despite the increased economic realism introduced by his study of political economy, is shown very clearly in the final stirring paragraph of the quotation from the *Critique of the Gotha Programme*, concerning the 'higher phase of communist society'.

In that phase, we are told, the 'enslaving subordination of the individual to the division of labour' will have 'vanished', as will also 'the antithesis between mental and physical labour'. Above all, however, labour will have become 'not only a means of life but life's prime want'. With that clause in particular we are right back to the earlier philosophical ideas on 'alienated labour' and to a vision of human liberation which views such liberation as consisting in the ability of everyone in society to work productively and creatively in a manner befitting their own aptitudes, for their own enjoyment and self-development as well as for the benefit of others.

It is true that some scholars – Michael Evans is one – have suggested that in his mature years Marx abandoned the idea that under communism the division of labour would be abolished (what we might call the *'German Ideology'* vision), for a view which recognized that 'a technical division of labour must remain', but that it would be 'functions rather than persons' which would be specialized. In other words, in communist society automated machines would undertake a wide variety of specialist functions, but they would be supervised and controlled by 'generalists with a polytechnic education'. Indeed, it would be through equipping everyone with an all-round scientific, artistic, and humanistic education (necessary both for supervising production and for partaking in decisions about what should be produced) that the 'antithesis between mental and manual labour' would be overcome, since, argues Evans, 'few are so lacking in intelligence that they can do no mental work'.[28]

Evans also quotes a sentence from the *Grundrisse*, in which Marx says:

[that] labour becomes attractive work, the individual's self-realization ... in no way means that it becomes mere fun, mere amusement, as Fourier ... conceives it. Really free working, e.g. composing [music] is at the same time precisely the most damned seriousness, the most intense exertion.[29]

Evans uses this quotation to suggest that Marx also abandoned the 'butterfly-like' conception of amateur pottering in various activities ('hunt in the morning, fish in the afternoon, rear cattle in the evening, criticise after dinner') found in the *German Ideology* vision of communism as pastoral idyll.

Thus Evans would read the '*Gotha Programme*' vision of communism as suggesting that 'the *enslaving subordination* of the individual to the division of labour' would be abolished, not necessarily that the division of labour *itself* would be abolished.[30] So, set free by automated machinery, the individual could choose to devote her whole life to one activity (composing music for example), but this would precisely be a *choice*. It would not have been forced upon her by her need to fulfil some position in the division of labour in order to subsist. 'Life lived in order to work creatively, not uncreative work undertaken in order to live', this is Marx's communist inversion of capitalism.

Well, Evans may be right here, and certainly it is true that the speculations about the possibilities inherent in automation which are found in the *Grundrisse* are interesting and surprising for those who had only known the *German Ideology* picture of communism as Marx's picture.

But however this may be, there is still a massive 'catch' even with the *Gotha Programme* conception of communism. Indeed it is the same catch as with the 1844 and 1846 conceptions. 'Society', we are told, will inscribe upon its banners 'From each according to his abilities to each according to his needs.' But who is to decide what an individual's 'abilities' or 'needs' are? Again there are two possible answers to this question. The first is, *the individual himself or herself will decide*. Thus, under communism 'I' decide what my abilities are, and 'I' decide what my needs are. But if that is the answer then the same question arises as we have already discussed. For how can it be guaranteed that I will not think that I have abilities which I do not in fact have (and so undertake some role in society to which I am totally unsuited)? Moreover, how is it to be guaranteed that I (or anybody else) will not think that I have needs greatly in excess of everybody else's but which I am entitled to have met if I am to receive 'according to' my 'needs'?

Suppose, for example, that I decide that my needs include two country houses with 200 servants each, three yachts and a private jet aircraft? If these are my 'needs' honestly and conscientiously stated after due introspection, then why should I (or anybody else with the same needs) not have them met?

Again Marx has two choices here. He can either say that such needs are 'artificial' ones produced by the material acquisitiveness of capitalism and that they will disappear with that mode of production (which I think is what he would have said, though I am not sure). Or he could set up a distinction between wants and needs, and say that, e.g. country houses and private jet aircraft may be part of my 'wants' but they are not part of my 'needs'.

But if he opts for this second alternative then we are back to the same question in a slightly different form. That is, *who* is to draw the line, make the distinction, between wants and needs?[31] Clearly now it cannot be *me* for myself (or anybody else for themselves) since I have already defined as part of my needs some things which Marx has assigned to my 'mere wants'. But if each individual is not to be allowed to make this distinction for themselves, then it follows (and this is the second alternative) *that somebody or something is going to make that distinction for them and enforce it upon them whether they like it or not.* Who or what is this something or somebody?

Marx's answer is 'society'. 'Society', says Marx in *The German Ideology*, 'regulates the general production'. Each worker, says Marx in the *Critique of the Gotha Programme* 'receives a certificate from society' to show what labour he has provided and to allow him to draw from 'the social stock of the means of consumption' that to which he is entitled through his labour input. 'Society', he says in the same text, inscribes upon its banners 'From each according to his abilities to each according to his needs.'

But who or what is this 'society'? It clearly is not everybody taken *individually*, making their own individual decisions, or at least if it is, we are back to the problems above. So it must be either 'everybody' gathered in some *collective* decision-making body, or it must be some *representatives* of society as a whole gathered in such a body.

If it is the first ('everybody' in society gathered in a collective decision-making body or assembly of some sort) then Marx must be conceiving communist society as a whole as made of *very small* self-governing communities, of a few hundred people at the most, otherwise of course such an idea would be impracticable.

If it is the second (some representatives or delegates of society gathered in a decision-making body) then we are talking about a *state* (albeit a democratic state) making crucial decisions about production and consumption, about abilities and needs *on behalf* of 'society' and Marx ought to say that and not talk obfuscatingly about 'society' itself making such decisions.

Which of these alternatives does Marx choose? What does he mean by 'society' in this crucial context? Perhaps the most extraordinary thing about Marx's entire life's work, his entire *oeuvre*, is that having read it, one can still be very uncertain what Marx did mean by this crucial term. For in fact he wrote very little about the actual decision-making process, the actual process of planning under socialism and communism. Indeed there is only one of Marx's texts in which these issues are touched on, even in a peripheral way, and that is his analysis of the Paris Commune, the text called *The Civil War in France* written in 1871.

The Civil War in France

In 1870 France and the German state Prussia went to war, a war which ended very quickly with a Prussian victory, and in fact with an invasion of France by the Prussian army. The official French government under the Prime Minister, Thiers, sued for peace on humiliating terms. But the population of Paris refused to accept the peace treaty and in a revolutionary uprising declared Paris an independent state, a 'Commune', opposed both to the Prussians and to the collaborating French government at Versailles. Paris was then put under military and economic seige by Prussian and French troops, a siege which lasted for over nine months and produced increasingly desperate shortages and terrible suffering among the population of Paris.[32]

Both Marx and Engels were enormously inspired by these events, and *The Civil War in France* is in fact a glowing tribute to the Commune and to the heroism of the ordinary people of Paris written as an address by Marx to the General Council of the First International in May 1871.

For our purposes, however, the most important point about the text is that in it Marx argues that the form of state, the form of government of Paris, thrown up 'spontaneously' by the Parisian population in the course of their revolutionary struggle, might provide a model for the socialist state of the future. Marx thought that the Paris Commune was a living example of a revolution 'smashing' and then restructuring the machinery of the state in a way which 'broke' state power and 'restored' to 'the responsible agents of society' those powers which the state had 'usurped' in asserting its 'pre-eminence *over* society itself'. In other words, the Paris Commune was for Marx a form of state which broke down the distinction between the state and civil society, a distinction to which he had objected twenty-seven years earlier in his *Critique of Hegel's Philosophy of Right*.

Let us therefore examine the structure of the Paris Commune. Marx enumerates five revolutionary features of it:

1. There was *direct election* of the Paris municipal assembly (the Commune) by universal suffrage of the entire population of Paris.
2. The Commune assembly *combined executive and legislative power* in its own hands. In other words, the assembly both made the laws and implemented them.
3. *The police and the standing army were abolished* within the boundaries of Paris and they were replaced by a popular militia.
4. *The church* (in the French case, the Roman Catholic church) *was disestablished* from the state, and the Commune created a system of free secular education throughout Paris.
5. And probably most importantly to Marx, *all public servants*, all officials, judges, magistrates, *were directly elected by the Commune*, were paid only 'average workmen's wages' and were revocable at the will of the Commune.

The implication of this fifth point was that a state bureaucracy, as a distinct, hierarchical and salaried occupation of administrative specialists, as a distinct part of the social division of labour, disappeared under the Commune. All those charged with implementing the Commune's laws were both directly elected by, and responsible to, the Commune assembly. It was this point – the disappearance of a professional bureaucracy and the wielding of such legitimate functions as it might have had by elected delegates of the people – which for Marx represented the overcoming or suppression of the distinction between the state and civil society which had allowed the state elsewhere in Europe to *dominate over* civil society.

Marx also noted that 'in a rough sketch of *national* organisation which the Commune had no time to develop', it had envisaged the whole of France being made up of thousands of such elected assemblies (in each village and town) linked by a 'Communal Constitution'. Under this constitution the village assemblies of communes would have sent mandated delegates to 'an assembly of delegates in the central town' and the latter in turn would have sent delegates to a 'National Delegation of Communes' in Paris. And Marx added here:

> The few but important functions would still remain for a central government were not to be suppressed, as has been intentionally mis-stated, but were to be discharged by Communal and therefore strictly responsible agents. The unity of the nation was not to be broken, but, on the contrary, to be organised by the Communal Constitution and to become a reality by the destruction of State power which claimed to be the embodiment of that unity independent of, and superior to, the nation itself, from which it was but an excrescence. While the merely repressive organs of the old government power were to be amputated, its legitimate functions were to be wrested from an authority usurping pre-eminence over society itself, and restored to the responsible agents of society.[33]

And that, to all intents and purposes, is it. That is all that Marx himself ever had to say about the form of state which in the same text he hails as 'Communism; impossible Communism' in germ, and which Engels regarded as the model of what 'the dictatorship of the proletariat' would be like.[34] Yet it is obvious that such an account begs a mass of questions. For instance:

1. The Paris Commune lasted for only nine months before the siege of Paris finally ended in its bloody suppression by French and Prussian troops. During that brief period the Commune was the form of government of a single city which was fighting for its life against overwhelming opposition and having to withstand a desperate military and economic siege. Such extraordinary circumstances are hardly conducive to a judgement about how the Commune would have fared as a long-lasting 'normal' form of government of a state at peace.[35]

2. The national 'Communal Constitution' drafted by the Paris Commune was never in fact implemented (since the rest of France was under the control of the Prussians and of the French

provisional government which they dominated) so it is impossible to say whether it would have worked in practice as a form of national government.

3. The 'laws' which the Paris Commune made were in fact restricted to assigning military tasks and to rationing stocks of food, medicines, and other supplies in Paris in a siege situation. It is just possible for a single body to exercise legislative and executive powers in this extraordinary and restricted situation, but very hard to see how such an arrangement could apply to the day-to-day running of a complex industrial society and economy.[36]

4. Similarly, because the administrative functions of the Commune were so limited, it was possible to entrust them to directly elected individuals paid only 'average workmen's wages'. Buoyed up by a self–sacrificing nationalist fervour and working with a population extraordinarily unified by extreme adversity, such individuals probably did perform their restricted range of tasks well, even heroically, for as long as the Commune lasted. But again, one would perhaps be unwise to rely on such altruism for the normal day-to-day conduct of public policy in a complex society at peace.

5. Although Marx talks about 'the few but important functions' which the central 'Delegation of Communes' would have taken on as the – hypothetical – central government of revolutionary France, he does not tell us what those functions would have been. So one is left profoundly uncertain how the division of powers and functions between local communes and the national commune would have worked.

In my view, this fifth and last point is at the heart of a fundamental contradiction in Marx's fragmentary vision of the communist society. For on the one hand he seems to desire an almost *anarchist* form of state, that is a state composed of small self-governing communities of villages and small towns in which all citizens are known to each other and therefore almost total power *can* be entrusted to an assembly of delegates elected from their number. In fact I think that the model of a kind of modernized Periclean Athens, an 'Athens' in which the citizens depend not upon slaves but upon automated machines for their subsistence, is never far from Marx's mind.[37]

On the other hand however, Marx clearly recognized the need for a 'national' controlling or planning authority of some sort in a modern industrial society. As we have seen, he applauded the fact that through the Communal Constitution 'the unity of the nation was not to be broken' and indeed later in *The Civil War in France* he describes communism as 'united cooperative societies ... [which] ... regulate *national* production upon a common plan.'[38]

But there is, to say the least, some tension between these two aspects of Marx's vision of the communist society. For the greater the functions and powers of the national planning authority (be it a National Delegation of Communes or whatever) the more restricted the autonomy of the local communes. Conversely, the greater the autonomy of the local communes, the weaker the planning powers of the national authority.

Moreover, the emergence of communism from a revolution against advanced capitalist society (which is what the *Critique of the Gotha Programme* explicitly assumes, as we have seen) presupposes a society with large-scale industrial production, with a complex and developed economic infrastructure of railways, roads, water, sewerage, and power systems, etc. Such a society would also have a highly developed division of labour involving mass production and important 'economies of scale' (as economists call them). In other words, capitalism develops high-productivity automated machinery precisely in order to cater for mass national and international markets.

However, if we imagine communism as a world of small, self-governing, *self-subsistent* communities, then we imagine a world in which such mass markets have disappeared. In which case the automated machinery (which we also have to assume as noted above) would either be redundant or would not be working most of the time under communism. This in turn means that it would be producing very high-cost products.[39] On the other hand, if one imagines that such mass markets would remain in being during communism, then the automated machinery makes economic sense, but there would need to be national, or even world-level, planning bodies to ensure that the masses were supplied with their material needs through that machinery (because of course Marx assumes that the 'market mechanism' would no longer be doing this). Such national and international planning bodies would however severely restrict the economic autonomy of the local face-to-face communes simply by their mere existence.

In other words – and to reiterate a point which has been made frequently even by sympathetic critics of Marx – it is very difficult to see how his desire for a society of small, self-governing, directly democratic communities can be squared, in any real situation, with his desire to maintain economies of scale in mass production and high–level planning authorities.[40]

Moreover, if we assume a continuing day-to-day planning of a complex industrial economy and society, the question immediately arises of who is to do this. Anyone familiar even with the working of British local government might be very sceptical of the capacity of an assembly of elected delegates to do this unaided (and I do not mean their *intellectual* capacity, I mean their *practical* capacity to do it unaided, given the likely complexity of the task and its size). But if we assume that they could not do it unaided, then we must postulate the existence of a specialized, trained group of people whose role in the division of labour would be to help plan and administer production and consumption. In other words we are back to *bureaucrats* again.[41] The problem of bureaucracy (a continuing concern of Marx's writing on the state) reasserts itself, as of course it has done in the USSR and elsewhere.

Personally, I think that this particular gap or incoherence in Marx's vision of the communist society, this unanswered question about how democracy and planning are to be squared (a question which is fudged by his convenient reference to 'society' as the body which both controls and is controlled) is the most serious weakness in Marx's thought. It is so serious, because in the real world, in real socialist societies, the gap must be filled, the question must be answered, if such societies are to be viable at all.

We know only too well the bureaucratic and authoritarian way in which the question was answered in practice in the USSR, but since this book is restricted to an analysis of Marx's own thought, I have neither time nor space to go into that issue here. Suffice it to say that I believe that in reality the gap does have to be filled by a bureaucracy, but it does not have to be filled by an *authoritarian* bureaucracy, and for some further ideas on that readers are referred to my *Rethinking Socialism* (Methuen, 1983).

CHAPTER 6

MUCH ADO ABOUT COMPARATIVELY LITTLE: CLASS, STATE, AND IDEOLOGY

We fail to get away from the idea that using a sentence involves imagining something for every word. We do not realise that we *calculate*, operate with words and in the course of time translate them sometimes into one picture, sometimes into another. Wittgenstein *Philosophical Investigations*, para. 449.

As philosophy finds in the proletariat its material weapons, so the proletariat finds in philosophy its intellectual weapons. Marx, *Towards a Critique of Hegel's Philosophy of Right*: Introduction

INTRODUCTION

It seems that no introductoy book on Marx – indeed no book on Marx – would be complete without at least a section devoted to Marx's views on class and class struggle. Indeed in the eyes of many people the concepts of class and class struggle are synonymous with Marx. They are the words most closely associated with his thought, to the point indeed where anyone drawing attention to class divisions in society or even using the term 'working class' may be accused of being a Marxist, or of having Marxist sympathies.

To suggest therefore, as I am going to do, that the importance of these concepts to Marx has been rather overestimated, may seem somewhat surprising and certainly in need of demonstration. To suggest in addition, that since Marx's death, far too much fuss has been made about his so-called 'theories' of 'ideology' and 'the state' may seem even more contentious. It is however what I intend to argue.

The first and most obvious point to make by way of such a demonstration, is the one most often made, only – in most cases – to be bemoaned, that is that in the whole of Marx's writings one finds nothing which can be dignified with the title of a 'theory' of class, state, or ideology. That is, one finds no set of detailed, coherent propositions relating to any of these subjects. All that one does find is a series of scattered references, ideas, and allusions which other, later, Marxist scholars have tried to arrange into coherent theories or (in other cases) have tried to demonstrate are incoherent or inconsistent in various ways.

It is true that in the various schemes for his major life's work (of which *Capital* as we have it today was merely a part) Marx did plan a section on 'the categories that constitute the internal structure of bourgeois society' and on 'the fundamental classes. Capital, wage-labour, landed property'.[1] It is also true that the famous incomplete chapter on 'Classes' in volume III of *Capital* may have been intended as Marx's authoritative statement on the matter. But the fact is that this chapter *is* incomplete, and that Marx *did* give priority to his 'critique of political economy' over these other aspects of his planned life's project.

In other words, for Marx the development of coherent theories of class, state, or ideology obviously came a long way second to a lot of other concerns, both to his political activities and to other intellectual tasks. But this fact, though often noted, is never, I think, given the significance it deserves. Its significance for this author is quite simply this; that since Marx makes abundant *use* of the concepts of class and ideology in most of his writings, and since he also frequently addressed himself to issues of politics and the state, without ever 'bothering' to present 'general theories' of the state, of ideology, or of class, it is clear that he did not believe that his use of these concepts was in any way dependent upon his having such a theory of them.

Indeed it is useful to ask what a 'general theory' of class, of ideology, or of the state would be supposed to accomplish. Presumably the aim would be to make the meaning of these terms absolutely clear or unambiguous, most probably by means of a definition. 'In Marxism classes are identified by their relationship to the means of production', 'the state is an executive committee for managing the common affairs of the bourgeoisie', or 'ideology ... consists in explaining human behaviour in terms of consciousness rather than in terms of material reality',[2] etc. But it is well known that Marx himself rarely provided definitions of these terms in this way. More-over, his uses of them in the total corpus of his work are far too variant and shifting to be captured by any single definition including those he himself provides.

The question however is whether this constitutes a 'problem' in Marxism. Those Marxists and other social scientists who adhere to a particular conception of science, who believe that 'exactitude' and 'rigour' of conceptualization are central to the scientific enterprise, and who also believe that such exactitude or rigour is attained primarily by tight *definitions* of terms, do tend to think that it is a problem. They therefore endeavour to solve this problem either by trying to find definitions of these terms which will capture all of Marx's uses of them, or – more commonly – they offer definitions of their own and argue for their superiority over others in capturing what Marx 'really' intended or should have said.

The reader will already have gathered that this is a book replete with ideas about what Marx 'should have said', so I am hardly in a position to criticize the legion of others who engage, or have engaged, in the same enterprise. But there is reason to doubt whether, especially in the case of these three terms, this task is best undertaken by means of definitions. It is this frequently encountered method of 'correcting' or 'developing' Marx's work which I shall criticize in this chapter, not the enterprise itself. Doing so will however involve me in an initial detour into rather specialized philosophical issues, which the student of social science, in particular, may at first find rather tangential. However, I hope that the patient reader will find his or her tolerance rewarded when, later in the chapter, insights generated through this detour are subsequently applied to Marxist theory.

WORDS AND THINGS

Consider these three questions:
1. What are classes?
2. What is the state?
3. What is ideology?

The first point to note about all three is that they revolve around the verb 'to be'. We are being asked to say what things *are*, or the way they *are*. And this is indeed the first and most fundamental problem, that this form of question requires, demands – given the semantics of our language – an answer which *identifies a thing*. In a word, this form of question is itself reificatory.

How do we identify a thing? Well, if it is a physical or material thing we can identify it in a number of ways. If, for example, I am asked 'what is an iguana?' and I happen to possess an iguana or know someone who does, I can show or point out an iguana to my enquirer. 'Look, here is one, quite immature as yet, only about a foot long. No, don't put your finger too near the wire, he bites!' On the other hand, if I do not possess one, nor know anyone who does, I may be able to find a book or some other source which contains a photograph or drawing of an iguana. 'Look here's one, not a very good photograph, doesn't capture the colouring very well, but. . . .' Or finally, I can get a dictionary and read out the definition of the word 'iguana'.

Philosophers would call 'showing' or 'pointing out' an iguana, either in the flesh or in a picture, an example of the *ostensive definition* of words (definition by 'showing') which is to be contrasted with *lexicographical definition* (definition by means of other words), and there are some theories of language learning which stress the importance of ostensive definition in the way children learn the fundamentals of language. However, more recent writing on this subject has suggested that ostensive definition is both much more limited and much more complex as a tool of language learning than one might at first suppose. For example, it may be a relatively simple process in the case of certain *nouns*, especially those which function as the names of physical objects. But it is a lot more complex and problematic process in the case of the learning of verbs, adverbs, and adjectives, as well as in the case of classificatory nouns and abstract nouns of various kinds.[3]

In fact, even the 'iguana' example above has many complications hidden behind its apparent simplicity. For showing someone an iguana would not be of much help to them unless they could recognize a lizard when they saw one, that is unless they *already knew* what a lizard was. But in that case, they would probably be wanting to see an iguana or a picture of an iguana, not because they did not know that an iguana was a lizard, but because they were interested in the *particular characteristics* of an iguana as a *type* of lizard. But if this was so, they would probably not have asked the question 'what is an iguana?' at all. They would probably have asked something like 'are you sure an iguana always has a mottled underbelly?'

Conversely, if they had wanted or needed to know what an iguana *was*, it is very probable that this would have been in a context in which they would have neither wanted or required an ostensive definition, but would have been content with the simplest lexicogaphical variety. For example:

A So all in all it was a really lousy day. And then to cap it all, when I got home I was bitten by an iguana.

B But I thought you said that you put a whole lot of insect repellant on you.

A An iguana is not a bloody insect you fool, it's a lizard!

So what this suggests is that ostensive definition of terms is used very infrequently among adult language users. In fact, among adults themselves it is used only for rather exotic or technically specialized nouns. It is used more frequently by adults in communication with small children, though even then often in ways which are a lot more complex and subtle than simply 'pointing at things'.

However, one very important 'residue' of ostensive definition for adults is that *it inculcates a particular understanding of one use of the verb to be*. This is that, even as adults, we tend to understand 'what is . . .?' or 'what is a(n) . . .?' questions as questions which are at least capable of being answered ostensively, even if in fact we choose to answer them lexicographically.

Thus – and here we return to the point – if I hear the question 'what is a social class?' or 'what are classes?' or 'what is the state?' or 'what is ideology?' I will probably answer that question lexicographically. 'A social class is a large group of people who share certain basic economic interests in common', 'the state is an organ of class rule', 'ideology is any set of ideas which endorse or support the social or political status quo'. And what I will think of myself as doing when I offer these answers is 'pointing out some*thing*' or 'defining some*thing*'.

But suppose I am challenged to provide an ostensive definition. Suppose someone says '*show me* a social class', '*show me* the state', '*show me* some ideology'. I have to confess that I would be a little stuck in the face of such a challenge – a little stuck but not totally stuck. In the case of social classes for example I might take my challenger for a conducted tour around a council estate with which I happened to be familiar, or perhaps for a walk around Mayfair or Kensington. In the case of the state, I might make a detour through Whitehall, or show him/her some pictures of American or British air bases, or show him/her my passport. In the case of ideology it gets much more difficult, but I might perhaps read aloud from Hegel or Adam Smith, or refer him/her to the *Bad News* books on television news,[4] or thumb with him or her through some copies of *The Sun* newspaper.

But even supposing that I did some or all of this, and even supposing that my challenger was impressed by what I said or 'pointed out' as we went through these activities together, my 'showing' would still be open to one obvious objection.

'Well yes', it might be said, 'you have shown me particular aspects or manifestations of class, of the state, of ideology. But you have not shown me the thing itself. You have not shown me the whole of the state, the whole of the British class structure, the whole of ideology. In short, you have not shown me what these things *are*.'

How am I to reply to such a challenge? As long as I stick to the idea that there is something that I could 'show', but for reasons of practicality or time I cannot do so, but can only show 'aspects' or 'manifestations' of it, then I have to acknowledge the force of this objection. I have to say, somewhat apologetically, 'Yes, well of course, in practice, that is all one can do.'

However, there is another way to deal with this kind of objection. This is to say that though social classes, states, and ideologies are 'things', they are not the kind of things which can be 'shown' or 'pointed out' ostensively. Thus, one cannot 'show' someone a social class, one can only 'show' them a manifestation or aspect of class. But this only replaces one kind of puzzle with another. For if classes, states, ideologies are not things which can be 'shown' or 'pointed out', what kind of things are they?

My reply to this question is to say that 'classes', 'the state', 'ideology' are ways of *conceiving* or *representing* human social activity. In other words, they are ideas which Marx used, and which contemporary Marxists use, to understand or make sense of human activity.[5] They are ways of describing or classifying that activity, of simplifying it in order to make it comprehensible. If this is so, it follows that I can only 'show' you what class is by pointing out to you, or directing you towards, the intellectual discourses in which the words 'class', 'state' or 'ideology' appear.

But here one might be tempted to think that if classes, states, ideologies are 'only ideas', then they are not real. But classes, states, ideologies *are* real, they really exist, they are not just ideas! However, the temptation to say this – that they are 'only ideas' and therefore not real – only arises because we are understanding 'real' as 'sensual'. What is 'real' is what can be seen, heard, smelt, touched. 'Mere ideas' cannot be seen, heard, smelt, touched, therefore ideas are not real.

This is a very persuasive way to think, and it is especially persuasive to many traditional Marxists who think of themselves as materialists (chapter 7 tries to explain why it is so persuasive). Despite this however, it is fundamentally misleading, for if taken seriously it would make certain quite commonplace activities incomprehensible. For consider two points:

1. If ideas – any ideas – are to be communicated to or understood by more than one person (the person who has the idea) then they must be either (a) spoken, or (b) written down, or (c) 'represented' in some other way, that is in drawings, paintings, film, video, radio programmes, etc. And from this moment of representation ideas *can* be heard and seen. In other words, ideas in society – social ideas – are not just thoughts. The idea that ideas are not 'real', are not 'material', is persuasive only so long as one equates ideas with *introspectively known thoughts*.

2. But in addition ideas like 'class', 'the state', 'ideology', function in the public realm of communication so as to make possible certain descriptive or explanatory *practices* which would be impossible, or at least a great deal more difficult, without them.

Imagine for example that two people are standing outside an imposing Victorian building in Whitehall. They have come there because one of them (whom we shall call A) has demanded an ostensive definition of the word 'state', and the other (whom we shall call B) is endeavouring to supply this.

A What's that building?
B The Department of the Environment.
A Who are those people going in and out?
B Not sure. Some of them look like civil servants.
A They work here?
B Yes.
A They are employed by the Department of the Environment?

B   No, not really. They move departments from time to time. They are really employed by the government.

A   The government?

B   Yes, the government . . . the state . . . you know . . .

A   Where's the government, show me the government!

B   Er . . .

Or imagine the same two characters in search of class, with B having now brought A to a local council housing estate.

B   So here we are then. This is the main shopping area.

A   There aren't very many shops. Not for all the people who must live here'.

B   No, there aren't.

A   They look pretty ropey too. One rather run-down Spar supermarket, a rather seedy hairdressers, a newsagent, and what looks like a betting shop.

B   Yes, that's the lot.

A   Well, where do people go if they need to do any other shopping?

B   In to town.

A   And how far is that?

B   About five miles.

A   Oh, so you would have to go by car.'

B   Yes, except that 60 per cent of the households on this estate don't have a car.

A   So what do they do?

B   Get a lift, take a taxi, or go by bus.

A   How often are the buses?

B   Every two hours.

A   And what does it cost?

B   £1.50 each way.

A   Jesus!

B   Quite.

A   And all the houses are falling apart for want of a coat of paint.

B   I know. Most of them haven't been painted for ten years; cuts in housing department finance.

A   What a dump. I'm surprised that anybody goes on living here.

B   Most of the people here don't have any choice. There are very few other council houses available locally and mainly they can't afford to buy a house of their own.

A Why not?
B Because most of them are at the poorest end of the working class, that's why not!
A Working class? Show me the working class!
B Er . . .

In the first dialogue above, the word 'government' was used synonymously with the word 'state', and in the second dialogue B might perhaps have said 'socio-economic class V'[6] or 'lower-income group', rather than 'poorest end of the working class'. But even so the problem would have been the same. Faced with the – admittedly rather curious – challenge to 'show me' the working class, lower-income group, government or state, B would have been similarly 'stuck', similarly unsure what s/he could do by way of such 'showing' that they had not already done, similarly unsure indeed what A could conceivably be after.

In other words, what both these dialogues suggest is that the concepts 'state', 'government', 'working class' are invoked, in specific situations and contexts *to explain something*. In the first case, the word 'government' was used to help explain how or why civil servants could be employed in more than one department of state. In the second case the words 'working class' were used to help explain limited household income and the constraints on mobility which this imposed.

Here is another dialogue:

A I hope we win.
B So do I.
A He is going to be very difficult to control though.
B Who? Maradona? Yes he is. He is a great player, one of the greatest.
A Yes. But I think that if we play it really tight in the midfield and push him deep . . . We've got to win! You can imagine them going really barmy if they beat us. Especially after the Falklands.
B Oh come on! It's just a football match.
A Don't you believe it. They are really out to get us. According to *The Sun* they are saying that this will be their revenge for the Malvinas.
B Oh for God's sake! You don't buy all that nationalist crap do you?

A I know you think it's all a load of ideology, but I take it
   seriously.

B I thought you had more sense.

In this third dialogue, the word 'ideology' is being used to
disparage a particular newspaper story, or more exactly it is
being used by A to show his recognition that the story could be
disparaged or discredited, but that he believes it to be accurate
despite this.

In short, what all three of these dialogues do is to draw
attention to an important characteristic of language use as a
human activity; that words can be very useful to us – indeed
they can be vital or irreplaceable for us – even if they do not
'name' or 'stand for' any*thing*.

The words 'state', 'class', 'ideology' are nouns, and we are
used to thinking of nouns in particular as *names* of something or
things. But if we look at these three dialogues we can see that in
cases 1 and 2 explanations could be provided (of why civil
servants work in more than one department, of why tenants
could not leave a council estate) and in case 3 the possibility of
doubt could be recognized ('I know you think it's all a load of
ideology') without the speaker having to be able to give a definition – either ostensive or lexicographical – of 'state', 'class', or
'ideology'. All that the speaker (and the hearer) had to be able to
do was to recognize that this occasion and context was the kind
of occasion and context (one of many) *where such words could be
used*. Being able to recognize contexts as appropriate ones for the
use of a particular word is a part – a large part – of what one
means when one says that a person 'understands the meaning
of a word. To understand the meaning of a word is *to exercise an
ability*, and being able to define the word is only one way and –
as an adult – a rather infrequent and untypical way in which one
exercises that ability.[7]

And this is why, in the first two dialogues, A's reiterated
demand of B to 'show me' the state, working class, etc. seems so
odd when one reads it. For the conversation up to this point is
apparently naturalistic, so that when A makes this demand for a
further ostensive definition, he or she seems, as it were, to step
out of character, to become in effect a suddenly incompetent
speaker of the English language. In fact, when we read these
demands to 'show me' we are apt to think 'but nobody would
ever say *that* in that context', and this is surely correct. Nobody

ever would. But I shall suggest, as I go on, that those Marxist and other social theorists who insist on the importance or essentiality of the prior *definition* of concepts to be used in social science discourse *are*, in effect, subject to A's linguistic delusion or incompetence. However, they can be so because they tend to be working in 'abstract', 'study-bound' contexts which make it possible to be linguistically incompetent or naïve without realizing it, indeed while thinking it the height of theoretical sophistication. In other words, alone in the study, they do, they can do, what they never do, never could do, either in the streets or even in the living-room with their families.[8]

I am suggesting therefore that a way to avoid this kind of theoretical naïvety, a way to begin to make Marxist theory as sophisticated theoretically as the linguistic and social *practices* with which it purports to deal, is to start thinking of abstract words like 'class', 'state', or 'ideology' not as names of theoretical *objects*, but as linguistic *tools* or *instruments* available to be put to a wide variety of uses in a wide variety of sentences and propositions.[9] Thinking of all nouns on the model of names of objects leads one to attach undue importance to the role of definitions in meaning, and taken in conjunction with a certain use of the verb 'to be' tends to reproduce constantly the illusion that classes, states, ideologies *are* things 'out there' graspable by either ostensive or lexicographical definition, rather than being *forms of representation*[10] of human activity, forms indispensable to human purposes.

SOME OBJECTIONS

I will have more to say about 'forms of representation' in the next chapter, but here I wish to deal with one rather obvious objection to what has been said above.

'Surely' (it could be objected) 'you have failed to take account of one point. It is true that if I say "No, they don't work for the department, they work for the state", or if I say "because most of them come from the poorest end of the working class", I may not be able, if challenged there and then, to come up with some coherent watertight definition of "state" or "class". But none the less the fact that I can use the word correctly shows that subconsciously I am in command of such a definition and could come up with one if given time, or could recognize one or endorse one if it was put before me. Thus, if someone defined the state as "the organized form of power and authority in society" or if someone defined the working class as "skilled, semi-skilled, and unskilled manual workers" I might recognize such definitions as encompassing most, if not all, of my uses of these terms.'

At first sight this is a persuasive objection, but only at first sight. Supposing, for example, that I accept the definition of 'the state' as 'the organized form of power and authority in society' put to me by a helpful social sientist friend. I then walk back to my car from a guided tour of Whitehall and find that I have been given a parking ticket. I explode, 'this is a typical piece of petty state oppression!' and I tear up the ticket in a rage and throw it at a passing policeman (whereupon I am promptly arrested).

Did my 'accepting' that earlier definition in any way prepare me for this use of the term? Did that definition somehow 'incorporate' or 'presage' this particular use of it? Certainly not. The abusive use I have just made of the term 'state' *is not incompatible* with the definition I have just accepted (and it would *not be incompatible* with a number of other definitions of the state – (including 'an executive committee of the bourgeoisie'), but it was not, in any meaningful sense, 'incorporated' or 'presaged' by such definitions.[11]

This example draws our attention to an important point, not just about these words, but about all words; which is that *knowing their definitions does not tell one how to use them*. Definitions seldom – perhaps never – rigidly confine the *use* of words. This is an obvious point about language use, which, once it has been brought to one's attention, can be confirmed by a moment's reflection upon one's own most basic or commonplace linguistic practices. But again it is a point often overlooked by Marxist and other social theorists obsessed by a particular notion of conceptual 'rigour' or 'exactitude' supposedly obtainable through definitions.

That our use of words is continually more various than can be grasped by any definitions of them, is explicable, as Wittgenstein stressed, by reference to the way in which all human beings *learn* language.

Although this is a complex matter to which I cannot do justice within the scope of this text, it suffices to say that human beings do not – mainly – *learn* the meaning of words through learning or remembering definitions (either lexicographical or ostensive) at all. To put it very broadly, human beings learn language through *living*. To live means to experience billions of situations and contexts in the course of one's life and to learn the language appropriate to such contexts *in* such contexts.[12] Moreover, since human beings are creative creatures they continually create new contexts and situations (that is human beings always have both a *history* and a *future*). To allow for this, the meanings of words within language are always 'open', are never rigidly confined, are always 'extendable' or 'projectable' to fit the evolving needs of a creative creature, of a creature which 'makes its own history'. In the next chapter, we will examine some particular 'analogical' or 'metaphorical' uses of language, some particular 'extended' meanings of words which are absolutely central to Marxism. We shall also see the problems that have arisen for the Marxist tradition as a result of these uses of language, problems which have derived from the fact that the implications of these uses have not been adequately grasped even – indeed especially – by those who have perpetrated and perpetuated them.

For the moment however we can simply use these reflections to reject the view (intuitively attractive though it may be) that when we use words we have some kind of 'implicit' definition of those words subconsciously or semi-consciously in our minds.

But if this is not the case then how is our use of words controlled? Why can one not use any word in any context? The answer to this is, in broad terms, clear enough. All use of words is, as it were, *socially* controlled.

Consider, for example, the following alternative ending to our third dialogue:

B Oh for God's sake! You don't buy all that nationalist crap do you?
A I know you think it is all a load of micro-computers, but I take it seriously.
B I thought you had more sense.

We would now understand the last line of this dialogue in a way very different from before. We would now take B not to be commenting adversely on A's *views* but on his/her *sanity*! That is, B would be saying that he did not understand A's previous remark, and we could imagine him/her going on to say 'What do you mean "micro-computers"? Have you gone mad or something!' In other words, in human society we are all checkers and guarantors of each other's meanings. The stability, reproducibility and consistency of meaning in language, as well as the continual process of meaning change, is socially controlled. It is not controlled by any one language speaker, and indeed there is reason to doubt whether any single or isolated individual could either construct or maintain the stability of meaning which a language requires.[13] So, in short, that we use the 'right' word in the 'right' context is something that is socially or inter-personally guaranteed. It is not guaranteed subjectively in the mind of any individual language user, and it does not therefore require such users to carry sets of 'correct' definitions of words around in their heads.

But are there not occasions when the linguistic social consensus breaks down, when there is genuine doubt or uncertainty, genuine *disagreement* about what is the 'right' word to use in any given context? There most certainly are, and these occasions, these disputes, are often the ones which interest or concern the sociologist most, especially when such disagreements have ideological implications.

For example, in our first dialogue, speaker B employed the words 'state' and 'government' interchangeably, and in that context s/he was not challenged. But s/he might have been challenged, either in that context, or in some other, by someone who had reason to insist upon a strong *distinction* between 'state' and 'government'. Or in dialogue 2, speaker B spoke of 'the poorest end of the working class', but s/he might perhaps have said 'because most of them have very low incomes' or 'because most of them are in a very low income group'. And in dialogue 3, speaker A might have said 'I know you think it's a load of propaganda' or 'I know you think it's just a prejudice but ... '. S/he did not *have* to use the word 'ideology'. There were a number of other words which would have been just as appropriate here.

So what determines which words we use when there are alternatives open to us? What determines which word or words we regard as 'most fitting' for any particular context or situation? We may ask this question both for 'ordinary' language users and for social theorists like Marx, for the broad answer is the same in both cases. It is the *purposes* of the speaker or writer which determines which of several 'possible' words s/he uses in a particular context.[14] Marx represents human activity in society in terms of the concepts of 'class', 'state', and 'ideology' (among others) because these forms of representation suit his particular purposes very well. So our next analytical task is to discover what precisely were Marx's purposes with regard to class, state, and ideology.

MARX'S PURPOSES: THE PHILOSOPHY OF PRAXIS

We will begin with class, regarded by many as the quintessential Marxist concept. Yet Marx himself said, we remember:

> the merit of having discovered either the existence of classes in modern society or the class struggle does not belong to me. Bourgeois historians had presented the historic development of this struggle of the classes, and bourgeois economists the economic anatomy of the same, long before I did. What was new in what I did was 1) to demonstrate that the existence of classes is tied only to *definite historical phases of the development of production* 2) that the class struggle necessarily leads to the *dictatorship of the proletariat* 3) that this dictatorship is only a transition to the *dissolution of all classes* and leads to the formation of a classless society.[15]

And this is indeed correct. Marx was not unique in regarding late eighteenth- and nineteenth-century European societies as class divided. The number of thinkers, from Adam Smith to Max Weber, who took the same view are legion. Nor was he unique in paying particular attention to the division between capitalists and workers as a division fraught with potential and actual conflict. He was not even unique, nor the first, in perceiving a relationship of exploitation between the capitalist class and the working class and developing a theory to explain this.[16] Moreover, Ronald Meek has even suggested that Marx may have, unwittingly, claimed too much for himself in claiming that he was the first to 'demonstrate that the existence of classes is tied ... to definite historical phases of the development of production', for Meek has found forerunners in doing this among the thinkers of the eighteenth-century 'Scottish Enlightenment'.[17]

However, where Marx was unique was in two of the respects which he himself enumerates in the quotation, that is in believing that the 'class struggle' under capitalism would end in a 'dictatorship of the proletariat', and that this would be a transitional form of government leading to the classless society (communism). In other words, the significance or importance which Marx attaches to classes and to class struggle in his representation of capitalist society derives from his belief that *he had found in the working class or proletariat an historical agency of human liberation*. For Marx the proletariat was the 'universal class' because its liberation from oppression would simultaneously bring about the liberation of all humankind.

Now the philosophical importance of this point is that, as we saw in chapter 1, Marx had formed his conception of human liberation (as the overcoming of 'alienation', as the creation of a society in which all activity would be creative 'species activity' expressive of the human essence) before he became either a theorist of the 'class struggle' or a political activist among the working class, indeed before the categories of political economy (of which 'class' was one) had begun to dominate his thought at all. In other words, Marx first reached the philosophical position that the 'de-alienation' of human life had to be a material or social process, not simply an intellectual one, and he *then* went looking for a material or social agency for that process and found the proletariat.[18]

And I would argue that this is a perfectly acceptable – indeed essential – methodological procedure for the study of society. Marx was clear what he wanted to see happen to human society and he was clear why he wanted to see it happen (he had clarified these matters philosophically) and he *then* asked himself two questions. Firstly, what social forces or groups have an interest in bringing this change about? Secondly, what social forces or groups have an interest in preventing it coming about? His answer to the first question was 'the working class or proletariat'. His answers to the second question were more various, being (a) the capitalist class, (b) the state organizations which represent the interests of the capitalist class, and (c) intellectuals and other 'ideologists' who propagate ideas favourable to the continuing dominance of the capitalist class over the working class.

So we can see then that given Marx's purposes (to see the realization of a particular conception of human liberation) his interest in and his analyses of (a) classes and the class struggle, (b) the state, and (c) ideology *all 'fit into place'* logically. But conversely of course it follows that neither (i) classes themselves, nor (ii) their struggle under capitalism, nor (iii) the forms and functions of the capitalist state, nor (iv) Marx's critiques of Hegelian philosophy and classical political economy as 'ideology', would be of any interest or significance 'in themselves' to Marx outside of the logical framework provided by his philosophical and political purposes.

This in turn has a most interesting implication, or rather set of implications, which should be made explicit. For had Marx been convinced by others, or had he convinced himself that either (a) his conception of human liberation was unrealizable; or that (b) the working class was *not* an agent of that liberation; or that (c) the capitalist state was *not* an impediment to the realization of a classless society; or that (d) there were *no* bodies of ideas ('ideologies') whose acceptance was impeding that liberation, then his life's project would have been seriously damaged or undermined. Clearly acceptance of point (a) undermines it totally. Acceptance of point (b) would require that another agency of that liberation be found. Acceptance of point (c) would have made 'the state' and 'theories of the state' totally uninteresting *to Marx* and acceptance of point (d) would have meant that Marx would never have spoken of 'ideology' at all.

It is vital to say this, because a great deal of modern Marxist writing, on class, on the state, on ideology, proceeds on the assumption that somehow or other 'scientific' theories of the state, or of class, or of ideology can be constructed *in abstraction* from any set of political or philosophical purposes. But this, I am arguing, is an epistemologically untenable position, which renders such theories formless, that is without any clear point or purpose.[19]

In other words, in Marx's own work, his analysis of class structure and class struggle, of the role of the capitalist state, and of ideology is all given force or point by an underlying commitment to a particular conception of liberation and to a particular agent of liberation (the working class). However, in more modern Marxist writing both these commitments have become attenuated. In particular, as advanced industrial capitalism has proved itself a more durable and stable form of society than Marx anticipated and the working classes in those societies have proved themselves less of a revolutionary force than he anticipated, there has been an ever-increasing tendency for Marxist analyses of class, of the state, and of ideology to be devoted, explicitly or implicitly, to *explaining* stability rather than to *aiding* revolutionary strategy.

Thus modern Marxist accounts of the class structure of

capitalism tend to concentrate on showing the way in which this structure has become more complex and fragmented since Marx's day, thus making working-class unity very difficult or impossible. Modern Marxist analyses of the role of the state under capitalism tend, similarly, to stress the increased role and power of the state both in stabilizing capitalism economically and preventing or impeding any revolutionary challenge to the system. Finally, a great deal of modern Marxist literature on the role of ideology tends to stress the power of 'ruling-class' or 'dominant' ideologies in modern capitalism, the acceptance of such ideologies by the working class, and the ideological 'hegemony' that this acceptance gives to 'bourgeois' ideas.

However, from the point of view outlined in this chapter, it must be doubtful how far any of this literature is actually in the spirit of Marx's original endeavour. For if the account of the logical structure of this endeavour given above is correct, it would seem that its logically primary element is a commitment to a particular conception of liberation, with Marx's commitment to the working class being a logically secondary commitment to a particular social agency of that liberation.

From this point of view then, it would be equally, if not more, in the spirit of Marx's original endeavour to retain the logically primary commitment to his conception of liberation, but to examine the possibility of there being *other* social agencies of that liberation in particular capitalist societies. Such agencies *might* be social classes related through ownership or non-ownership of the means of production, but they might equally well be status groupings or indeed single occupational groupings. They might be particular groups of young people, or particular gender groups, or simply alliances of individuals who, for a variety of reasons, were committed to socialist transformation.

In any particular capitalist society, or indeed in all capitalist societies, such a 'search' for a new or alternative revolutionary agency might be a failure. The (from the Marxist point of view) 'gloomy' conclusion might be reached that no such agencies could be found, or none strong enough or committed enough to carry through the process of socialist liberation.

However, from the point of view of the philosophy of praxis, this would *not* be the worst of all possible worlds. The worst of such worlds would be the maintenance of a 'formal' commitment to the working class as revolutionary agency, but a commitment which, in fact, is so vestigial as to have no theoretical impact on the *form of analysis* undertaken. For in these circumstances, Marxist accounts of 'class', of 'the state', or of 'ideology' are likely, in practice, to relapse into positivism. That is, the 'development' of a Marxist theory of class will come, in practice, to mean providing accounts of the class structure of advanced capitalism which are as 'descriptively accurate' as possible. The 'development' of the Marxist theory of the state will come to mean providing accounts of state institutions and their functioning which are as 'descriptively accurate' as possible. The 'development' of the Marxist theory of ideology will come to mean providing the most 'descriptively accurate' account of the origins of ideology and of its domination over society. In short, 'descriptive accuracy' and the development of 'concepts' to ensure such 'accuracy', will become *ends in themselves*.

But if the philosophical position outlined both in this chapter, and in earlier chapters, has any merit, it would suggest that this decline into positivism will not 'merely' mean a loss of a great deal of Marxism's political point, it will also mean a distinct loss even of its analytical strength. For the analysis above has suggested that *in themselves* concepts like 'descriptive accuracy' or 'conceptual exactitude' have no clear or coherent meaning. They must rather be given a meaning by an initial purposeful commitment of the observer. There is, as it were, no 'purpose-neutral' criterion of 'the most accurate' account of class structure, or of the state, or of ideology. That there can be such a criterion or criteria is in fact the central positivist delusion,[20] to which a Marxist social theory shorn of its liberation commitment can easily become prey.

AN ALTERNATIVE CONCEPTION OF LANGUAGE

Up to this point, my primary aim in this chapter has been to encourage the reader to think about words like 'class', 'state', and 'ideology' in a rather different way. Instead of thinking of these words as denoting things or theoretical objects (as being *names* in fact), I have sugggested that we think of them as tools or instruments, as ways of perceiving or representing the social world, and as being subordinate to the purposes of the person (in this case Marx) who uses them.

I have especially wanted to alert the reader to some of the misleading implications of certain uses of the verb 'to be', especially those uses which, by implicit analogy with uses we have learnt in childhood and early life, we associate with ostensive definition (definition by 'showing' or 'pointing at' something).[21]

Thus, for example, if somebody asks 'Is this (any) society class-divided?' we think this is a question with a simple 'yes' or 'no' answer which can somehow be discovered empirically. Whereas, I am suggesting, another and, from some points of view, more helpful answer is, 'It can certainly be perceived or represented as being so, for certain purposes.' Similarly, to the question 'Is this (any) state acting in the interests of the capitalist class?' an illuminating reply is 'It may usefully be represented as doing so for certain purposes.' Or finally, to the question 'Is neo-classical economics an ideology justifying capitalism as a form of economy and society?' a useful reply may be 'It may certainly be conceived as such for certain purposes.'

This way of thinking about such questions has one clear advantage. In contrast to the positivistic understanding of them (an understanding which always treats the verb 'to be' in such questions as having an empirical reference rather than a reflexive use) it can accommodate, and make sense of, 'yes and no' answers to such questions.

For, obviously, if for some purposes neo-classical economics may be thought of as an ideology of capitalism, then for other purposes it may not be thought of in this way. Similarly, any state may be represented as serving interests other than those of the capitalist class, and any society may be represented in ways other than as class-divided. In fact we often use a vocabulary analogically derived from visual perception to make this point. Some representations of society or of the state emphasize one 'aspect' of it (them), we say, while other representations emphasize another 'aspect', and this vocabulary is helpful here.[22]

But perhaps you are still not convinced by all this. Perhaps this way of looking at things seems plausible in the case of 'ideology', but perhaps it seems less so in the case of 'the state' and of 'class'.

Perhaps you are tempted to say something like the following: 'Look, if we are talking about the state in Britain now for example, then I can show you official statistics and other data describing the major institutions of government, the number of people employed by them, their backgrounds, official positions, and salaries. I can show you legislation specifying the duties and powers of each institution and of government as a whole. I can measure how much revenue the British state collects, describe how much money it spent, and on what, in any given period. I can even describe various official and unofficial state influences on the press and other mass media, etc. etc. Surely, therefore, since I can ostensively "show" you all this, I *can*, in a sense "show" you the state. The state *can*, in a sense, be regarded as a "thing" or "object" "out there".'

Similarly, in the case of the British class structure one might be tempted to say something like: 'Look, I can tell you very precisely how many skilled and unskilled manual workers there are in Britain now. I can tell you their average earnings and their earnings by various occupations. I can tell you how many are owner-occupiers, how many live in council houses and other rented accommodation, their average number of children, their educational levels, even a lot about their health status. And I could do the same for the middle and upper classes in this society as well. Surely therefore classes too *can* be regarded as things, as objects "out there" too.'

Moreover in both these cases one could add 'and I could do that *whoever* I was and *whatever* my purposes were. It is these sorts of facts, and not the purposes of the observer, which we refer to when we use the words "state" and "class".'

Again, this sort of objection seems very plausible at first sight. Yet its plausibility ends the moment that one asks the question 'Yes, but *why* would one do any of that? Why would one collect these data, these facts?' For the possible answers to that question are numerous and various, as numerous and various as human purposes themselves.

Perfectly acceptable answers in the case of 'class' include:

1. To demonstrate the prosperity of the British working class now compared with its predecessors of 100 years or 50 years ago.

2. To demonstrate its current disprivilege as compared with the middle or upper middle classes in British society.

3. As an exercise to improve a government's data base, or the data base of some academic institution.

4. As a governmental exercise to provide a basis for policy changes in the fields of education, health, or income distribution.

5. To show the efficacy or efficiency of some new social survey technique.

6. To provide some supporting data for a stiff letter to *The Times*.

7. To provide some supporting data for a stiff letter to *The Socialist Worker*.

I am sure that with a little imagination the reader could suggest a large number of other reasons for gathering such data on class. Similarly, the collection of data on the major institutions of the state, on the number of state employees, on their social backgrounds, official roles and salaries, on the legal duties and powers of each institution, etc., etc., could also be undertaken for a wide variety of purposes, some of them contradictory one with another. It should be noted, moreover, that each of these purposes is likely to produce variant forms of data collection on class or on the state. Different levels of detail, of aggregation, of comprehensiveness, etc., of data will be required for different purposes.

To reiterate, what all this tells us is that activities such as 'studying the class structure' (past or present) or 'studying the state' (past or present) or 'studying ideology' (past or present) are, like all other human activities, *purposive*. In the case of Marx we have already seen that his purpose in undertaking such activities was to enhance the realization of a certain vision of human liberation.

This is not to deny that such activities, once begun, are not interesting 'in themselves'. On the contrary, they often generate all kinds of intellectual and technical puzzles which may be deeply absorbing in themselves. But it is to say that Marx did not begin to study the state because an activity called 'studying the state' was in itself interesting to him. And certainly he did not do so in order to achieve some peculiar objective like 'having a proper or correct Marxist concept of the state' or 'having a correct Marxist concept of ideology'. Thus, that some contemporary Marxists can even imagine that they are doing something coherent when they are 'developing a proper Marxist concept of ideology' (or of the state or of class) and that they are surprised when such exercises prove sterile and formalistic, only shows how far certain forms of modern Marxist scholarship have drifted from the philosophy of praxis.

WORDS AND SENTENCES

This last reflection brings us to another, even more important. I began this chapter, and I have continued it to this point, with a focus on words, on concepts, and in particular on three concepts used by Marx: 'class', 'state', and 'ideology'. I have done so because, in a great deal of modern Marxist scholarship this is how the issue is posed. 'What is the correct Marxist conceptualization of the state?' 'How is the Marxist concept of class to be developed?' 'What is the Marxist theory of ideology?' These questions, and questions like them are the typical stuff of contemporary theoretical debate in Marxism.

I have already discussed the epistemologically misleading role of the verb 'to be' in such questions, and I will not repeat those points again. But it is clear that the effect of such questions is to focus analytical attention on *single words* – in this case on 'class', 'state' and 'ideology' – with their object-like connotations derived from their grammatical status as nouns.

However, the central thrust of this chapter, and indeed of this work as a whole, is to stress the quite fundamental *misunderstanding* of the working of language which is built into this 'theoretical' concentration on single words or 'concepts'. For if the view which I have been attempting to develop throughout this work is at all persuasive, and words like 'class', 'state', and 'ideology' are better grasped in analogy to tools or instruments of analytical purposes, rather than in analogy to names of objects, then it follows that theory should concentrate on the *sentences* and *propositions* in which these tools are put to use, than on these 'concepts' themselves.[23]

Thus we best grasp Marx's concept of class not by asking 'what is class?' or 'what is Marx's theory of class?' but by asking 'has industrial development in the west during the last fifty years seen a marked deskilling of certain sections of the working class?' or by asking 'do the interests of finance capital always coincide with those of industrial capital?' or by asking 'when does the bourgeoisie act as a single class, and when is it more productive to conceive it as made up of more than one class?' and so on.

You may still be tempted to reply to this that it is impossible to understand, let alone answer, these more specific, complex questions until the 'basic' 'conceptual' questions are clear. However, my answers to this objection should by now be clear: 1. This is just not true. You, the reader, and I *do* understand these more specific types of questions, and we understand them without having to provide the *definitions* which are the only 'answers' we can give to the 'conceptual' questions.

2. We are not only not required to provide such definitions in order to understand the sentences and propositions in which these words are used, such definitions would do us only limited good anyway, because *no definition of a word can determine or constrain the use of a word.*

3. By 'the use of a word', one means precisely its use in sentences, in propositions. It is the use of a word, its active working in a given context that gives a word (any word) an exact meaning (if such a meaning is needed *there*) or a vague meaning (if such a meaning is needed *there*). Words live in sentences and propositions, and context is the oxygen which keeps them alive. Take away the grammatical context of other words, and individual words lose a great deal of their life, a life which can only very partially be returned to them by a definition. That this is so both explains and is explained by the way in which we all learn language, as children, that is that we learn not individual words, but whole phrases or sentences, whole contexts, at one time.[24]

4. Thus – and this is the most important point of all perhaps – the reason why one does not need to master a definition of the word 'class', in order to know what a question like 'will a government sympathetic to the working class be elected?' means, is that one *learns* what the word 'class' means by hearing, seeing, asking and answering questions such as that (and thousands of other 'contextual' questions like it) *not* by asking, or answering, the question 'what is class?' And the same of course goes for 'state', 'ideology', etc.

SUMMARY

So let me now summarize the argument of this chapter to this point:

Many of the problems, and much of the debate, about Marxist theories of 'class', 'state', and 'ideology' would be entirely re-cast, and much of it would appear empty, if these concepts were understood as *tools* or *instruments* of Marx's analytical purposes, and not as *names* of things or objects (even 'theoretical' objects).

Marx's analytical purposes were themselves a sub-set of his broader philosophical and political purposes (the philosophy of praxis and the vision of human liberation derived from it) and obtain their power and force from this fact. Marx's vision of liberation therefore gives a profound analytical and descriptive strength to his scholarly work, and is not in itself in contradiction to his aspiration to science. Certain essentially positivistic theories of science, to which much of twentieth-century Marxism has been an unconscious heir, can suggest that there is a potential or actual contradiction here, but this suggestion should be resisted.

That the points made in the two previous paragraphs are not understood by many contemporary Marxists, derives from their fundamental misunderstanding of the working of language, a misunderstanding based essentially on the misapplication of the notion of ostensive definition which leads all nouns to be understood on the model of names of objects. This misunderstanding is a hallmark of both positivist and realist theories of science, both of which rely on some version of a correspondence theory of truth. For this theory in turn always rests, in one way or another, on a 'reference' theory of meaning, that is on the theory that the meaning of words is given by the things or objects to which they refer.

This mistake in turn, leads to a tendency – commonplace both in contemporary Marxist social theory and in contemporary social theory in general – to concentrate on individual *words* ('concepts') as the fundamental constituents of language rather than on *propositions*. It is however through propositions that words live, and that language moves or is active. Or, to put it more accurately, it is through making propositions about the world that human beings actively appropriate the world. Whereas a concentration on individual words or concepts, and on the definition of such individual words or concepts, both reflects and reinforces an implicitly *passive* or *contemplative* picture of language which sees it as simply 'mirroring' the world in certain ways.[25]

It may be said in this context that the fundamental weakness of Marx's philosophy of praxis, as it was formulated in the mid-1840s, was that Marx failed to 'follow it through' with an appropriate theory of language, despite a few passages in *The German Ideology* and elsewhere where the rather diffuse raw material of such a theory may be found. Marx's failure to see the linguistic implications of the 'activist materialism' outlined in the *Theses on Feuerbach*, led both him, and Engels, in later life, to 'fall back' into theories of language and of truth which were implicitly 'reflective' or positivistic, and this in turn led them to some very 'deep' misunderstandings of their own method (see chapter 7). It is hardly surprising therefore if such misunderstandings have been echoed in later Marxist thought, in which nearly all attempts to make Marxism more 'scientific' and 'rigorous' have perpetuated, and indeed exacerbated, the linguistic naïvety of the founding fathers.

However, Marx's failure to develop an 'actively materialist' theory of language to underpin his philosophy of praxis cannot be said to be severely culpable, since such a development was not really possible until what has been termed 'the linguistic turn' in twentieth-century philosophy. It is my view that one of the pioneers of this 'turn' – Ludwig Wittgenstein – developed, in his later philosophy, a picture or theory of language which can been seen as the linguistic completion of Marx's philosophy of praxis, and which can be used to explode some of the essentially fallacious notions of 'scientific rigour' which are at the heart of many contemporary realist and neo-realist versions of Marxist social theory.

An application of Wittgenstein's later philosophy to Marxism holds out the possibility of developing a philosophical account of Marxist analytical and explanatory method which is as sophisticated in theory as some of the best Marxist scholarship is in practice. This would mark an advance on the current situation where even the best explicit accounts of 'historical materialism' appear as parodies of the best Marxist scholarly practice, especially in the field of history.

HYPOTHESIS FORMATION

One of the most significant methodological points which may be derived from the conclusions above concerns the process of hypothesis formation. For hypotheses are of course themselves types of sentences or propositions. Indeed hypotheses are an important propositional instrument in the activity called 'seeking knowledge of the world'. In addition however there is a dialectical relationship between the possession of a clear set of purposes for studying the world and the process of forming hypotheses. Put simply, that relationship is that hypothetical propositions cannot be formulated without a clear set of purposes for study, but the treating of propositions *as* hypotheses, that is as capable of verification or falsification, is itself the *activity* which prevents *only* that knowledge being acquired which will suit the purposes of the observer.

It is important to say this because an insistence that Marx's study of class (or of the state or of ideology) was logically ancillary to his philosophical commitment to a particular vision of human liberation, could appear to reduce Marxism to a totally voluntaristic subjectivism. For example, it could appear from this perspective that Marx could simply 'choose' to concentrate only on those aspects of working-class activity which would give credence to his view of it as a revolutionary force, or that he could 'choose' to emphasize only the repressive aspects of the state, or that he could 'choose' to focus only on the ideological functions of certain sets of ideas or beliefs in supporting the status quo, etc. In other words, it might seem to be implied from this perspective that Marx could simply neglect or ignore any or all other aspects or characteristics of all these phenomena which did not suit his purposes.

There is no psychological or emotional reason why something like this *cannot* happen, and it is indeed arguable that it did happen from time to time in Marx's own work, and has been an ever-present danger in the Marxist tradition as a whole. But an important logical and psychological safeguard against this kind of 'wishful thinking' or 'wishful analysis' is the constructing of clear hypothetical propositions on the basis of one's purposes.

Thus one may say 'if the working class is a revolutionary force it will act in a certain manner (for example, it will form a revolutionary political party). Is it in fact doing so?' Or one may say 'if this is an ideology supportive of the status quo, it will present the present form of society as 'natural' and therefore as unchangeable. Does it in fact do so?' Or one may say 'if the capitalist state is an agency supportive of capitalist interests it will act to suppress workers' movements. Does it in fact do so?'

Moreover, more subtle or modulated questions can be derived from these hypotheses. For example 'in what ways, or to what extent, is this (any) working class a revolutionary force, and in what ways, or to what extent is it not?' or 'to what extent is this (any) state supportive of capitalist interests?' or 'to what extent does this (any) body of ideas support the status quo, and is that all it does?' Also, of course, the answers one obtains to these questions may be highly variant, both from one capitalist society to another at any one point in time, and in any one capitalist society through time. Moreover, the answers one gets may also not be the ones for which one had hoped or which one had expected. Marxists, like all other human beings, may be disappointed. Their purposes may not be realized or realizable.

But the point to note here is that *without a clear set of purposes for knowing, hypotheses cannot be formulated at all*. It is only if one knows what one wants or expects to find, that one can (a) know what to look for and (b) know that one has *not* found it.[26] One can only come to know that 'things are not as simple as I thought' if one knew what one thought, that is if one had a clear set of hypotheses for testing based upon a clear set of purposes for knowing.

In short then, the insistence that the pursuit of knowledge is always a purposive activity, that it is always the desire to know something for some purpose, does not have to lead to a radical subjectivism. Indeed, in so far as the possession of a clear set of purposes is a logical prerequisite of the formulation and testing of hypothetical propositions, such purposes can, paradoxically, be the best safeguard against wishful thinking. Only those who know clearly what they would wish to be the case, can probe the world in a precise enough way to discover that it is not the case.

Finally, it should be noted in this context that to speak of Marx's analysis of society as being logically ancillary to his philosophical and political purposes, leaves open the question of the origins of these 'purposes' themselves. How did Marx become committed to his particular vision of human liberation and to the industrial working class as the agency of that liberation?

In my view there is no single or simple answer to this question. One may of course refer to the intellectual influences of Hegel, Feuerbach, the Young Hegelians, etc., but this hardly suffices as a sufficient answer, since many students of Hegel were or became conservatives, and most of the Young Hegelians did not become Marxists. One may refer to the class divisions of nineteenth-century Europe, to the material sufferings and struggles of the new industrial working classes etc., but there were many other observers of those divisions and of that suffering who did not become revolutionaries. Finally, one may refer to the characters and personalities of Marx and Engels themselves, but no specific political or philosophical doctrine can be explained on the basis of such psychological analyses alone, no matter how suggestive these may be in a more general way.

We are driven therefore to the conclusion that the 'Marxism' of Marx or Engels is not to be explained as the product of intellectual influences, of social conditions, or of personal psychology and biography, rather it is to be explained as a *creative* synthesis of all these things. In other words, Marx's philosophy of praxis applies as much to his own work as to everything else. Marx's 'Marxism' was the product of a whole complex creative life's *activity* on his part. The fundamental purposes of Marxism were actively *produced* (see chapter 1 on 'production') by two men on the basis of their particular psychologies and personality structures, observing a particular set of social and historical conditions, and being influenced by a particular set of intellectual forerunners. Marxism was something that Marx and Engels *did*.

SOME OTHER NON-ISSUES

There are two other issues around 'class' which have generated a great deal of debate and a great deal more heat than light. These are:

1. The relationship between class structure and the forces of production. In other words, is it changes in the forces of production which change a society's class structure or is it changes in the class structure which produce a change in the forces of production?

2. The issue of classes as social subjects. For while much non-Marxist social science recognizes classes as objects or as social 'things' and is perfectly happy to use the terminology of class in this way, Marxists speak of the working class 'doing' X or 'achieving' Y or 'failing to do' Z. They also speak of the bourgeoisie and other classes (past and present) as 'doing' X or 'achieving' Y or 'failing to do' Z. How far is this way of talking and writing legitimate? Are classes active social subjects?

Let us take these two issues in order:

Class structure and productive forces

This issue can be fairly rapidly dealt with, for the key issue here is *the division of labour*, Adam Smith's great theoretical contribution to classical political economy and to social science in general, which was taken over by Marx and a host of other nineteenth-century thinkers.[27]

If anybody (Marx or any other social theorist) observes a given society at any given moment in time, he or she will observe (a) a certain form of technology, or a certain level of development of the forces of production and (b) a certain pattern of the social division of labour. In some societies – and Marx himself gave most attention to European feudalism and capitalism, as we remember from chapter 2 – that division of labour will, at a certain moment in time, take a class form. That is to say, there will be a class of owners of means of production (feudal lords, slave masters, industrial capitalists) and a class of direct producers (serfs, slaves, industrial proletarians).

Now all these concepts – 'forces of production', 'relations of production', 'class structure' – are, like the division of labour itself, 'snapshot' or 'synchronic' concepts. In other words, and as already stated, they are used by Marx to describe a social situation *at a given moment in time*, either an historical or a contemporary moment. However, for this very reason, they are not concepts which are very useful for analysing *change* through time, or social *processes* in time. Indeed, one may go so far as to say that, as used in Marx's own work, these are not mainly 'change' or 'process' concepts at all. Therefore to ask a question like 'is it changes in the class structure which causes changes in the forces of production, or changes in the forces of production which cause changes in the class structure?' is to ask a question which is already misleading, because neither of these concepts is useful in analysing change at all, and neither should be associated with 'cause' at all.[28] Rather, if we want to be clear headed about questions of change or causes of change in society, we have to use both these 'snapshot' concepts as dependent variables and say that changes in both are 'caused' by creative human activity.

CLASS STRUGGLE

One can say however that class *struggle*, or human activity which can be categorized under this head, is a cause of structural social change. Hence what helps to change both class structure and productive forces are such *activities* as 'enclosing peasant land', 'introducing an outwork system', 'conquering colonial peoples', 'resisting colonial conquest', 'raising wages by forming unions', 'substituting capital for labour in the production process', 'smashing guild controls', etc. But it should also be noted that similarly important in explaining changes in the class structure and in productive forces are activities which may not

be categorizable as 'class struggle' at all, for example 'developing a sedentary agriculture', 'creating trading cities', 'inventing
the wheel', 'inventing the spinning jenny', 'inventing the micro-
chip', etc.

Seen in this way then, the problem disappears, or can be seen
to be a false one. We are not forced to choose between 'the
productive forces' (with their associations of 'economism' and
'reductionism') on the one hand, and 'the class structure' on the
other, as explanations of structural social change, for the simple
reason that *neither of these concepts is meant by Marx to be used
in explanations of change at all*. They are meant to be used in
descriptions of a given society at a given moment in time. Class
struggle can however be used (and should be used) to explain
social change, but only because it is one type of creative human
activity which is the only 'thing' that changes any human society.

Classes as subjects

Some people take exception to Marxism because they object to
sentences such as 'The bourgeoisie, during its rule of scarce one
hundred years, has created more massive and more colossal
productive forces than have all preceding generations together',
or 'The proletariat . . . cannot stir, cannot raise itself up, without
the whole superincumbent strata of official society being sprung
into the air', or 'The French bourgeoisie balked at the domination of the working proletariat; it has brought the *lumpenproletariat* to domination . . . the bourgeoisie kept France in breathless
fear of the future terrors of red anarchy . . . '[27]

The objection here is that in such sentences millions of individual people, sometimes people who are all alive in one
period of history, sometimes people from different periods (as
in the first sentence above) are being 'lumped together' into one
entity – a 'class'. And not only are they being lumped together
in this way, they are then being talked about as if they were a
collective person', as it were, as if a 'class' could be an *active
subject*, capable of 'doing', 'wanting', 'achieving', 'failing', 'wish-
ing', etc., as individual human beings are. But, it is said, classes
are not active subjects at all. Only individual human beings are
active subjects in this sense, and this kind of aggregation is
illegitimate.

Now Marxists usually reply to such objections as if – once
again – what was at stake was purely some kind of empirical

issue. We see the bewitching influence of the verb 'to be' once more, with the 'are' (in 'are classes active social subjects?') being understood ontologically rather than reflexively. So the question then becomes one about 'how far' a class 'really *is*' like an individual, that is how far it has a 'common consciousness' or some sense of a common objective or purpose which 'it' is pursuing.

Marx himself encourages others to discuss this question in a purely empirical way through his distinction between classes 'in themselves' (that is, a group of people who shared a common relationship to the means of production or a common material situation) and classes 'for themselves' (that is, groups of such people who, on the basis of their shared material situation, did develop a 'common consciousness' and/or a common political activity or programme, perhaps through a political party).[30]

This empirical issue is certainly important, although it can be very difficult to determine, and becomes the more difficult the further back in history one goes, and/or the sparser the data on class consciousness and political organization.

But, more importantly, it is a mistake to think that the empirical issue is the only one at stake here. For to treat the issue as if it were *purely* an empirical one, is, once again, to give inadequate attention to 'class' as an instrument of analysis, as a way of seeing or representing society. For the fact is that 'class' is only one of many aggregative concepts which we use to describe and analyse human activity. There are innumerable others: think of 'family', 'community', 'state', 'government', 'economy', 'clan', 'tribe', 'caste', 'district', 'city', etc., and we need such concepts for the same reason that we need class, that is that we could not handle, or would not find helpful or useful, a representation of human activity which dealt exclusively with individual human beings.

To understand this, we might return to the first 'class' sentence quoted above, from Marx's *Communist Manifesto*, 'The bourgeoisie, during its rule of scarce one hundred years, has created more massive and more colossal productive forces . . .' etc. Now Marx was writing this in 1847, so let us take him exactly at his word and suppose that he is referring to a set of social and economic changes taking place between 1747 and 1847. How could we replace this 'class subject' sentence by a set of descriptions couched in purely individual terms? Well, one might have something as follows:

1. 'In 1747, across the world, the following 150,782 people, whose names appear below, were responsible for small improvements in forces of production in 8,247 different activities also enumerated below. These changes occurred in 5,672 locations on the earth (specified to the nearest square mile). In addition another 41,863 people, whose names appear below, introduced organizational innovations in transport, communications, and commerce in the manner specified in the appended computer printout. Of this total of 192,645 persons, data on social standing, income level, and political and social attitudes have been extensively compiled on 191,283 and also appear below. They appear to justify the broad designation 'bourgeois' in describing these persons.'

2. 'In 1748 . . . ' etc.

3. 'In 1749 . . . ' etc., etc. (up to 1848).

Now this description, or something like it, may represent the ideal form of social science from some people's point of view. But quite apart from the 'contingent fact' that data like these are not available for most periods of human history, the fact is that even if they were, and even if human beings had developed the computer capacity to store them all *they would simply not be usable or possible to handle by human beings in this form*. Data, in this form, on this scale, would simply overwhelm the human capacity to, as we say, 'make sense' of them.

We could read information like this, page after page after page of it, but very soon we would have no idea what it 'meant', and to get an idea of what it 'meant' we would have to simplify it, pattern it, which means, in fact, to *aggregate it* in some way, on the basis of some principle or principles. Once again a visual analogy is useful. Research on visual perception has shown that a human being, any human being, does not observe 'everything' which is in his/her field of vision at any given moment. On the contrary, the human activity which we call 'visual perception' involves a very strict but subtle *selection* of particular objects or movements out of those present in the field of vision at any one moment. In other words, to 'observe' something visually is simultaneously *not to see, not to perceive* other things which we could see if, as we say, we 'switched our attention' to them.

In short then, those who object to *all* sentences or propositions about society in which classes appear as active subjects, are, in effect, objecting to a particular way of representing society, to a particular way of seeing it, looking at it, a way which embodies certain purposes, broadly purposes of simplification in pursuit of comprehension. They should therefore be asked to proffer an alternative form of representation or aggregation of human activity, which can serve the same purposes as 'class subject' sentences and propositions, but which does not have the same or similar problems.

It should be noted in this context that one of these problems may be more apparent than real. For not all 'class subject' sentences *do* postulate a conscious class actor, as is sometimes assumed. For example, Marx's 'bourgeoisie' sentence above does not imply that the creation of 'massive and colossal productive forces' was a result of the conscious combined activity of the bourgeois class. It was rather the unintended *outcome* of the activity of thousands of different people who may all, in some sense or other, have been 'bourgeois', but who are not represented in this sentence as having done this 'creation' as any kind of consciously shared class project. By contrast, the sentence from *The Eighteenth Brumaire* beginning 'The French bourgeoisie balked at the domination ... ' does impute some common consciousness, some common, consciously pursued class project, and is the more problematic – and open to empirical questioning – for this reason. In fact, it would be most interesting to comb through the corpus of Marx's work and clearly distinguish to those 'class subject' sentences and propositions which do impute or require a conscious class project, and those which do not. *A priori* it might be hypothesized that sentences which use non-psychological or behavioural verbs, 'the proletariat succeeded in ...', 'the bourgeoisie failed to ...', 'the declining petty bourgeoisie tried to ...' would, in most cases, not necessarily postulate a common consciousness, while those which impute a collective psyche of 'desires', 'aims', 'wishes', 'dreams', 'fears', etc., would usually do so.

So then in both these cases – in the case of the relationship between class structure and productive forces and in the case of classes as subjects – I have endeavoured to recast what are frequently treated as empirical issues or pseudo-empirical issues, into questions about Marxism as a *form of representation* of human activity. I have then tried to discuss the advantages and limitations of this form of representation and the complex set of purposes which it serves. I have done this by drawing attention, reflexively, to the language of Marxism, by drawing attention not to what is seen through these particular linguistic spectacles, but to the characteristics and structure of the spectacles themselves.

I have done this because I am convinced that both Marx and Engels themselves, and, even more, much modern Marxist social theory, is trapped into a peculiarly reified conception of language, a rigid, static conception, in which words are treated primarily as names of objects and in which, because of this, 'scientific rigour' is continuously associated with a ponderous cult of the definition of individual theoretical 'concepts'.[31] I have sought to challenge that conception of language at its root, to suggest that it is mistaken, but *profoundly* mistaken, mistaken in a 'deep' way which is not at all easy to understand or to escape from. It is such a profound mistake because it derives from the misapplication or misleading extension of some of our most basic linguistic practices (especially ostensive definition) into other areas of language which are in practice (praxis) much more sophisticated and subtle than can be grasped by this 'naming' theory of language. Thus this theory, and the conceptions of theoretical rigour and exactitude which it underpins, continually rigidifies and traps the intelligence of those who are in thrall to it. My crusade for a liberation, a freeing of Marxism from this rigidity in the name of an all-encompassing creative, moving appropriation of the world, continues actively in the next and final chapter, in which more is said about 'forms of representation'.

CHAPTER 7

MARX'S DUBIOUS LEGACY: A PICTURE OF REALITY

> A *picture* held us captive. And we could not get outside it for it lay in our language and language seemed to repeat it to us inexorably. Wittgenstein, *Philosophical Investigations*, paragraph 115

This final chapter is rather different from the ones which have preceded it. Whereas they were concerned primarily with an exposition and evaluation of the leading ideas in Marx's own thought, this chapter is concerned with something rather different. For in it I shall analyse what I take to be Marx's most important and influential intellectual legacy.

That legacy has been so profound and pervasive, both for Marxism and for thinking about human society in general that its importance can scarcely be overestimated. I know of no one who has been touched by Marx's thought, even in a peripheral way, who does not show its influence. Yet it is hard to describe, and still harder to bring into the light of day. It is even hard to categorize. It is not exactly part of Marx's formal philosophy or epistemology and indeed in some ways is directly at odds with it. Neither can it be said to be part of his explicit economic or political theory, though it underlies them both. The nearest that Marx ever came to a formal statement of it is his famous 1859 Preface (examined at length in chapter 2), and yet the Preface is by no means an exhaustive statement of it. I am not even sure that its totally pervasive influence is due to Marx alone, for it draws on analogies and metaphors about human society which are certainly far older than Marx's own thought and whose compulsive hold clearly has very deep roots. The most that Marx can be said to have done was to overlay or combine certain pre-existing pictures or images of human society and human life, pictures or images which obtained still greater power and reinforcement by that combination.

I have opted to call this – Marx's most important intellectual legacy – a *picture of reality*, using that term in the sense pioneered by Ludwig Wittgenstein.[1] I will argue that Marxists and others have been long 'held captive' by that picture, a picture which lay deep in the language of Marxism, and has been 'repeated inexorably' by that language, so that there has seemed no escape from it. Indeed, all attempts to escape the grip of that picture have merely succeeded in reproducing it again and again in endlessly variant forms. Moreover, I will suggest that in a sense that picture *is* inescapable. We probably cannot think about human society and human thought without some variant of it. Yet at the same time it can be confining, cramping of our thought, and can even be utterly subversive of it, if we are not self-aware about it. We need, I shall argue, to be aware of the complexity and confusion which underlies the picture's apparent simplicity and obviousness, and aware too that like all metaphorical pictures it has its uses and its place, but can easily bewitch and confuse if not continually seen in the context of the purposes which underlie it and give it its point.

HUMAN SOCIETY AS SPATIAL OBJECT

Since I want to talk about a picture, or rather three overlaid and mutually reinforcing pictures, I shall begin not with words but with drawings.

A preliminary note

The first point to make about these drawings is that to a degree they destroy what they purport to represent. For to an important extent the power of the intellectual representations which I have tried to make palpable in these drawings depends upon their *not* being made palpable, upon their not being made explicit. Indeed to a degree they are defiled, or at least rendered embarrassingly banal, by the mere act of trying to capture them or render them exact, rather as the imagined characters of a novel or a radio drama can be robbed of their magic by their 'realization' in TV or cinema.

In this case particularly, the power and force of these intellectual representations depends upon certain conceptual elisions or semi-conscious confusions occurring constantly. So once one renders those representations graphically those confusions and elisions are both harder to make, and, more importantly, appear obviously as such, and may thus be indignantly denied.

I have therefore to ask the reader for both indulgence and honesty in reading what follows; indulgence in bearing with explorations of metaphors and analogies, explorations which may appear at times almost insulting to the intelligence in their dogged literalness, and honesty in considering how far he or she does make the connections, conflations, elisions, and leaps which these conceptual pictures facilitate.

Comments on the pictures

FIGURE 7.1

The first and most obvious point to make about figure 7.1 applies also to figures 7.2–7.4. This is that all these representations, of people, of society, and of human activity depend upon a notion of *distance*, and in particular of distance between top and bottom.

Representations of people can of course make use of a non-metaphorical concept of distance (of distance in Euclidian space in fact), and certain forms of sculpture may even reproduce the physical dimensions – including height – of the human model. Drawings of people however are usually not 'to scale' and, being two-dimensional, also depend on certain conventions of projection to which the human eye becomes accustomed by continuous exposure to representational drawing. However, the relative naturalness and ease with which Euclidean dimensions can be incorporated into representations of people may facilitate the transition to extended or metaphorical notions of distance in representations of human society and social activity (figures 7.2 and 7.3).

Note also how figure 7.1 introduces other connotations related to or flowing from notions of distance from 'top' to 'bottom'. Thus the head is both the source of confusion and mystification (we get confused 'in our heads') but it is also the point of control over the body. The head is indeed 'at the head' of the body, in control of it. However, the distance between the head and the body also creates the possibility that head and body may

Figure 7.1 A picture of people

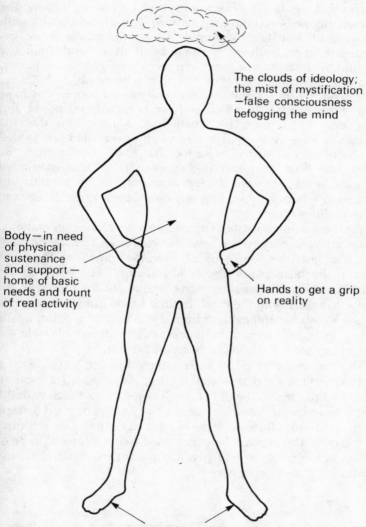

The clouds of ideology;
the mist of mystification
—false consciousness
befogging the mind

Body—in need
of physical
sustenance
and support—
home of basic
needs and fount
of real activity

Hands to get a grip
on reality

Feet: on the ground;
in touch with basic reality;
anchored, grounded

become 'out of touch' with each other. In particular the head may get out of touch with reality. And this notion introduces others that figure 7.1 does not capture very well. Because the human figure is standing up only its feet are in contact with the ground. But if, for example, it were to become dizzy, get confused, then perhaps it could bend down and *touch* the ground with its hands, even support its weight on its hands, and thus 'get a grip' on or 'get in touch' with reality in that way. Moreover, figure 7.1 reminds us that whatever people may *think* with their heads, their bodies have certain basic needs and functions which must be satisfied. It is important that the human head is aware of this reality, otherwise the head as well as the body will suffer. Note too that ideas coming from the head, may float away even higher, even to the 'mist-enveloped regions' of religion,[2] but the feet are firmly on the ground, and will soon – hopefully – bring our figure back to earth, back to basic realities again.

Yet these same polarities can and do have other connotations. Thus the head may be the source of confusion or mystification, but it is also the source of all 'elevated' pursuits. The head thinks, the head plans, the head imagines. The body merely continues with its basic functions, and as for the feet, well the feet are just stuck in the mud. In their heads human beings can aspire to 'higher things' and from a good starting point, heads being, in human terms, the highest things already. We should not let our more basic instincts drag us down.

So even in the physical representation of the body distance can carry *threat* (of disassociation), but also *promise* (of escape). The head can indeed be out of touch or get out of touch with the body, but this can be either bad (loss of reality) or good (escape from restraint). Moreover if the head is 'at the head' or in control of the body this too can be either good (we don't want to be or get out of control) or bad (we don't want the head to be too 'controlling' and 'repressive').

FIGURE 7.2

This is fairly familiar to us. The representation of society as a triangle or pyramid with the wealthy and most powerful at its apex, the poorest and most oppressed at its base, and the 'middling ranks' between them is a very familiar metaphor in social science. It can be used to represent various forms of pre capitalist society as well as capitalist and/or industrial societies.

Figure 7.2 A picture of society

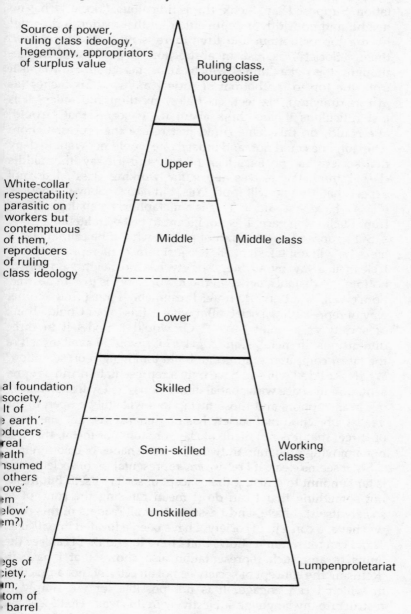

Source of power,
ruling class ideology,
hegemony, appropriators
of surplus value

Ruling class,
bourgeoisie

Upper

White-collar
respectability:
parasitic on
workers but
contemptuous
of them,
reproducers
of ruling
class ideology

Middle — Middle class

Lower

al foundation
society,
lt of
e earth'.
oducers
real
ealth
nsumed
others
ove'
em
elow'
em?)

Skilled

Semi-skilled — Working
class

Unskilled

egs of
ciety,
m,
tom of
barrel

Lumpenproletariat

But suppose that I/you/one just refuses this spatial representation. Suppose I say, 'Look, this is ridiculous, "Society" has no height, and no width or depth either for that matter. It does not have a top or bottom and thus there is no distance between them. "Society" is just an abstraction, a product of human thought, it is not a "thing" which can be measured. How far is it from the top to the bottom of society anyway? Six inches (as in this drawing), six feet, six miles, six thousand miles? It is just ridiculous if you think about it.' It seems that I could, one could, do this. One could just refuse the representation. After all, one could not, and indeed one would not want to deny that society has no Euclidean height, and if I say 'the middle classes think themselves above the working class', I do not expect that anyone will reply 'Yes, but *how far* above? About 3' 6"?' We have just said it. This is a metaphor, an analogy drawn from Euclidean space. It is not meant to be taken literally!

But suppose I am the kind of person who, if he cannot take it literally, will not take it at all. I *do* just refuse the representation. I clean it away by saying, 'society has no height, no top or bottom, no distance between them. "Society" is just an abstraction.' Well, what do I do now? Presumably I must find another way of representing society. But what is this to be? Could I think of society as a point ($\rightarrow \cdot \leftarrow$)? Or would I model it in three dimensions, in metal, stone, or clay? Or would I avail myself of the latest computer graphics to build a moving representation? Whatever I do I will still have only a representation and a representation in space with spatial dimensions. So I will still be dealing in metaphors and those metaphors will still be open to the 'realist' objection that society has no dimensions, not one, two, or three, that it is not made of clay, or stone, or metal, that it is not a moving hologram in twenty-seven shades of colour, etc.

So, it seems clear. If I refuse *any* representation of society, that is tantamount to refusing the concept of society itself. But this is not something that I can do (I mean refusing the concept of society itself). I have, and I assume that all readers of this book will have, a concept of society. I have been educated into its use. That I can represent it shows that I have it, and that I can see the limits of any such representation also shows that I have it. 'Refusing the concept of society' is not an activity, not a practice, in which I can engage. It is not possible for me simply to restructure my language subjectively in this way. That I feel at a loss when I 'refuse the representation' and that I am forced to

Figure 7.3 **A picture of human activity**

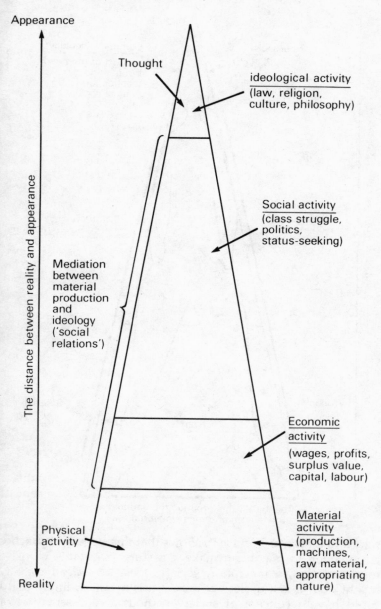

Figure 7.4 Superimposition: a gripping picture

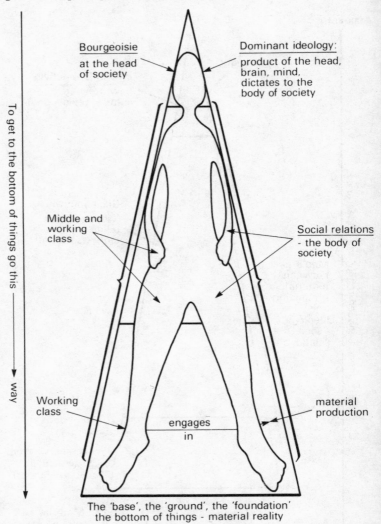

Bourgeoisie
at the head
of society

Dominant ideology:
product of the head,
brain, mind,
dictates to the
body of society

To get to the bottom of things go this ———→ way

Middle and
working
class

Social relations
- the body of
society

Working
class

engages
in

material
production

The 'base', the 'ground', the 'foundation'
the bottom of things - material reality

return to it even as I refuse it, shows that this subjective practice
is not open to me. I can make a gesture ('look this is just a
representation, a metaphor, society does not *really* have any
height') but it is a useless gesture if it is meant to imply that I
could have a concept of society without a representation or
representations of it, and without the limits or shortcomings

Figure 7.5

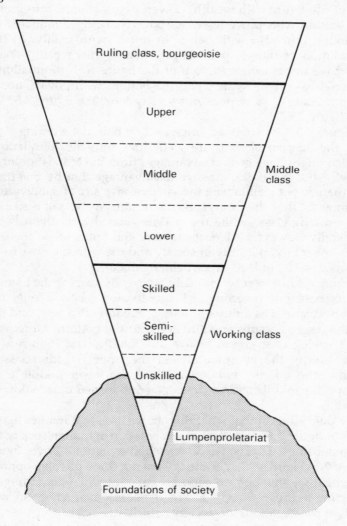

which all representations have.[4]

Yet one may still usefully ask 'Yes, but why this *particular* representation?' and this is not merely a useful, but a very important question ('why any representation at all?' is by contrast neither a useful nor an important question). In asking 'Yes, but why this *particular* representation?' I would, for example, be asking why we analogically associate the Euclidean top of the figure with wealth, power, domination, control, and the bottom with powerlessness, poverty, being dominated or exploited (but also with being 'in touch' with reality, at the foundation of things, providing the basic, real wealth). Why could we not associate the top of the figure with foundations, material base, real wealth, and the bottom with power, domination, control? Why does not society look like figure 7.5? Or like figure 7.6?

Figure 7.5 has certain advantages. In it both the working class and the *lumpenproletariat* are well stuck into the foundations (which might have certain advantages from the Marxist point of view!).[5] But it has the massive disadvantage that by inverting the triangle but maintaining the same relative size of subdivisions it suggests that the bourgeoisie is of almost the same size as the working class, while the middle class dwarfs them both. Generally however, Marxists require the bourgeoisie to be a clear, even tiny, minority in society and the working class to be a considerable, indeed overwhelming majority.

Figure 7.6 however seems really bizarre. By keeping the triangle on its base but inverting the sub-division labels it puts the *lumpenproletariat* as a tiny minority at the top of society, and the bourgeoisie as a substantial minority at the bottom. Moreover, the working class comes 'above' the middle class (which is in turn 'above' the bourgeosie) and the upper middle class is 'below' the middle middle class and the lower middle class 'above' the middle middle class. 'A world turned upside down'[6] indeed!

I would suggest that what this shows us is that neither figure 7.5 nor figure 7.6 is a *possible* representation of human society for human beings. That is, we do not 'choose' figure 7.2 over figure 7.5 or 7.6. Figures 7.2, 7.5 and 7.6 are not three possible options of which we 'happen' to choose figure 7.2 while discarding or rejecting figures 7.5 and 7.6. We just *cannot* use, *cannot* operate with representations of society which dissociate the tops of figures from wealth, power, control and the bottom from domination, powerlessness, exploitation, foundations. And if we ask why this is, why this pattern of analogical or metaphorical association is *compulsory* for us as human beings, the answer is in part to be found in figure 7.1 in the natural fact that human beings' heads and brains are at the top of their bodies and their means of balance and rootedness to the earth are at the bottom.

Figure 7.6

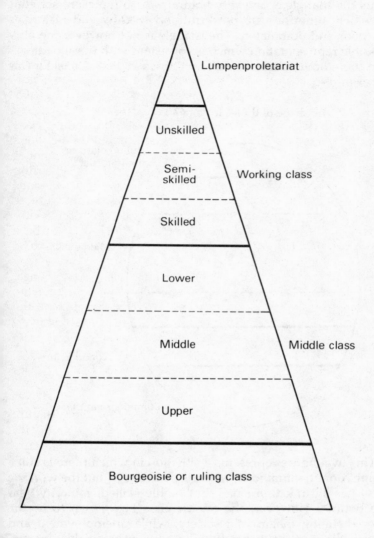

It also has to do with the fact that all physical edifices built by human beings have their foundations in the ground.[7] Also the physics of our earth is such that smaller numerical sets of any given physical entity cover a smaller Euclidean space than larger sets, therefore we 'naturally' represent minorities by smaller geometrical areas and majorities by larger geometrical areas. Thus the triangle is one very natural way to represent societies in which minorities are powerful and wealthy and majorities are poor and dominated. The triangle is not however the only possible representation which is consistent with these natural – and therefore unchosen – patterns of association. Consider this for example.

Figure 7.7 The shape of things to come?

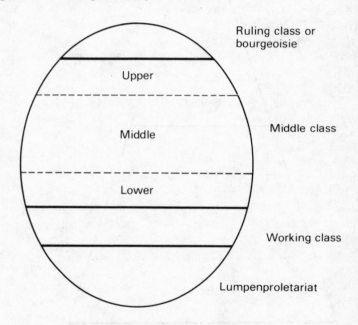

This oval figure represents a situation in which there is still a ruling, dominant minority at the top of society, but the working class has shrunk to a small, but highly skilled, minority near the bottom. However, the middle class has grown to be the overwhelming majority in society, while unemployment and marginalization have produced a very considerable *lumpenproletariat* at the very bottom of society. It seems not at all impossible that many western capitalist societies may look something like this at the end of this century or the beginning of the next. However, while the triangular shape has been dispensed with in this representation of society, the oval still maintains the connection between 'topness' power and dominance and 'bottomness' poverty and exploitation. Thus it is still natural and acceptable to us as a possible representation of society, irrespective of whether it proves predictively accurate or not.

In what circumstances would society be represented in a *totally* different way? Well, if, for example, we imagined that there were thinking creatures who lived not on a planet in the solar system, but in a weightless environment in space, and if we further imagined that these creatures had no vertebrate structure of any kind, but were spherical glutinous masses with their thinking organ (their equivalent of our brain) in the centre of that sphere, then:

1. They would have no existential connection between cognitive control and 'topness' (that is, they would have no heads).

2. Since they would not live in a gravitational environment these creatures would have no association between 'bottomness' and rootedness or foundation. They would not build as we build – if indeed they 'built' at all – so none of our extended metaphors from construction would be of any use to them (in other words they would not have this set of meanings).

3. If these creatures fought, they would not associate victory in such a fight with 'getting on top', nor would they associate defeat with 'being driven down' or 'being driven into the ground', metaphorical associations which are deeply embedded (as we say, but they would not) in our representations of power, domination, and control in society.

In other words then, certain metaphorical or analogical associations in our representations of society are *inescapable* for us, are not a matter of choice for human beings, because of what Wittgenstein calls certain 'very general facts of nature'. Such facts include (a) our living on a planet which has the physics that it has, (b) our being physically constructed, as creatures, in a certain way, and (c) our engaging in activities which are as they are and not otherwise.[8] For example, human beings do not have fights in which the winner ends up on the bottom and the loser ends on top, and this 'natural fact' is what determines some of the limits of the use of the noun 'fight' and of the verb 'to fight'. It also enters importantly into the analogical extensions of 'winning' and 'losing'; winners come top of the league but losers come bottom.

It is to this, and things like this, that Wittgenstein is referring in his famous aphorism 'the limits of my language are the limits of my world'[9], where what is misleading in the aphorism is the personal pronoun (with its 'subjectivist' associations). From this point of view he might better have said 'the limits of (human) language are the limits of the (human) world'.

Still, that these associations (of 'topness' with power, wealth, domination, control and of 'bottomness' with poverty, power-lessness, defeat, foundation, reality) are *inescapable* for us, are part of human nature, of the human condition, does not mean that they cannot mislead us, confuse us, inhibit our understanding.

To begin to grasp the subtle but profound ways in which we can be misled by this web of metaphors, we must first observe that at its centre is the hegemony or dominance of Euclidean space and spatial relationships over human thinking.[10]

In human thought everything is conceived as having a *location*, which means that everything is conceived on the model of, or in analogy with, physical objects in space. To understand this think of such questions and assertions as, 'where in society is the dominant ideology to be found?'; 'how are we to reach the truth?'; 'that is really beyond me, I cannot get a grip on it at all'; 'the whole set of events proceeded so quickly'; 'its consequences could not be foreseen'; 'getting to the centre of state power is a difficult business': 'all that is behind us, we must look ahead': 'in this society coercion stands nakedly in the place of consent', etc. Again, none of this is avoidable. If human beings did not live in Euclidean space and did not themselves occupy such space, they (whoever or whatever 'they' were) would not have this spatially metaphorical epistemology. But they do, so they do.

However, one very important and potentially confusing complication is that human beings also *move*, both in space and through time. This being the case their stock of epistemological analogies and metaphors must also have a place for movement, for dynamism, for change, as well as for fixed locations. So, we have a language in which we 'reach' the truth, but the truth can also 'change' or 'shift'. We have a language in which the centre of state power may be 'located', but it may also 'alter'. We have a language in which we seek a 'clear overall' view of the matter, but in which a lot also depends on 'the perspective' one is taking or 'the aspect' with which one is concerned.[11]

In fact human language has somehow to do a very difficult dual job. It must reflect the universal human fact that 'nobody can be everywhere at once or do everything at once' so that a great deal of the world *is* fixed and unalterable for most of us, most of the time. But it must also reflect the fact that human beings do, both physically and conceptually, 'change their positions' or 'change their perspective' on things in ways which 'make them look very different', and they also actively change the world, both physically and socially, so that things not merely look different, they *are* different. So human language, and indeed other human forms of representation of the world, must embody fixity *and* flux, stasis *and* movement, structure *and* agency. And they do so. We have vocabularies, webs of metaphors, similes, analogies in human language to do both jobs.

Yet the job is not done without strain, and the strain shows itself in language primarily by way of conflicts, or apparent conflicts, between metaphors, images, representations. In our language we have a vocabulary of human *society* which stresses its fixity, its 'structure', its rigid constraints (straight lines), its immutable continuity of functions, and we also have metaphors, images, similes of human *activity* which stresses its dynamism, unpredictability, creativity, as well as the freedom of choice and personal responsibility which is the concomitant of voluntary, uncoerced, activity.

Thus when we notice the very different and apparently conflicting pictures of the human condition which these different sets of metaphors are used to construct, we are apt to think that we have encountered an empirical question, that is, 'which of these accounts is correct, which is the true account?' But if both pictures and the constituents of both pictures are available to us in our language, then this might suggest, at least *a priori*, that we are dealing here, not with an empirical question about the 'true' nature of human society, but with a question about the different human *purposes* which are served by these different vocabularies. In other words, it might be more productive here to ask not 'which of these accounts is true?' but 'when, or on what occasions, do we use one, and when or on what occasions, do we use the other?' For if it turns out that the purposes and occasions on which we tend to opt for the vocabulary of fixity and structure are very different from the purposes and occasions on which we opt for the vocabulary of activity, movement, change, creativity, then we may not have to 'choose' at all. We can quite happily accept both these gifts of our language.[12]

However, all this may become clearer if we turn to an analysis of figures 7.3 and 7.4. For it is in figure 7.3 that we first begin to encounter real signs of strain in the metaphor or form of representation which we are considering here, that is human society as pyramid or triangle.

FIGURE 7.3

The strain is signalled in the very title of the figure, 'A picture of human activity'. For here the triangle itself and its sub-divisions are representing not physical parts of the human body (as in figure 7.1) nor physical groups of people (as in figure 7.2) but 'activities'. Thus the top of the triangle represents 'ideological' activity, the next segment 'social' activity, and the bottom two 'basic' segments represent 'economic' and 'material' activity, or to be more precise, economic and material production.

Now we are happiest with spatially fixed representations of things in the world, if those things are themselves conceivable as 'fixed' in some way. Thus heads are always drawn at the top of human bodies, because heads always *are* at the top of living human bodies, while feet are always at the bottom and stomachs always in the middle, etc. Similarly the metaphor of society as triangle is most 'natural' and 'obvious' to us when bits of the triangle which are in fixed relationships to each other spatially are representing social groups which are in socially and economically 'fixed' relationships to each other in society. (In many cases these social groups may be in physically fixed relationships to each other too, living in different parts of cities or in different regions, etc.).

But when a small triangle at the top of figure 7.3 represents, for example, ideological *activities* or *practices*, then we are 'stuck' (a good word here) with a fixed location representing something which has no fixed location in society. Of course ideological practices in the law may take place in spatially 'fixed' law courts and barristers' offices, but they can also take place in solicitors' homes, clients' homes, on moving buses, trains, aeroplanes, etc. And the same remarks would apply equally to the 'social' activity or practices represented in figure 7.3.

The representation may seem, at first sight, somewhat more satisfactory in the case of economic and material production, in so far as it is thought of as taking place in fixed factories or workshops. But of course capitalist production is production of commodities, commodities which are consumed as well as produced and which, in order to be consumed, must 'circulate' through society, along with money (that dual circulation which enables 'surplus value' to be 'realized', profits to be appropriated, and capital to be accumulated). Therefore, the representation of material and economic production by a fixed, bounded space seems no more satisfactory, on reflection, than such representations of social and ideological activity. Moreover, and more importantly, that any human activity takes place in a fixed location does not, in itself, fix *it*. Our language is such that when we think of activity we think of movement. Even if movement occurs in a place, movement is not a place.

Moreover, these are not the only complications with figure 7.3. For in this particular use the triangular hierarchy may smuggle in other implications which we might wish to reject. Thus, for example, the fact that ideological activity is located 'at the head' of society, at a considerable distance from economic and material production (which takes place 'at the base') can very easily suggest that ideological activity is at such a distance from, is so different from, material activity *because the former involves thought, but no physical activity, and the latter involves physical activity but no thought*.

In earlier chapters, we strenuously rejected this 'vulgar materialist' interpretation of Marx's thought, and argued that he too would have rejected it as incompatible with his philosophy of praxis. But note how the shade of figure 7.1 can hover here and reinforce by metaphorical association this very interpretation. Thought takes place in the human head, ideology is thought perpetrated 'at the head' of society by groups utterly divorced from the 'reality' of basic production, etc.

Of course one then 'remembers' that a human act is only an *act* because it involves thought and purpose. One also 'remembers' that just as material production takes place in a physical location with physical plant and equipment, so religion takes place in churches, law takes place in law courts, and philosophy takes place in academics' studies and in university buildings and involves books, paper, word processors, etc. In short one remembers that *all* human activity, including intellectual activity, is both physical *and* mental and must take place in physical locations. But before, as it were, one remembers all this, the bewitching influence of mixing and merging representations and images has done its damage. Ideology and production, thought and production have been separated (spatially and conceptually separated), and that has been implied, inferred *in a certain pattern of use* of our language which would never have been asserted or defended as an explicit position.

The question is however why, how does this happen? How does our use of language persuade us of something of which we have not, as it were, been explicitly convinced?

FIGURE 7.4

I think an answer to this question may lie in figure 7.4 which brings together the previous three pictures into a composite picture of reality. As will be seen, the power of this picture derives from its *superimposition* of human physical and sensual attributes on to an ontology of the world. Thus we can conceive of the dominant ideology in society (perpetrated by the bourgeoisie or some other ruling class) as made of completely different 'stuff' from material and economic production, because we are aware that others can see our feet anchored to the ground (and we can *feel* them anchored there) but nobody can see (or hear, smell, touch) our thoughts. In other words this composite representation *invites us to understand ideology in society on the model of our own subjectivity.*[13] But, though tempting, this model of ideology is seriously misleading. For,

1. Ideology in society is a material practice. It is found in the material forms of books, newspapers, films, videos, theatrical drama, etc.; and
2. It is also a practice undertaken by perceptible human beings in physical locations (law courts, churches, television studios, etc.). Hence,
3. Ideological practice is a material practice and it involves thought, but it does not involve thought any more than any other human practice. Thus,
4. The essence of ideology is *not* thought and in so far as the composite figure 7.4 tempts us to conceive ideology in this way it is seriously misleading.

More generally, this composite picture of the base, ground, foundation of society in material production obtains its persuasive power from what can only be described as *an elision of gravity and empiricism.* That is, for reasons ultimately anchored (ahem) in the physics of our earth, human language metaphorically extends much of the language of spatial 'bottomness' – ground(s), foundation, base, bottom, source, origin – into the language of causal or logical priority. Thus, we 'get to the bottom' of things, we 'get back to basics', we seek 'the source of our errors' and 'the origin of the difficulty'. For ultimately the same anthropological reasons, the ground, the earth, is an important metaphor of *solidity* or *reliability* in all human languages.[14] If human beings become dizzy, lose their balance, they fall to the ground and can then feel its comforting reality throughout their body. In war, under enemy bombardment, safety is sought on or below the ground. We anchor, found, all our buildings in the ground, and an earthquake is therefore a favourite metaphor of insecurity.[15]

Now when one adds to these images and connotations of 'bottomness' others (such as 'getting one's hands dirty' as the ultimate way of 'keeping in touch' with reality) then we can see how easy is a metaphorical or image elision of the working class, manual labour, material production and ontological priority ('basic' reality) in a single concept of the 'foundation' of society. Ultimately, this elision works, as figure 7.4 as a whole works, not by appeal to our intelligence, but *by an inviting appeal to our senses*. Perhaps that is why it *is* so persuasive, is so much a part of the language of popular Marxism (and other sympathetic socialist creeds) and often permeates and subverts the day-to-day speech even of Marxist intellectuals who in other places (books, articles, lectures) know better. This is, as one might say, Marxism of the hands and feet, not Marxism of the mind.

But the complications are not over yet. For in figures 7.3 and 7.4 not only is a fixed spatial hierarchy being used to represent a hierarchy of activities, but the elaborations of those activities in both diagrams may also seem rather odd. Thus in figure 7.3 social activity is elaborated as 'class struggle, politics, status seeking', but economic activity is elaborated as 'wages, profits, surplus value, capital, labour' and material production is elaborated as 'machines, raw materials, labour process, appropriating nature'.

Now quite apart from the fact that many of these labels are nouns rather than verbs (and thus appear to name things rather than describe activities) it may also be objected that what is being represented here is not human activity as such, but a particular conceptualization of that activity, that is, the Marxist conceptualization. In addition, it may be objected that fixed graphical spaces are a particularly inappropriate way of representing the fluid categories of human thought. The first of these objections is not of any real significance in itself, because human activity can only be represented if it is not being undertaken. In other words no representation of human activity whether in language or graphics or in any other medium can be a *reproduction* of that activity, so that the concept of 'human activity as such' (above) can be given no useful meaning. The Marxist representation of human activity may well have its limitations but in itself this does not make it one whit different from any other representation. The important thing therefore is not that it is limited. The important thing is to specify the *particular* limitations of the Marxist representation and to see whether other representations can help compensate for those particular limitations.

The second part of the objection is more serious however. For earlier in this book I myself drew attention to the fluidity of the categories of human thought and in chapter 6 I argued that the meanings of words in any human language are never rigidly fixed but always have a certain openness, a certain indeterminacy, which cannot be eliminated by definitional exercises. Indeed I argued that the pursuit of linguistic exactitude through fixed definitions, which is a hallmark of much modern Marxist and non-Marxist social science, represented the confused pursuit of an objective which would not be desirable even if it were attainable, but which language in fact makes unattainable.

These reflections on the fluidity of the categories of human thought – these recognitions that thinking is itself an activity in which words and sentences are actively used to impose meanings upon the world – make figure 7.3 seem a doubly inappropriate form of representation. For here is a fixed, static figure representing an active, changing conceptualization, and a changing conceptualization of that which is itself moving, dynamic – human activity. Moreover, it is creative human activity that makes human societies themselves *change*, that produces social change. Since, as I have already noted, human language is so constructed that when we think of activity or change we think of movement, all these reflections lead me to want to put some *movement* into my graphical representation of human society too. For now not merely figure 7.3 but all my triangles (7.1–7.4) seem far too static.

So would figure 7.8 be better?

Figure 7.8

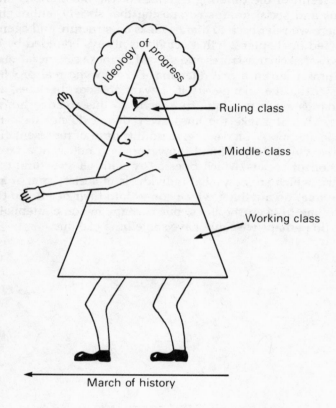

No, I do not feel that this really does the trick. By giving society arms and legs and putting it into motion this figure does – rather crudely – capture the notion of social change, but of course by keeping the bounded triangular form and going in for caricature anthropomorphism, it has all of society moving together in one direction. This is because I am still relying on a representation of the human figure in motion, and human beings possess the physical limitation of only being able to move in one direction at one time. Hence this representation easily lends itself to a unilineal notion of historical or social progress.

But in any case, any notion of creative human activity in society draws attention to the possibility of discrete movements of all parts of society, both individuals and social groups. It also implies that when there is general or total social change this is the result of the differing activities of the multifarious individuals and social groups composing that society, although – and here we refer back to Marx's ideas on structure and agency discussed in chapter 2 – that activity is always bounded by inherited social circumstances and shaped by those circumstances.[16]

So now I am in a real dilemma. For now the real problem seems to be the triangle itself. I want to take the lines, the boundaries away to allow 'free reign' to this creative human activity. But If I take the lines away then I do not have my triangle any more. I have to give up this form of representation entirely. On the other hand, however, I do not want a representation of society which does away with all structural constraints, which suggests that individuals in society can, at any given time, do anything which comes into their heads. So this tempts me to keep the lines, but perhaps in some attenuated form. So perhaps we could have something like this:

Figure 7.9

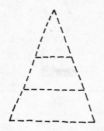

or this

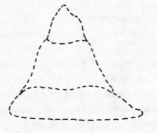

or this

No, none of this works. And why not? Because if I remain within a static graphical representation of society I can only have boundaries or not have boundaries. It is true that I can have continuous boundaries or broken boundaries. I can have straight lines or curves. With more sophisticated graphics I can even have moving boundaries. *But I cannot both have boundaries and not have boundaries*, which is really what I want. In other words I have here reached the limits, the logical limits, of the graphical representation of human society.

Human society both has boundaries and has no boundaries, it both has constraints and has no constraints. Or, in other, better words, there are purposes from which it makes sense to conceive of human societies in both these ways. But there are no purposes from which it makes sense to conceive of Euclidean spaces in both these ways (which is why a non-Euclidean geometry is required to describe 'space/time'). In other words Euclid, and all our numerous metaphors and analogies deriving from Euclidean space and extended to non-spatial phenomena *break down here*. We should not worry about this. All metaphors, all analogies break down 'somewhere', otherwise they would not be metaphors or analogies. The important thing is to be able to recognize when, where, they have broken down and not to mistake a breakdown in a form of representation for a breakdown in reality.

HUMAN SOCIETY AS CREATIVE ACTIVITY

'Human society both has boundaries and has no boundaries.' The proposition may sound profound, but it is not very illuminating. In fact, despite its appearance, this is not primarily a proposition about human society at all. Rather it is the kind of paradox which signals the limit, the breakdown, of a particular metaphor, of a particular form of representation. One exits from a form of linguistic representation by means of just this kind of paradox. The paradox does not tell us that there is anything wrong with human society. It tells us that there is something wrong, or at least limited, in this way of describing it.

So what other form of representation should we seek? Well it is clear that it must not be any form of representation which portrays society as an object, a thing, because as soon as we opt for that questions arise such as 'where is it?', 'what are its boundaries, its limits?', even 'what does it look like?', and then of course we are back to Euclid, and triangles, and tops and bottoms, and the problems which we have just encountered and are trying to escape.

But if one gives up the metaphor, the image, of society as object, as thing, entirely, is one not then forced to give up the concept of society itself? Does not society now simply disintegrate into discrete social groups, or even into a mass of individuals. I think not. And I think not because 'society-as-object' uses are not our only uses of the concept 'society'. However, to clarify what I mean here I must deal in specifics, and I will do so through two quotations. The first is from Engels:

> Marx discovered the law of development of human history: the simple fact ... that mankind must first of all eat, drink, have shelter and clothing, before it can pursue politics, science, art, religion etc.; that therefore the production of the immediate means of subsistence and consequently the degree of economic development attained by a given people or during a given epoch, form the foundation upon which the state institutions, the legal conceptions, the ideas on art, and even on religion, of the people concerned have been evolved, and in the light of which they must, therefore, be explained.[17]

And this is Marx himself:

> Men are the producers of their conceptions, ideas etc. – real active men, as they are conditioned by a definite development of their productive forces and of the intercourse corresponding to these, up to their furthest forms. Consciousness can never be anything else than conscious existence, and the existence of men is their actual life-process. If in all ideology

men and their circumstances appear upside down as in a *camera obscura*, this phenomenon arises just as much from their historical life-process as the inversion of objects on the retina does from the physical life-process.

In direct contrast to German philosophy, which descends from heaven to earth, here we ascend from earth to heaven. That is to say, we do not set out from what men say, imagine, conceive, nor from men as narrated, thought of, imagined, conceived, in order to arrive at men in the flesh. We set out from real, active men, and on the basis of their real life process we demonstrate the development of the ideological reflexes and echoes of the life process. The phantoms formed in the human brain, are also, necessarily, sublimates of the material life process, which is empirically verifiable and bound to material premises. Morality, religion, metaphysics, all the rest of ideology and their corresponding forms of consciousness, thus no longer retain the semblance of independence. They have no history, no development; but men, developing their material production and their material intercourse, alter, along with this their real existence, their thinking and the products of their thinking. Life is not determined by consciousness, but consciousness by life.[18]

I wish now to analyse these two quotations closely and with particular regard to the way in which they deal with *processes in time*. For this is one aspect of human society which spatial representations necessarily omit.

Fixed graphical representations of society – like our triangles – can be amended to incorporate spatial movement (through the animated cartoon for example, or through computerized graphics). But even then they find time, and particularly long time-spans, very difficult to incorporate. In fact they can do so only to the extent that (a) they themselves have a duration (10 minutes, 30 minutes, 1 hour, etc.) and to the extent that (b) they incorporate temporal symbols in the graphics (dates etc.). They can also combine these two forms of representation. Thus with computerized graphics one could produce diagrammatic representations of – say – social structure at time t_1 which is then slowly mutated, through shifting images, into social structure at times t_2, t_3, t_4, etc. Even here however the representation of social processes is defective in so far as timed 'end-states' can be shown, but not the processes which produce them. Thus for example, a series of diagrams dated at intervals between 1880 and 1980 could show stages in the decline of the manual working class as a proportion of the total population of the UK, but they could not in themselves show the continuous processes which have brought that decline about. To show these, resort usually has to be made to other forms of representation, archive film with narrative 'voice-over', analytical comments from interviewed 'experts', supplementary diagrams, etc.

Now this problem with time, or more exactly with social processes occurring in time, is rather obvious when one is focusing on spatial or graphical forms of representing society, but it takes altogether more subtle and confusing forms when one is concerned with language, written or spoken. For language handles processes in time primarily through the use of *verb* forms, often – though not always – through verb forms metaphorically or analogically derived from physical movement in space. Thus, think of 'to slow', 'to quicken', 'to rise', 'to fall', 'to merge', 'to separate', 'to grow', 'to decay', 'to increase', 'to decrease', etc., etc. (Once you have the idea you should be able to think of hundreds of other examples). However, because nearly all analogical verbs of social process do have physical movement or physical activity uses too, they can easily, effortlessly, seduce the writer or speaker who uses them back into the spatial world, a world whose vocabulary is, as we have seen, replete with a fixity which might best be avoided, especially if one is attempting to describe or analyse processes in time. Let us now watch Friedrich Engels and Karl Marx being so seduced.

According to Engels, Marx's 'law of development of human history' is a 'simple fact'; the fact that 'mankind must first of all eat, drink, have shelter and clothing before it can pursue politics, science, art, religion etc.'. Well that *seems* pretty clear. We are dealing with processes in time here. Taking any society as a whole, basic material needs must be satisfied *before* other pursuits can be entered into (not least, one supposes, because if they are not, nobody would be alive to 'pursue politics, science, art, religion etc.').

But all is not quite what it seems, because further reflection suggests that Engels cannot strictly be thinking about temporal sequence here. He clearly does not mean that all human societies 'first' concentrate on satisfying basic material needs and then 'get on' to politics, science, etc., *later*. He means that unless a society is productive enough to satisfy the basic material needs of, at least some, people, they will not physically survive to engage in other activities. In other words what is being outlined here is a functional condition, not a temporal sequence. The 'time' language ('first of all', 'before') is doing logical not chronological work. First complication. Let us go on.

'Therefore' (he says) 'the production of the immediate means of subsistence and consequently the degree of economic development attained by a given people or during a given epoch form the foundation ... ' Now here we have a real pot-pourri. Literally, this sentence says that 'the *production* of the immediate means of subsistence' (a process) and – consequently – 'the degree of economic development attained by a given people' (state of affairs) or 'during a given epoch' (a process) *come together* to 'form' something which is apparently a 'foundation'. So it is very clear, two processes and a state of affairs form a foundation!

The reader may or may not agree, but to the author this imagery seems positively surreal in its contradictoriness. And surreal too in that whatever world there may be in which two processes and a state of affairs form a foundation, it is clearly not our world. Engels *cannot* mean what he says here. In fact his 'therefore' is spurious, as spurious as everything which follows it. Engels is not drawing a logical conclusion (which is what the 'therefore' might suggest) *he is just repeating himself*, and that rather badly. In other words, all this sentence up to 'foundation' says is (again) that 'unless the basic material needs of, at least some, people are met in any given society, then people will not survive to engage in other activities'.

But we have still not finished. Because Engels then tells us that 'upon' this 'foundation' (composed of two processes and a state of affairs) 'the state institutions, the legal conceptions, the ideas on art, and even on religion ... have been evolved', and therefore it is in its 'light' that they must be 'explained'. So now we have a foundation (object) 'upon' which things 'evolve' (process) but which apparently 'sheds light' (process) in which things can be 'explained' (process)! I have always thought of foundations as rather dark and gloomy places, hardly designed to shed light on anything, but since this foundation is composed of two processes and a state of affairs, it is no doubt capable of performing this surreal wonder as well.

We should remember that this quotation is from Engels' speech at Marx's graveside. There are therefore very good reasons why he might not have been at his best when he wrote it. But that is really not the point here. My aim is not, by means of a close analysis of crazily mixed metaphors, to pillory or ridicule what Engels is saying. As I hope to show, I think it is perfectly clear what Engels *means* to say, and I find what he means to say very clear, although still open to doubt and debate. I am rather concerned here with the way in which the language on which Engels is drawing has, in important ways, subverted even what he means to say. Moreover, since this language is in many ways the quintessential language of Marxism – the kind of language in which 'historical materialism' has trafficked from Engels' day to our own – an analysis of the way it can confuse and mislead those who make use of it is, I think, of continuing relevance.

It is the final part of the quotation which is particularly important in this respect. Engels arrives at his 'foundation' by way of 'production' (of 'the immediate means of subsistence') and by way of 'the degree' (of 'economic development') attained by a given people. Now production is also a physical process – houses are produced and a first stage in their production is the laying of foundations – and degrees are after all classically Euclidean measures of spatial relationships (angles). So both 'production' and 'degrees' can translate Engels effortlessly from time to space, from process to objects, and in so doing they allow 'the production of the immediate means of subsistence' and 'the degree of economic development' to become *fixed objects* ready made to become 'foundations'. But Engels has not quite forgotten that it is not objects but processes with which he is concerned and so, rather confusedly, things (objects) like 'state institutions', 'legal conceptions', 'ideas on art' and 'ideas on religion' *'evolve'* (perhaps they should rather revolve!) on this foundation.

In other words, the verb 'evolve' is a kind of hapless reinvocation of movement, a sort of gestural attempt to unfix what is threatening to become totally concreted. But by now it is too late. The whole grammar of that final sentence completely fixes and reifies 'legal conceptions', 'ideas on art', and 'ideas on religion' as *things*, things resting on, and therefore above, 'foundations'. The damage has been done. The base is back, 'topness' and 'bottomness' are back. Whereas, of course, all that Engels means to say is that just as the means or processes by which a society attains its material subsistence change, so its state institutions, its legal conceptions, its ideas on art, and even its religious beliefs change. It is also clear that Engels thought that this was some kind of causal relationship, that changes in 'the production of the immediate means of subsistence' *caused* changes in state institutions, legal conceptions, etc. and I have already outlined, in chapter 2, my reasons for doubting this. But I also tried to show that a rather different, and less problematic interpretation of these relationships can be provided in which changes in material production as much as changes in legal conceptions, ideas on art, etc. are treated as the result or outcome of *creative human activity*. Thus, as human societies develop, creative human actors, building on the achievements of previous generations of such actors cause changes in material production *and* legal conceptions *and* ideas on art, etc.

Thus at any given point in time a whole set of social institutions (from forms of material production to forms of state and art) can – retrospectively – be categorized separately from the set of such institutions existing in the same society at an earlier point in time. But the *process*, the dynamic *process*, which produces the changes which can be intellectually captured as a series of static 'sets' of institutions (and called 'feudal society', 'capitalist society', etc.) is a process fuelled, powered, driven (better verbs, these) by human creative activity, not by *things* called 'forces of production', 'relations of production', etc.

But what makes a 'set' of institutions into a coherent set? Is this just a unity imposed by the Marxist observer? Not quite. For 'the degree of economic development', to use Engels' phrase, does act as a constraint in so far as certain things are just not possible if certain material conditions are not present. Thus political and moral debate about nuclear power *could not* go on under feudalism, nor did the theological issues raised by genetic engineering worry medieval theologians. Also, as we have already suggested, mass starvation is a moral problem in 1987 in a way in which it was not, could not be, in 1387.[19] State control over the mass media becomes a political issue only when there are mass media. Twentieth-century jurisprudence has reason to be concerned with the law of copyright in a way that twelfth century jurisprudence had no reason to be.

In other words, scientific and technological developments 'enable' much that is neither scientific nor technological; political, moral, and religious debate or speculation on new issues, new legal concerns, new forms of social control and communication, even new forms of art. (Thus the photographic camera both enabled new forms of representational art, and raised new issues for representational painting as an art form, issues still unresolved.)[20] But note a logical point. To say that B (a political, ideological, legal or artistic phenomenon) *could not have occurred* without A (a scientific or technological development) is not to say that if A occurred B 'had' to occur (for B might be only one of a number of possible responses to A), or that B was *caused* by A.

This latter point is particularly crucial. The art form called 'photo-montage' could not have existed without the invention of the camera, but both the camera and photo-montage are caused by, or (we should better say) are a product of human creativity. Photo-montage was not 'necessitated' by the camera. It still had to be invented. Similarly, science fiction is not necessitated by science, though it is impossible without it. Political activity to control state uses of computerized information on a citizenry is not necessitated either by computers or by state information systems, though it would not happen without them.

Here I can get close to giving a meaning to my earlier paradox that 'human society both has boundaries and has no boundaries'. At any given point in time it has boundaries in that certain things (innumerable unknowable things) are not possible, are not occurring, because the conditions for their occurring are not present (and when I say 'things' I mean thoughts, feelings, conceptions, speculations as well as material production and social activities). Very frequently it is scientific and technological developments which 'allow' new things to happen, which create new possibilities. But that scientific and technological development itself occurs is due only to human creativity. Thus social possibilities are limited only by human creativity itself. I do not know what the limits of this creativity are (the future will show), and neither does anyone else. Hence that creativity can be treated as limitless, or at any rate, as of indeterminable limit.[21] Hence boundaries and no boundaries. *At any given time* in the development of human society many things are not possible, but in the history and future of human society conceived *as a process through time*, who is to say what is impossible?

Thus I think that neither the image of spatial boundaries nor the image of 'foundations' (the 'limit' of the building is that it must 'fit' on the foundations, or can only be as 'heavy' or as 'high' as the foundations will allow) helps us to understand the notions of the technological limits *of possibility* and the breaking through of those limits by human creativity which I have been trying to outline above. And in that sense Engels' language is disastrously misleading, not merely of himself, but of many later Marxists seeking to grasp historical materialism. When he needs movement he is seduced into stasis, when he needs flow, he gets stuck in concrete. Above all (and more exactly) when he needs to minimize space and object language and to maximize movement and process language, he fails disastrously to make this change.

Thus a very delicate *logical* issue, the issue, to be precise, *of necessary but insufficient conditions*, of the capacity of scientific and technological development to make possible what was previously impossible (but its equal incapacity to 'necessitate' anything) is lost. It is lost in the 'heavy' imagery of 'base' and 'superstructure' with its philosophically disastrous implication that thought is somehow less 'real', less 'material', less 'basic' than production, when both are equally real, equally 'physical' and 'mental', when both are, in short, just different forms of human creative activity.

Let us see now whether Marx does any better.

He begins well:

Men are the producers of their conceptions, ideas, etc. – real active men, as they are conditioned by a definite development of their productive forces and of the intercourse corresponding to these, up to their furthest forms. Consciousness can never be anything else than conscious existence, and the existence of men is their actual life-process.

But then we have:

If in all ideology men and their circumstances appear upside down as in a *camera obscura*, this phenomenon arises just as much from their historical life-process as the inversion of objects on the retina does from the physical life-process.

This is *The German Ideology*, so 'all ideology' probably refers to left Hegelianism. The rest of the sentence then develops one of Marx's favourite images in dealing with that ideology, the image of *inversion*. In all ideology 'men and their circumstances' appear 'upside down', and he (Marx) aims, as he says elsewhere, to put them 'the right way up'.[22] But here he is just making the point that in so far as some form of inversion – not specified – occurs in ideology, this too 'arises from' the human 'historical life-process', 'as much' as the inversion of objects on the retina of the eye 'arises from' the physical life-process.

Now Marx has yet to tell us what ideological 'inversion' involves precisely, but the switch to visual imagery, with the explicit evocation of cameras and eyes, is somewhat worrying. It is worrying partly because spatial 'topness' and 'bottomness' are already very near again and partly because the phrase 'arises from' is used in such a way as to suggest a *direct parallel* between logical inversion and image inversion. But clearly the way in which ideology 'arises from' the historical life-process is very different from the way in which the inversion of objects on the retina 'arises from' the physical life-process. The verb which is hovering here (and which is found explicitly in other passages of Marx dealing with these issues) is the verb 'to reflect'.[23] The implication clearly is that ideology *reflects* the historical life-process in the way in which the retina *reflects* light from the physical world, that is as an inverted or mirror image.

But this is dangerous talk, because it suggests a 'directness' or 'automaticity' of relation between human life and ideology which is quite misleading. Ideology (if we take this in *The German Ideology* sense of more or less coherent systems of thought) is produced, consciously constructed, by human beings. It is most assuredly not a non-conscious process (like the reflection of light in a retina). Therefore, the way in which it is linked to the historical life-process of the individuals or social groups who produce it is likely to be a lot more complex and subtle than can be grasped by the visual imagery of 'reflection' and 'inversion'.

As so often in these writings of 1846–7 Hegel is clearly dominating Marx's conception of ideology here. Indeed, as we have already seen (chapter 1, pp. 25–6) Marx's critique of Hegelian philosophy accepted Feuerbach's view that Hegel had logically 'inverted' subject and object in his philosophy. But even if this image does justice to Marx's critique of Hegel (and I do not believe that it does), it is certainly unwarranted to generalize it to 'all ideology'. It would not even (for example) be helpful in understanding Marx's critique of classical political economy as ideology (which centred on the tendency of the classicals to think of both a particular form of society – capitalism – and of their own analytical categories as *eternal*).[24] So there is reason to worry here. And as Marx continues the worries grow:

In direct contrast to German philosophy, which descends from heaven to earth, here we ascend from earth to heaven. That is to say, we do not set out from what men say, imagine, conceive, nor from men as narrated, thought of, imagined, conceived, in order to arrive at men in the flesh. We set out from real, active men, and on the basis of their real life process we demonstrate the development of the ideological reflexes and echoes of the life process. The phantoms formed in the human brain, are also, necessarily, sublimates of the material life process, which is empirically verifiable and bound to material premises.

Oh dear. The danger signs above were indeed danger signs. A clear deterioration has set in. We should probably ignore the first sentence as a conscious flight of metaphorical fancy. But when Marx unpacks the metaphor (from 'That is to say' onwards) the worst does indeed come to the worst. For firstly, Marx claims to 'set out', not from what men say, imagine, conceive (fair enough) nor 'from men as narrated, thought of, imagined, conceived' but from 'real active men'. Now this latter contrast cannot be valid. There are no 'real active men' in *The German Ideology*, nor are there in *Capital* either. My copies of both these works are far too small and compressed for any 'real men' (even the smallest) to live and breathe in there. In fact all there is in my copies of these works is words, written language. So, in so far as there are 'real men' or women in either of these works, they *are* 'men', people, as represented, conceived, narrated, in language. So Marx is misleading us. As writer, as intellectual, he does, like the Hegelians, 'set out' from 'men as narrated, thought of, imagined, conceived'. But he narrates them, thinks of them, imagines them, conceives them *in a different way* from the German philosophers' and this is what he should say. But he does not say it, and in his desire to emphasize the difference between his conception of 'men' and the Hegelian, he flirts – indeed more than flirts – with the most crude empiricism and naïve materialism.

This becomes even clearer as he proceeds. For 'on the basis' (the phrase 'the real basis' occurs over and over again in *The German Ideology*) of 'men's' 'real life-process' Marx is going to 'demonstrate', 'the development of the ideological reflexes and echoes of the life-process'. For 'the phantoms formed in the human brain' (that is thoughts presumably) are just 'sublimates' of the 'material life-process', this latter being 'empirically verifiable and bound to material premises'. Now the implication of these two sentences is very clear and very disastrous. *It is that while ideology involves thought* (the 'phantoms' found in the human brain, the 'reflexes' and 'echoes' of the life process. See my earlier comments on 'reflection'. They also apply here to 're-flexes' and 'echoes'.) *the material life process somehow does not involve thought.* Figure 7.4 is back with a bang. The 'head' of society may have all kinds of 'disembodied' 'cloudy' notions in it, but its 'material life-process' is very 'feety', very automatic, very basic, very anchored in the mud of reality. Moreover, while one cannot see, touch, smell or hear thoughts in the head, one can see, hear, touch, even smell the feet and all their doings (their 'basic' processes).

Now of course this is not what Marx means. Remember that he has just said that 'Consciousness can never be anything else than *conscious* existence, and the existence of men is their actual life-process.' So 'men's' actual life process is a conscious, thought-filled process. Indeed elsewhere in the same work we read:

> Language is as old as consciousness, language is practical consciousness that exists for other men, and for that reason it really exists for me personally as well; language, like con-sciousness, only arises from the need, the necessity, of inter-course with other men. Where there exists a relationship, it exists for me: the animal does not enter into *'relations'* with anything, it does not enter into any relation at all. For the animal, its relation to others does not exist as a relation. Consciousness is, therefore, *from the very beginning* a social product, and remains so as long as men exist at all.[25]

But the fact remains that in his desire to differentiate his own position sharply from idealism, Marx continually adopts formulations and an imagery which makes the 'basic', 'material', 'real' life process sound as if it was the life process of an auto-maton, a process somehow driven blindly by physical need or some other automatic stimulus which renders thought redundant. How this is to be squared with a conception – also found in *The German Ideology* – of the historical process as the continuous production of new needs by human beings[26] is not at all clear. In fact it cannot be so squared. Marx does not conceive the 'material life-process' as a process devoid of thought. On the contrary, for him, because it is a human *practice* it is a process permeated with thought, with consciousness. Marx means only that what 'men' think, what they say, must be analysed in the context of their whole life activity, and not treated as autonomous (as, he believed, it was treated in Hegelian philosophy).[27] Yet the fact remains that this is *not* what he says here. What he says here can give comfort and credence to the most naïve empiricism and materialism, the most naïve juxtaposing of 'thought' to 'reality'.

However, Marx has by now touched bottom, and proceeds to get better:

> Morality, religion, metaphysics, all the rest of ideology and their corresponding forms of consciousness, thus no longer retain the semblance of independence. They have no history, no development; but men, developing their material production and their material intercourse, alter, along with this their real existence, their thinking and the products of their thinking. Life is not determined by consciousness but consciousness by life.

This is better because it abandons, at least temporarily, the spatial metaphor of a 'stratosphere' of ideology and a 'base' of material life process. In its place comes a series of verbs including thought *in* practice. Thus 'morality, religion, metaphysics' etc. 'no longer retain the semblance of independence' not because they have no spatially separate realm of existence, but because their history *is a part* of the material history of human beings. This is a history in which 'men' 'alter, *along with* . . . their real existence, their thinking and the products of their thinking'. Thus, by implication, 'along with' the active alteration of 'their real existence' men also actively alter their moral, religious, metaphysical, etc. thinking.[28] As already suggested above, such an idea can be given a coherent meaning which does *not* involve treating changes in 'material production and . . . material intercourse' as a prime (uncaused) *cause* of changes in morality, religion, etc.

However, though an improvement, this conclusion to the quotation is by no means ideal. For first of all the phrase 'no longer retain the semblance of independence' can be read in a quasi-spatial or metaphorically spatial way which provides an image of an area or realm being annexed to or incorporated into another more 'basic' realm (the process often called 'reductionism').[29] More importantly, however, the final sentence –

variants of which occur frequently in Marx – is especially unfortunate.

'Life is not determined by consciousness but consciousness by life.' The clear implication of this is that there is one 'thing' (object) called 'life' and it 'determines' another separate 'thing' (object) called 'consciousness'.[30] But in whole sections of *The German Ideology* Marx precisely denies this distinction. 'Consciousness can never be other than conscious existence, and the existence of men is their actual life-process.' Indeed the whole Part One of *The German Ideology* is a continual polemic against the 'idealist' attempt to separate something called 'consciousness' from 'life' (human practice, activity) and to make it 'determining' of the latter. However, at least in part I think because of the bewitching influence of the 'inversion' analogy, Marx constantly slips from a – proper and brilliant – *denial* of this separation into a *reproduction* of it (but with the determination reversed). This slippage is extremely unfortunate, because, at times at least, Marx does seem to say, and to want to say, not that 'consciousness is determined by life' or (in the 1859 Preface) by 'social being', but that consciousness is *inextricably woven with*, is *an integral part of*, is *not to be conceived separately from*, 'life' or 'social being'. It is the denial of the separation which is so brilliant and has the capacity to illuminate so much, especially when it is related to a conception of human *language* as 'spirit burdened with matter', as 'practical consciousness' or consciousness in practice, in activity. However, to proceed beyond the denial, and to reproduce the split between 'spirit' and 'matter' as a split between a realm of thought ('ideology') and a 'material' base, is to evacuate human thought and activity from the 'material' and thus to construct a 'materialist' theory of history which can easily be understood as devoid of creative human agency.[31]

CONCLUSIONS

I have no way of knowing whether the reader will be convinced by the analysis of Marxist language offered in this chapter. The chapter began, after all, with some graphical representations of 'society' and of 'reality' which do not appear anywhere in the works of Marx or Engels, and it then went on to a detailed (some might say nit-picking) discussion of two brief passages from their works, both of which it is possible to dismiss as 'untypical' or as 'taken out of context'.

But I hope that, taken in conjunction with the chapters which have preceded it, and especially with the analysis of other Marxist texts which are found in those chapters, this chapter will be seen to be in no way a pastiche. I believe that in *The German Ideology*, *The Poverty of Philosophy*, *The Communist Manifesto*, *The Eighteenth Brumaire of Louis Bonaparte*, *The Grundrisse*, *Capital*, *Socialism Utopian and Scientific*, *Anti-Duhring*, *Ludwig Feuerbach and the End of Classical German Philosophy*, and in innumerable letters, both Marx and Engels *do* proffer the picture of capitalist society (and of several pre-capitalist societies) inextricably interwoven with an ontological picture, a picture of 'levels of reality', which has been the focus of analysis in this chapter. Indeed this dual, superimposed picture of society and reality is what Marx and Engels themselves, and most subsequent Marxists, have referred to as 'historical materialism'.

And as 'historical materialism', as a picture of society and a picture of reality (*and* indeed as a methodological prescription), this picture continues to live in the intellectual imaginations and in the political practices of many present-day Marxists and Marxist-influenced political groups and parties. Even the briefest perusal of the *Socialist Worker* or the *Morning Star* (not to mention the pages of the *New Left Review* or *Monthly Review*) will quickly reveal it as alive and well.

Indeed the aim of this chapter has been to suggest that the intellectual potency, tenacity and persuasiveness of this dual Marxist picture, its capacity to survive innumerable critiques and would-be revisions, and to maintain an instant intuitive appeal to generation after generation of people who first encounter it, is in no way surprising. For I have argued that it is anchored deep into our consciousness, far deeper in fact than can be reached by logic and rational argument alone. Indeed I am convinced that there is no purely intellectual critique which can reach those levels, if by 'reach' one means totally to *erase* or *eradicate* this ontological picture and replace it with another.

For, as I have repeatedly suggested in this chapter, this dual picture – or at least many of the fundamental (ahem) elements of it – are anchored in, derive from, nothing less than the physics of the human species and of the planet earth. I have speculated in a very Wittgensteinian way about the kinds of creatures who would have no use for such a picture, for whom it would have no meaning. They were, you remember, glutinous spheroids floating in space. But we are not glutinous spheroids floating in space, so there are certain ways of thinking which distinguish *homo sapiens* as a species, and which will end only when the species and/or the earth itself ends.

If this is the case, if the 'philosophical anthropology'[32] presented in this chapter does explain the hold of the Marxist picture of reality upon us, does explain its endless capacity for resurgence, even when we think we have dispensed with it, then clearly there are certain respects in which there is no point, no sense, in trying totally to dispense with it. Human beings require both a picture of the social groupings in which they live and an onto-logical account of the world which they inhabit, for they cannot live, be practically active, upon the earth now without them. The point rather is to be aware that *any* representation of 'society' and of 'reality' has its uses, but also has its limits (ahem). Let us see what the classical Marxist picture of reality is good at doing:
1. It captures relationships of *power* and *dominance* in society very well, and has a good vocabulary for both describing and analys-ing such relationships.
2. It draws attention to certain *material constraints* on what human beings can do at any point in time.
3. It is very good for making intellectuals and other 'mental labourers' in society feel (a) useless or peripheral and (b) guilty because useless or peripheral. This is clearly of some political and psychological utility in mobilizing both intellectuals and (in a different way) manual labourers to the Marxist cause.

However, it is very bad for:
1. Incorporating processes in time, and therefore
2. Understanding the precise *logical* structure of material con-straints on social possibilities. Moreover,
3. It can easily facilitate a 'vulgarly materialist' or 'vulgarly empiricist' Marxism, which outside of academia is indeed the most common or dominant form of Marxism in the world.

I have already suggested that the 'static', 'hierarchical' aspect of the Marxist picture of reality is its most damaging aspect from the point of view of the Marxist intellectual project. For the essence of that project – or at least of Marx's own project – is the understanding of both human society and human thought as dynamic *practices* or *activities* in time. Indeed, I think it could fairly easily be shown that Marxist historical scholarship (which in my view has always been the richest vein of Marxist scholarship) has been at its best when it has either implicitly or explicitly *ignored* the ontology of 'historical materialism' or understood it as an account of the material limits of social possibility in the manner outlined earlier in this chapter. In short, historians have often made the best Marxist scholars because they have insisted on, as it were, pushing time through Marxist structural concepts, even if that has meant partially washing them away! Even then however this 'dynamization' of Marxist concepts has often been more a feature of the professional *practice* of Marxist historians than of their explicit attempts at theorization of that practice, when they have often either reverted to orthodoxy, or undertaken but partial and guilt-ridden revisionism. Engaging in a professional practice which is more intellectually sophisticated than its theorization is in fact very likely to coexist with a trained inability to either recognize or express that sophistication formally or explicitly, especially as historians are not typically long-suited in philosophy.

In short then, I am suggesting that Marx and Engels did not think very clearly about the logic of processes in time, and to that degree they did something of a disservice to the intellectual tradition which they founded. But this is not surprising, for time is very hard to think about. Indeed I have been aware in this chapter, in introducing the notion of 'human society as creative activity' (in time) of skirting yet deeper philosophical depths, depths inhabited by Kant and Einstein among others, and depths in which I might very easily be submerged. When *I* think of time my language resources are very conventional. I tend to resort to verbs of flow, to images of running water or sand.[33] As befits a human being untrained in modern physics and bound to this planet, I have no functioning vocabulary of 'space/time'.

But I find that I do have the language resources to talk about particular social processes in time with some ease. 'Skilled workers formed themselves into trade unions much more rapidly in the 1850s.' 'The twentieth century has seen a major fall in Third World death rates.' 'The British share of the international car market fell sharply from the 1950s onwards.' 'They have not really been happy as a couple since his illness made him so irritable' etc., etc., etc. And we have simply to be aware that this descriptive and analytical competence with which our language provides us in dealing with a myriad of discrete social processes or activities in time *is all that we need*. We do not need a coherent picture of 'human society as creative activity' to set alongside or to counterbalance our picture of 'society as spatial object'.

Indeed, if one thinks about it, it will be immediately apparent that not only do we not *need* such a picture, we cannot have one. Because social processes in time defeat the capacities of pictorial representation in important ways. In other words, the metaphor of 'picture' itself breaks down here. Human beings cannot have 'a picture of time', for 'a picture of time' is a self-contradictory notion, as is 'a picture of process'. We must avoid what Wittgenstein calls our 'craving for generality' here. So do not seek for a picture of 'society as creative activity', just 'go with the flow'. What is it that you were wanting to say about how Melanesian sexual mores changed in the 1950s? Trust your language. You *already have* the capacity to say it.

But we 'already have' something else. We have already, as adults, and usually *long before* we become students of social science, or professional intellectuals, what has illuminatingly been called the 'tangled undergrowth' of our language.[34] We 'already have' (if we have English, or French, or Swahili, or Tamil) the extraordinarily complex and interwoven sets of metaphors, images, similes, which constitute the basic infrastructure of our language. They are a truly wonderful descriptive and analytical resource, but they are also extraordinarily hard to become conscious of, to bring into critical scrutiny and focus. For of course you have to use the language to scrutinize the language, and thus even to analyse a particular use of language one often has to perpetuate that use. If the reader has any doubt about that, let him/her play a game with this last chapter.

I have said that human language is so structured that there is *nothing* one can talk or write about without making use of 'spatial', 'object', and 'visual' analogies. If this is true, it should be the case that even in the sections of this chapter when I am discussing the limits of those analogies I had to make use of them, and the reader will find that this is so. S/he should also be able to see that I have just done it again (and again)!

And of course if the above is true of everybody, it must also have been true of Marx and Engels. They were fluent in German long before they were fluent in historical materialism, and they too got tangled in the luxuriant undergrowth of metaphor and image in their language. This was particularly subversive, I have suggested, of their attempts to describe a Marxist epistemology, a Marxist *method* for the study of society. It was much less damaging – indeed hardly damaging at all – of their attempts to describe and analyse particular societies at particular times (see, for example, Marx's *Eighteenth Brumaire*).

In other words, I have suggested in this book that in important ways Marx and Engels *misdescribed their own method*. I am not sure how much they are to be personally blamed for this, or how much this misdescription was built in to the stock of intellectual tools upon which they had to draw in their own time. But it has certainly been harmful to Marxism as an intellectual tradition, especially when, within that tradition, certain classical descriptions of the Marxist intellectual method (say the 1859 Preface) were taken as gospel. It is doubly harmful when such descriptions are first taken as gospel and then rejected as gospel (as in some recent 'structuralist' renderings and then 'post-structuralist' rejections of Marxism).[35] For these too – both the 'gospels' *and* their rejections – have rested, as did the classics of historical materialism themselves, on a fundamentally flawed under-standing of language, and especially of how exactitude is attained in language. And in that flawed understanding Euclid, geometry, space, objects, and visual analogies have once more been the culpable grammatical pucks. But that, as they say, is another story, the story not of 'society' but of *concepts* as 'objects' with 'boundaries' to be 'defined'.

CONCLUSION

This book has surveyed and analysed the major ideas developed by Karl Marx over some sixty years of intellectual and political activity. Its conclusions on the validity of those ideas have been distinctly mixed. It has suggested that Marx's theory of history, while enormously suggestive and stimulating in certain ways, was expressed in a manner which could easily lead to it being understood (wrongly in my view) as a deterministic stage theory of history. It has examined the core of Marx's lifetime intellectual effort – his political economy – and found it seriously flawed, most notably with regard to the theory of class exploitation which Marx attempted to erect upon the Ricardian foundations of the 'labour theory of value'. Marx's writings on revolution and communism were found to be more varied and multi-dimensional than is commonly supposed, but his vision of communism was found to be distinctly question-begging in a number of ways and appears to have an unresolved contradiction (between democracy and planning) at its centre. Finally, what is, arguably, Marx's most fundamental and influential legacy to the study of society – his superimposed picture of society and reality often referred to as 'historical materialism' – was found to rely on certain metaphors and analogies which, while deeply embedded in human language and probably unavoidable for human beings, are not the most appropriate ones for communicating the dynamic processes with which Marx and Engels were concerned, nor for elucidating at all clearly the logic of those processes.

In so far then as Marxism is thought of as a set of ideas, as a set of propositions which may be be evaluated and then either believed or disbelieved, the conclusion of this book must be that the corpus of ideas which is Marxism is seriously flawed and must either be abandoned altogether, or revised in major ways if it is to continue to have any credibility.

However, this book will have been seriously misunderstood if that is the major conclusion which is drawn from it. For the aim of the whole analysis in the previous seven chapters, and in particular of the theses put forward in chapters one and six, has been to stress that Marxism is not *primarily* a set of 'ideas' at all. The logic of the philosophy of praxis in Marxism, if applied to Marxism, is that to be a Marxist is not, first and foremost, a cognitive commitment at all, is not first and foremost a commitment to *believing* anything. It is, first and foremost, a commitment to *doing* something, namely to realizing, or helping to realize, a certain vision of human liberation. Marx's logically primary commitment was (and, in the view of this book, the logically primary commitment of every Marxist should be) to that vision of liberation. Moreover, 'logically primary' here has a fairly specific meaning. It means, as this book has argued, that *everything else* in Marx's work is logically subordinate to that initial commitment. Neither Marx's theory of history, nor his economic theory, nor his vision of revolution and communism, nor his ideas about classes or the state or ideology, make any sense unless it is appreciated that they are all designed to assist in the realization of a certain conception of human liberation. However, while the corpus of Marx's intellectual work is logically dependent upon the vision of liberation (in the sense that that entire corpus is meant as an intellectual tool or instrument to achieve, or to assist in achieving, the realization of that vision and thus has no significance apart from it), the truth or falsity of that corpus, or any part of that corpus, does not depend upon the vision of liberation. In other words, one could hold *all* of Marx's ideas to be false and still be committed to his vision of liberation. Conversely, one could hold a large number of specific factual or theoretical propositions in Marx's work to be true but consider them individually or collectively *insignificant* or trivial because one did not share the vision of liberation to which they are subordinate. However, as noted earlier in a different context, if one is not committed to his vision of liberation one probably would not, and probably should not, spend any time or effort trying to determine the truth or falsity of Marx's ideas, for if one is not so committed it *does not matter* whether Marx was right or wrong about anything or everything.

It may be objected however that the above account is flawed. If, for example, one rejects some or all of the ideas which make up Marxism, but is still committed to Marx's vision of liberation, there still remains the question of the grounds on which one is so committed. If, for example, I say that Marx was committed to the realization of a world in which every individual could make the maximum use of their creative capacities in a positive way, and if I say that I too am committed to the creation of such a world, then surely this *is* a cognitive commitment. It is, in fact, a commitment to believing that a sentence such as 'a world or society in which everyone makes the maximum use of their creative abilities in a positive way is desirable' is true, and if I believe (as I do) that this sentence is true, I must have grounds or reasons for believing it, and if these grounds or reasons are not valid then it may be false.

I am happy to accept this objection. It is clear to me that Marx's commitment to his vision of human liberation was based on his acceptance of a proposition such as the above, and my commitment to it also rests on such an acceptance and to that extent it is a cognitive commitment. Moreover, a serious commitment to this vision of liberation also requires one to be able to say, at least in broad terms, what would be the institutional structure of a society which would be 'liberating' in this way, what practices would be encouraged in such a society and what would be discouraged, what values would be lauded and what shunned and so on, and all such propositions are open to challenge. What is equally clear however is that my belief in the validity of Marx's vision of liberation, in the conception of the 'creative' human essence which underlies it, and in the form of socialist society which I believe could realize it *is not based on my acceptance of any or all of the corpus of ideas known as 'Marxism'* and moreover *neither was Marx's*. In other words, Marx was a socialist before he was a Marxist (before he created Marxism as a variety of socialism) and one can be a socialist, in the sense that he was a socialist, without being a 'Marxist' in the sense that he (subsequently) created.

But if Marx's socialism did not rely on his Marxism (though his Marxism relied on his socialism) and if anyone's commitment to 'his' (Marx's) socialism does not have to rely on 'his' (Marx's) Marxism, what did it (does it) have to rely on? I think there is no single answer to that. In my case, my socialist commitment relies on my observations of people around me, on my assessment of the history and the contemporary strengths and weaknesses of the society in which I live and was brought up, on my assessment of the history and the contemporary strengths and weaknesses of the 'actually existing' socialist societies in the world, and on my hopes and dreams (some of the latter having, no doubt, psychological roots that I do not totally understand). In other words my socialist commitment is a creative commitment on my part *actively made* out of the diverse reality of my life and so, no doubt, was Marx's. The point is, however, that nothing in that diverse reality has led me to the view that Marx's vision of liberation is fundamentally flawed although it has led me to the view that some of his conceptions about the form of society which could realize it are fundamentally flawed. This being the case, I continue to call myself a Marxist. But that in itself, is an insignificant point. The much more significant point is that, if the analysis of the logic of Marx's world view proffered in this book is correct, a shared commitment to Marx's vision of liberation is first and foremost what it *means* to be a Marxist, since everything else in the corpus of Marxism is *meaningless* without it.

NOTES

INTRODUCTION

1 See however note 5 to chapter 6.
2 See for example K.T. Fann, *Wittgenstein's Conception of Philosophy* (Oxford, Basil Blackwell, 1969), p.46. Also Stanley Cavell, 'The Claim to Rationality' (Harvard University PhD thesis, 1961), pp. 164, 177, 259–61, 265, 267, 274, 295 and 310. See especially p.164, 'it is a central theme of my entire effort that the subject of self-knowledge, both as a phenomenon and as a source of philosophical knowledge, has been rudely neglected or damned in modern philosophy.'
3 See for example Hanna Fenichel Pitkin, *Wittgenstein and Justice: On the Significance of Ludwig Wittgenstein for Social and Political Thought* (Berkeley, University of California Press, 1972), pp. 21, 336–40. Also Cavell, 'The Claim to Rationality', pp. 129 and 274.
4 Two excellent texts dealing with Wittgenstein's ideas in the context of the philosophy of science, both of which concentrate on this point, are Derek L. Phillips, *Wittgenstein and Scientific Knowledge: A Sociological Perspective* (London, Macmillan, 1977) and David Bloor, *Wittgenstein: A Social Theory of Knowledge* (London, Macmillan, 1983).

CHAPTER 1: MARX, HEGEL, FEUERBACH, AND THE PHILOSOPHY OF PRAXIS

1 V.I. Lenin, 'The Three Sources and Three Component Parts of Marxism' (1913). Republished in MESW, pp. 23–7.
2 David McLellan, *Karl Marx: His Life and Thought* (London, Macmillan, 1973), pp. 456–7 ('Marx's Confession').
3 The *Oxford English Dictionary* gives 'demiurgos' or 'demiurge' as 'A name for the Maker or Creator of the world in the Platonic philosophy.' Marx is once more drawing on his background as a scholar of Ancient Greece. For a brilliant account of Marx's indebtedness to ancient Greek literature, see S.S. Prawer *Karl Marx and World Literature* (Oxford, Clarendon Press, 1976).

4 *Capital*, I, pp.19–20.

5 However, the following are good sources for an overview of Hegel's philosophy, as it influenced Marx. S. Avinieri, *The Social and Political Thought of Karl Marx* (Cambridge University Press, 1968), ch.1, pp.8–40. George Lichtheim, *Marxism: An Historical and Critical Study* (London, Routledge & Kegan Paul, 1961), ch.1, pp.3–12. Sidney Hook, *From Hegel to Marx* (University of Michigan Press, Ann Arbor, 1962), ch.1, pp.15–76. Herbert Marcuse, *Reason and Revolution: Hegel and the Rise of Social Theory* (Boston, Beacon Press, 1960). Also G.A. Cohen, *Karl Marx's Theory of History: A Defence* (Oxford, Clarendon Press, 1979), ch.1. W.L. McBride, *The Philosophy of Marx* (London, Hutchinson, 1977), ch.1. Among simpler introductions to Hegel's own thought are R. Plant, *Hegel: An Introduction* (Oxford, Basil Blackwell, 1983) and Peter Singer, *Hegel* (Oxford University Press, Past Masters Series, 1983). An interesting modern interpretation of Hegel is Charles Taylor, *Hegel* (Cambridge University Press, 1975). See also his *Hegel and Modern Society* (Cambridge University Press, 1979). Students who are brave enough to wish to try Hegel himself are probably best advised to begin with his *Philosophy of History* (translated by J. Sibree, with an Introduction by Professor C.J. Friedrich, New York, Dover Publications, 1956) which is the most immediately accessible of his works, and should then perhaps proceed to the famous Preface to his *Phenomenology of Spirit* (translated by A.V. Miller with an analysis of the text and foreword by J.N. Findlay, Oxford University Press, 1977).

6 Good sources for Lockean empiricism are J. Dunn, *Locke* (Oxford University Press, Past Masters Series, 1984); J.W. Yotton, *Locke: An Introduction* (Oxford, Basil Blackwell, 1985); and D.J. O'Connor, *John Locke* (London, Penguin, 1952). For a more advanced treatment see I.C. Tipton (ed.) *Locke on Human Understanding: Selected Essays* (Oxford University Press, 1977).

7 Kant's views on this matter are set out in his *Critique of Pure Reason* (London, Dent, Everyman's Library, 1969) especially the 'Introduction', pp.24–40, and the 'Transcendental Doctrine of Elements' pp.41–54, (on 'Time' and 'Space'). A clear introduction to Kant's philosophy and its influence is S. Korner, *Kant* (Harmondsworth, Penguin, 1955).

8 Ludwig Feuerbach, *The Essence of Christianity* (1841), translated by Marian Evans (George Eliot) (New York, Harper & Row, 1957), and David Strauss, *The Life of Jesus* (1835), translated by Marian Evans (George Eliot) (London, SCM Press edition, 1973).

9 For two contrasting views on Marx's conception of human nature see Eric Fromm, *Marx's Concept of Man* (New York, Frederick Ungar, 1961) and the sharply critical comments in Hook, *From Hegel to Marx*, especially the 'New Introduction', pp.1–9. See also Vernon Venable, *Human Nature: The Marxian View* (London, Denis Dobson, 1946) and the recent essay by Norman Geras, *Marx and Human Nature: Refutation of a Legend* (London, Verso, 1983). For a recent

persuasive argument that no consistent doctrine of human nature can be distilled from Marx since he did not possess one, see Kate Soper, *On Human Needs: Open and Closed Theories in a Marxist Perspective* (Brighton, Harvester, 1981), chs 5,6, and 7.

10 MECW, 3, pp.274–7.

11 *GI*, p.42.

12 *Grundrisse*, Notebook IV, p.453.

13 *Capital*, I, p.72, emphasis added.

14 This view is set out in Feuerbach's *Essence of Christianity*, and in his *Principles of the Philosophy of the Future* (1843), translated with an introduction by Manfred H. Vogel (Indianapolis, Bobbs Merrill, 1966).

15 The word 'praxis' is of ancient Greek origin and 'refers to almost any kind of acitivity which a free man is likely to perform; in particular, all kinds of business and political activity'. It played an important part in the philosophies of Aristotle and Kant as well as in Marx. For an excellent outline see the entry on 'Praxis' by Gajo Petrovic in Tom Bottomore (ed.) *A Dictionary of Marxist Thought* (Oxford, Basil Blackwell, 1983), pp.384–9. The phrase 'the philosophy of praxis' is well known mainly because of its use by Antonio Gramsci in his *Prison Notebooks*, where it is sometimes used simply as a euphemism for Marxism in general, but sometimes in a more specific sense which has parallels with the use employed here. Gramsci himself appears to have got the phrase from Labriola. See Antonio Gramsci, *Selections from the Prison Notebooks*, edited and translated by Quintin Hoare and Geoffrey Nowell Smith (London, Lawrence & Wishart, 1971), especially the Introduction, pp.xxi–xxii, and part III, pp.319–472. The secondary literature on the subject is vast, but see especially Kostas Axelos, *Alienation, Praxis and Technē in the Thought of Karl Marx* (University of Texas Press, Austin and London, 1976), and R.J. Bernstein, *Praxis and Action* (London, Duckworth, 1972), the first chapter of which, ('Praxis: Marx and the Hegelian background') is the best single reading on this topic known to me. Leszek Kolakowski, *Main Currents of Marxism: Vol.1, The Founders* (Oxford University Press, 1978) provides an interpretation of Marx's own thought informed throughout by this perspective, which is also well summed up in his essay 'Karl Marx and the classical definition of truth', chapter 2 of his *Marxism and Beyond* (London, Paladin, 1971). See also Richard Kilminster, *Praxis and Method: A Sociological Dialogue with Lukacs, Gramsci and the early Frankfurt School* (London, Routledge & Kegan Paul, 1979) for an examination of the role played by praxis in Marxist thought after Marx. John Hoffman, *Marxism and the Theory of Praxis* (London, Lawrence & Wishart, 1975) provides a critique of this approach from a stolidly orthodox perspective. S.S. Prawer, *Karl Marx and World Literature* also has an excellent fifth chapter on the subject.

16 *Capital*, I, p.178.

17 See David Rubinstein, *Marx and Wittgenstein: Social Praxis and Social*

Explanation (London, Routledge & Kegan Paul, 1981), chs 6–11 in which it is very persuasively argued that the philosophies of Marx and the later Wittgenstein coalesce in their refusal to analyse human thinking in abstraction from the broader practices in which it is always embodied. In the case of the later Wittgenstein this position is focused on a theory of meaning in language which was in turn developed out of the most detailed analyses of language use. In Marx, by contrast, the insight remains at the level of general formulations and propositions (mainly in *The German Ideology* and the *Theses on Feuerbach*) and is not linked to a theory of language. I argue later that it is the less secure and the more fitfully present in Marx's later thought for just this reason. Another secondary work on Wittgenstein's philosophy which focuses centrally on the role of 'practice' in his later theory of knowledge is Thomas Morawetz, *Wittgenstein and Knowledge: The Importance of 'On Certainty'* (Brighton, Harvester, 1980), especially chapter 1. See also Peter Winch, 'Im Anfang war die Tat' in Irving Block (ed.), *Perspectives on the Philosophy of Wittgenstein* (Oxford, Basil Blackwell, 1981), pp. 159–77. Winch is here elaborating on a remark in Wittgenstein's *Culture and Value* (Oxford, Basil Blackwell, 1980), p.31e, 'Language – I want to say – is a refinement, "in the beginning was the deed" (Im Anfang war die Tat).' Nothing could show more clearly that the later Wittgenstein was not a 'linguistic philosopher' or a 'philosopher of language' in the sense in which Gellner for example (Ernest Gellner, *Words and Things*, Harmondsworth, Penguin, 1968) treats him, a treatment which for a long time had a disastrous effect upon the appreciation of Wittgenstein by social scientists. Interestingly enough, 'Im Anfang war die Tat', a quotation from Goethe's *Faust*, also appears in chapter 2 of volume I of Marx's *Capital* (p.86). See the comments on this in S.S. Prawer, *Karl Marx and World Literature*, p.324.

18 MESW, pp.28–30.
19 On this: K.T. Fann, *Wittgenstein's Conception of Philosophy* (Oxford, Basil Blackwell, 1969), pp. 85–91; Hanna Pitkin, *Wittgenstein and Justice: On the Significance of Ludwig Wittgenstein for Social and Political Thought* (Berkeley, University of California Press, 1972) p.82; P.M.S. Hacker, *Insight and Illusion: Wittgenstein on Philosophy and the Metaphysics of Experience* (Oxford University Press, 1972), pp. 128 and 132–3; David Bloor, *Wittgenstein: A Social Theory of Knowledge* (London, Macmillan, 1983), pp.29–33; Stanley Cavell, 'The Claim to Rationality' (PhD thesis, Harvard University, 1961), p.258; and Thomas Moravetz, *Wittgenstein and Knowledge*, ch.4, pp.78–101.
20 On this see Richard Rorty, *Philosophy and the Mirror of Nature* (Oxford, Basil Blackwell, 1980), chs 3 and 4; Cavell, 'The Claim to Rationality', ch.5; Pitkin, *Wittgenstein and Justice*, chs 12 and 13; Morawetz, *Wittgenstein and Knowledge*, Introduction and ch. 1, and the essay by Rorty, 'Method, social science and social hope' in his *Consequences of Pragmatism* (Brighton, Harvester, 1982) ch.11.
21 Perfect examples of this would be the early philosophy of Louis

Althusser, especially his *For Marx*, (London, Allen Lane, 1965) and L. Althusser and E. Balibar *Reading Capital* (London, New Left Books, 1970); also the earlier works of Hindess and Hirst, especially B. Hindess and P.Q. Hirst, *Pre-Capitalist Modes of Production* (London, Routledge & Kegan Paul, 1975). Works with similar obsessions but somewhat different approaches to the Althusserian are Geoffrey Pilling, *Marx's 'Capital': Philosophy and Political Economy* (London, Routledge & Kegan Paul, 1980) and David Hillel–Ruben, *Marxism and Materialism* (Brighton, Harvester, 1977).

22 Must I not rather ask: 'What does the description do anyway? What purpose does it serve?' – In another context, indeed, we know what is a complete and what an incomplete description. As yourself: How do we use the expressions 'complete' and 'incomplete description'?

Giving a complete (or incomplete) report of a speech. Is it part of this to report the tone of the voice, the play of expression, the genuineness or falsity of feeling, the intentions of the speaker, the strain of speaking? Whether this or that belongs to a complete description will depend on the purpose of the description, on what the recipient does with the description.

Wittgenstein, *Zettel*, second edn, (Oxford, Basil Blackwell, 1981), paragraph 311. On this see also G.P. Baker and P.M.S. Hacker, *Wittgenstein: Meaning and Understanding* (Oxford, Basil Blackwell, 1980), ch.1.

CHAPTER 2: MARX'S THEORY OF HISTORY

1 MESW, pp. 181–2.
2 For the critiques see H.B. Acton, 'The materialist conception of history' *Proceedings of the Aristotelian Society* (1951–2), and *The Illusion of the Epoch* (London, Routledge, 1955). Also M.M. Bober, *Karl Marx's Interpretation of History* (Cambridge, Mass., Harvard University Press, 1948), especially his Conclusions in part V, pp.297–439. For two recent defences see G.A. Cohen, *Karl Marx's Theory of History: A Defence* (Oxford, Clarendon Press, 1979) and William H. Shaw, *Marx's Theory of History* (London, Hutchinson, 1978).
3 For 'sociological determinism' and the sin of 'historicism' of which it is just a part, see K.R. Popper, *The Open Society and its Enemies* (London, Routledge & Kegan Paul, 1945) especially vol.1, chapter 1, and vol.2, chapter 13.
4 *Capital* (1867), Preface to vol.I, pp.8–9.
5 ibid., p.10.
6 Marx, letter to Weydemeyer (1852), MESC, p.69.
7 Marx, *The Holy Family* (1845), MECW, 4, p.37.
8 Marx, *The Communist Manifesto* (1848), MESW, pp. 35–6.
9 Marx, GI (1846), pp. 57–8.

10 Marx, *The Holy Family* (1845), MECW, 4, p.93.
11 Marx, *Eighteenth Brumaire of Louis Bonaparte* (1869), MESW, p.96.
12 Marx, letter to Annenkov (1846), MESC, p. 35.
13 Engels, letter to Bloch (1890), MESC, p.417.
14 *Capital*, I, pp.18–19.
15 MESC, p.313.
16 Most of the seminal articles of the original debate on these matters are in Rodney Hilton (ed.), *The Transition from Feudalism to Capitalism* (London, Verso, 1978). See also the recapitulation of many of the same issues in the debate which followed the publication of Robert Brenner's 'Agrarian class structure and economic development in pre-industrial Europe', *Past and Present*, no.70 (February 1976), pp.30–75. See especially *Past and Present*, nos.78, 79, 80 and 85, and Brenner's reply to his critics in *Past and Present*, no. 97 (November 1982), pp.16–113. See also Perry Anderson, *Lineages of the Absolutist State* (London, New Left Books, 1974), especially chs 1–7 and the 'Conclusions', pp.397–431.
17 MESW, pp.612–14 and MESC, pp.413–25 (letters from Engels to P. Ernst, C. Schmidt and J. Bloch).
18 MESC, p.418 (Engels to J. Bloch).
19 MESW, p.29 (Marx's sixth thesis on Feuerbach).
20 MESW, p.182.
21 Pioneering essays along these lines were Rosa Luxemburg's 'The Russian Revolution' and 'Leninism or Marxism?', the latter originally published in 1904 and the former in 1922. They appear together in an edition edited and introduced by Bertram D. Wolfe, *The Russian Revolution and Leninism or Marxism?* (Michigan, Ann Arbor, 1961). See also Gwyn A. Williams, *Proletarian Order* (London, Pluto Press, 1975) and A.J. Polan, *Lenin and the End of Politics* (London, Methuen, 1984).
22 A classical English text in this vein is Maurice Cornforth, *Dialetical Materialism: An Introductory Course* (London, Lawrence & Wishart, 1954), vol.2. For the popular (or relatively popular) influence of this kind of Marxism, see Stuart Macintyre, *A Proletarian Science: Marxism in Britain 1917–1933* (London, Lawrence & Wishart, 1986), especially chapter 5.
23 GI, pp.43–6; *Grundrisse*, Notebook V, pp.484–7, and especially pp.497–8 and 502–14.
24 See Marx's articles on 'The British rule in India' and 'The future results of the British rule in India' (*New York Daily Tribune*, 25 June and 8 August 1853) in Eugene Kamenka (ed.), *The Portable Marx* (Harmondsworth, Penguin, 1983), pp.329–41. For more general discussions of Marx's work on pre-capitalist modes of production, see Eric Hobsbawm's 'Introduction' to K.Marx, *Pre-capitalist Economic Formations* (London, Lawrence & Wishart, 1964); B. Hindess and P.Q. Hirst, *Pre-Capitalist Modes of Production*; and Perry Anderson, 'The Asiatic mode of production', Appendix B of his *Lineages of the Absolutist State*, especially pp.462–95.

25 See R. Enmale (ed.), *Marx and Engels on the Civil War in the United States* (New York, International Publishers, 1937) for a good selection of material on Marx's views of US capitalism. For Marx's fluctuating views on the prospects for a socialist revolution in pre-capitalist Russia the best source is his four drafts of a reply, and his actual reply, to a letter of 1881 from the Russian revolutionary Vera Zasulich in which he was asked to 'set forth your ideas on the possible fate of our rural commune, and on the theory that it is historically necessary for every country in the world to pass through all the phases of capitalist production'. The drafts, together with much illuminating comment, can be found in T. Shanin (ed.), *Late Marx and the Russian Road* (London, Routledge & Kegan Paul, 1983). See also Marx's 'letter to the Editorial Board of Otechesvennye Zapiski', MESC, pp.311–13.

26 MESW, pp.180–1.

27 MESW, p.182.

28 See for example *Capital*, I, pp.14–15 and pp.76–81. An astute criticism of Cohen's thesis along these lines is Andrew Levine and Erik Olin Wright 'Rationality and class struggle' in *New Left Review*, no.123 (September–October 1980), pp.47–68.

29 See C. Wilson, *England's Apprenticeship 1603–1763* (London, Longman Green, 1965), especially chs 4, 7, and 9. See also 'Introduction' to David S. Landes, *The Unbound Prometheus: Technological Change and Industrial Development in Western Europe from 1750 to the Present* (Cambridge University Press, 1969), pp.1–40.

30 MESC, p.423 (Engels to C. Schmidt, 27 October 1890).

31 *Capital*, I, p.486.

32 *Grundrisse*, Introduction, p.104.

33 MESW, p.182.

34 For a development and particular application of this idea, see Angela Reidy and Gavin Kitching, 'Primary health care: our sacred cow and their white elephant', in *Public Administration and Development*, 6 (1986), pp.425–33.

35 On this point, see for example Harry Braverman, *Labor and Monopoly Capital* (New York, Monthly Review Press, 1974), chs 5, 7, and 8.

36 MESC, pp.417–25.

37 On this, see my *Rethinking Socialism: A Theory for a Better Practice* (London, Methuen, 1983), especially chs 1 and 2.

38 See for example C. Gill, *Work, Unemployment and the New Technology* (London, Polity Press, 1985).

39 For an interesting discussion of teleology in Marxism, see Paul Q. Hirst, *Marxism and Historical Writing* (London, Routledge & Kegan Paul, 1985) especially chs 1 and 5.

CHAPTER 3: MARX'S ECONOMICS: A PRESENTATION

1 David McLellan, *Karl Marx: His Life and Thought* (London, Macmillan, 1973), p.424. However this assertion has always been the subject of

some dispute. See for example Terrell Carver's entry on 'Darwin' in *A Dictionary of Marxist Thought* (Oxford, Basil Blackwell, 1983) p.113.

2 *Capital*, I, p.10. Subsequent quotations from, and references to, *Capital* have volume and page number after them in the text.

3 MESW, p.429.

4 For a good general account of Social Darwinism see G. Jones, *Social Darwinism and English Thought: The Interaction between Biological and Social Theory* (Brighton, Harvester, 1980). Also R.C. Bannister, *Social Darwinism: Science and Myth in Anglo-American Social Thought* (Philadelphia, Temple University Press, 1979).

5 See MESC, p.302 (Engels to P.L. Lavrov in London, 1875). Also MESC, p.128 (Marx to Engels in Manchester 1862).

6 As set out in Thomas Malthus, *An Essay on the Principle of Population* (1798) (Harmondsworth, Penguin Classic edn, 1970).

7 MESC, p.303 (Engels to P.L.Lavrov).

8 On this see S.S. Prawer, *Karl Marx and World Literature* (Oxford, Clarendon Press, 1976), especially ch.11 (although the whole work is centrally relevant to this issue). Also Diane Elson, 'The value theory of labour' in Diane Elson (ed.), *Value: The Representation of Labour in Capitalism* (London, CSE Books, 1979) has some interesting remarks on the use of biological and chemical metaphors in Marx. See especially pp.133 and 140–1.

9 The most well known modern statement of this view is probably Peter Winch, *The Idea of a Social Science and its Relation to Philosophy* (London, Routledge & Kegan Paul, 1958), but its most classical formulation is in Max Weber, *The Methodology of the Social Sciences* (Glencoe, The Free Press, 1949).

10 MESW, pp.429–30.

11 Good introductions to the classical economists are to be found in W.J. Barber, *The History of Economic Thought* (Harmondsworth, Penguin, 1967) and Phyllis Deane, *The Evolution of Economic Ideas* (Cambridge University Press, 1978). More advanced treatments are D.P. O'Brien, *The Classical Economists* (Oxford, Clarendon Press, 1975) and L. Robbins, *The Theory of Economic Development in the History of Economic Thought* (London, 1968). See also works by R.L. Meek, especially his *Economics and Ideology and Other Essays* (London, Chapman & Hall, 1967) and *Smith, Marx and After* (London, Chapman & Hall, 1977).

12 For a good overview see R.L. Meek, *Studies in the Labour Theory of Value* (London, Lawrence & Wishart, 1973), ch.1.

13 The major works of the classical economists are readily available in inexpensive modern editions. Adam Smith, *The Wealth of Nations* (1776) (Books I–III in Penguin English Library, 1976); Thomas Malthus, *An Essay on the Principle of Population* (1798) (Pelican Classic, 1970); David Ricardo, *On the Principles of Political Economy and Taxation* (1817) (Pelican Classic, 1971); and John Stuart Mill, *Principles of Political Economy* (1848) (Books IV and V in Penguin Classics, 1985).

14 This is not strictly accurate in that Ricardo does not have a concept

of 'abstract labour', but he was the first systematizer of the theory that, in his own words, 'the value of a commodity ... depends on the relative quantity of labour which is necessary for its production'. Ricardo, op.cit., ch.1, p.55.

15 *TSV*, part II, pp.399–404. See also *Capital*, I, pp.515–6 and 538–9.

16 See also Marx's 'Wages, Price and Profit', sections VII–X in MESW, pp.207–12.

17 Apart from *Capital*, a clear outline of these processes is contained in Marx's 'Wage Labour and Capital', MESW, pp.71–93.

18 Marx's 'Law of the Tendency of the Rate of Profit to Fall' is set out in *Capital*, III, pp.211–31.

19 *Capital*, I, pp. 312–21 and 621–8. On pp. 406–7 he says the following:

> Surplus value arises from variable capital *alone*, and ... the amount of surplus value depends on two factors, viz, the rate of surplus value and the number of workmen simultaneously employed ... however much the use of machinery may increase the surplus labour at the expense of the necessary labour by heightening the productiveness of labour, it is clear that it attains this result, only by diminishing the number of workers employed by a given amount of capital. It converts what was formerly variable capital, invested in labour power, into machinery which, *being constant capital, does not produce surplus value.* (emphasis added)

20 *Capital*, I, pp. 177–85 ('The Labour Process and the Production of Use Values') and the famous chapter 1, section 4, pp.71–83 ('The Fetishism of Commodities and the Secret Thereof') are two points at which Marx's philosophy of praxis meets with his political economy.

CHAPTER 4: MARX'S ECONOMICS: A CRITIQUE

1 For the purposes of this part of the argument I am assuming that Marx intended abstract labour as a tool of economic measurement, though personally I do not believe this. For conflicting views on this issue, see Ian Steedman, *Marx after Sraffa* (London, New Left Books, 1977), ch. 2; Anwar Shaikh, 'The Poverty of Algebra' in Ian Steedman *et al.*, *The Value Controversy* (London, Verso, 1981), pp.226–300; Lucio Colletti, *From Rousseau to Lenin* (London, New Left Books, 1973), pp.87–8; and Diane Elson, 'The value theory of labour' in Diane Elson (ed.) *Value: The Representation of Labour in Capitalism* (London, CSE Books, 1979), pp.164–7.

2 Again a great deal of debate centres on the significance of this point. Those who hold that market exchange solves the problem of 'abstraction' in reality (e.g. I.I. Rubin, *Essays on Marx's Theory of Value* (Montreal, Black Rose Publishers, 1973) ch. 14 and Diane Elson, op. cit.) tend not to believe in the necessity for the measurement of values anyway. Those who treat 'value' as a category for

economic measurement (Steedman and Shaikh among others) cannot remain content with this 'solution'. As will be seen below I tend to the view that value is not meant to be a category for economic measurement, so that the severe technical problems with it as such a measure are unimportant. But I do not think that this solves the really fundamental theoretical problems of Marx's economics.

3 J. Harrison, P. Armstrong, and A. Glyn, 'In defence of value – a reply to Ian Steedman', *Capital and Class*, no.5 (Summer 1978), pp.1–31.

4 For an outline of the severe problems with values interpreted as units of 'embodied labour', see Steedman, *Marx after Sraffa*, ch.2 and also his 'Value, price and profit' in *New Left Review*, no.90 (March–April 1975), pp.71–80. See also Geoff Hodgson, *Capitalism, Value and Exploitation: A Radical Theory* (Oxford, Martin Robertson, 1982), chs 6, 7, and 9, which is probably a more accessible version of the 'post-Sraffian' critique of value theory for the non-economist than Steedman, though essentially recapitulating the former's arguments. For an attempt to solve some of Steedman's problems within the assumption that values *are* meant as economic measures, see Harrison, Armstrong, and Glyn, 'In defence of value'. And for other attempts to rebut the post-Sraffian critique see S. Bowles and H. Gintis, 'The Marxian theory of value and heterogeneous labour: a critique and reformulation', *Cambridge Journal of Economics*, 1, no.2 (June 1977); E.O. Wright, 'The value controversy and social research', *New Left Review* , no.116 (July–August 1979); and S. Himmelweit and S. Mohun, 'The anomalies of capital', *Capital and Class*, no.6 (Autumn 1978). See Hodgson's replies to these attempts in *Capitalism, Value and Exploitation*, ch.8. Other contributors to the 1970s debate on value theory, were D. Yaffe, 'Value and price in Marx's *Capital*', *Revolutionary Communist* (January 1975); B. Fine and L. Harris, 'Controversial issues in Marxist economic theory' *Socialist Register* (1976), pp.141–78, and 'Surveying the foundations', *Socialist Register* (1977), pp.106–20. See also the reply to Fine and Harris by Hodgson, 'Papering over the cracks', *Socialist Register* (1977), pp.106–20.

5 Steedman, 'Value, price and profit'.

6 On this see A. Sen, 'On the labour theory of value: some methodological issues', *Cambridge Journal of Economics*, 2, no.2 (1978), pp.175–90; and Hodgson, *Capitalism, Value and Exploitation*, ch.6.

7 Harrison, Armstrong, and Glyn, 'In defence of value'.

8 On this see Michael Ellman, *Socialist Planning* (Cambridge University Press, 1979), especially pp.178–88, 198–221, and 246–57.

9 See for example David S. Landes, *The Unbound Prometheus: Technological Change and Industrial Development in Western Europe from 1750 to the Present* (Cambridge University Press, 1969) chs 1 and 8. Also Tom Kemp, *Historical Patterns of Industrialization* (London, Longman, 1978), ch. 4. Marx himself remarked, in the *Grundrisse*,

that 'all economics can be reduced in the last analysis to the economics of time'.

10 P. Sraffa, *The Production of Commodities by Means of Commodities* (Cambridge Universiy Press, 1960); Maruice Dobb, 'The Sraffa system and critique of the neo-classical theory of distribution' in E.K. Hunt and J.G. Schwartz (eds), *A Critique of Economic Theory* (Harmondsworth, Penguin, 1972), pp.205–21. The most accessible introduction to 'Neo-Ricardianism' and its relationship to Marxism is still Bob Rowthorn's article, 'Neo-Classicism, Neo-Ricardianism and Marxism', *New Left Review*, no.86 (July-August 1974), reprinted in his *Capitalism, Conflict and Inflation* (London, Lawrence & Wishart, 1980) with some qualifications to the original argument in the Introduction to the book (p.8). See also the critical comments in Hodgson, *Capitalism, Value and Exploitation*, p.21.

11 See for example G. Hodgson, 'The theory of the falling rate of profit', *New Left Review*, no.84 (1974), pp.55–82, and the excellent overview of the debate in P. Van Parijs, 'The falling rate of profit theory of crisis: a rational reconstruction by way of an obituary', *Review of Radical Political Economics* (Spring 1980).

12 The first attempt at empirical study of this issue was made by Joseph Gillman, *The Falling Rate of Profit: Marx's Law and its Significance to Twentieth Century Capitalism* (London, Dobson, 1957). His results are summarized in Meghnad Desai, *Marxian Economic Theory* (London, Grey-Mills, 1974), ch. XVIII, especially table V, p.109. Broadly speaking, using data from 1849 to 1952 and applying four different measures both of the rate of surplus value and of the rate of profit, Gillman found no evidence of decline, indeed by three of his measures the rate of profit showed a small upward trend over this period. Desai's own conclusion (p.107) is that

> On balance, one can say that the rate of profit as measured by Gillman in flow terms does not decline. When adjustments are made on a stock basis there is some tendency for a decline in the 1880–1919 period. If we accept unproductive expenditure as a deduction from surplus value then the period post-1919 also shows a decline. It must be said however that these tests are not decisive either way.

Hodgson, 'The falling rate of profit', pp.70–5, draws much the same indeterminate conclusion from a review of Gillman and some other empirical evidence. More recently data compiled by Armstrong, Harrison, and Glyn for manufacturing and business net profit rates in Canada, France, Germany, Italy, Japan, UK, and the USA *do* show a sustained downward trend between 1951 and 1981. However the authors do not argue that this was due to a rising 'organic composition of capital' (i.e. to C rising faster than V+S). See P. Armstrong, A. Glyn, and J. Harrison, *Capitalism since World War II* (London, Fontana, 1984), Appendix tables A1 and A2, pp.464–5. See also pp.254–8.

13 *Capital*, I, pp.316–21, 604–5 and 621–8.
14 This was the view of Joan Robinson for example – *An Essay on Marxian Economics* (London, Macmillan, 1974), especially ch.2.
15 Leszek Kolakowski, *Main Currents of Marxism: Vol.1. The Founders* (Oxford University Press, 1978), pp.412–13. See also Prawer, op. cit., ch.1, pp.1–31 and the quotation from the *Grundrisse*, Notebook III, p.361 reproduced at the beginning of this book.
16 'What economists therefore call the value of labour, is in fact the value of labour power, *as it exists in the personality of the labourer*, which is as different from its function, labour, as a machine is from the work it performs' (*Capital*, I, p.538, emphasis added).
17 Richard Bernstein, *Praxis and Action* (London, Duckworth, 1972), pp.55–66 makes this connection very powerfully, but perhaps without seeing some of its complexities from the economic point of view.
18 I. Steedman, 'Marx on Ricardo' (University of Manchester, Department of Economics Discussion Paper no.10, 1979) argues just this. See however the critical comments on Steedman's view in Hodgson, *Capitalism, Value and Exploitation*, pp.192–7.
19 ibid., p.211,

> What is being asserted here is that labour is the active agency in production. This involves a Marxian view of production as *a labour process* abstracting from the particular social relations in which it takes place. It is *not* being suggested that labour alone is productive of value, nor even that labour alone is productive of wealth; for capital goods can add to the value of the output, and nature can provide use values, i.e. wealth. What *is* being suggested is that production, by definition, is a *human* activity which, in its most abstract form, depends upon human labour within the environment of nature. It is not a *naturalistic* activity in which human labour and other resources have an equivalent status. Human labour is the subject, not an object of production.

With the exception of the historically question-begging equation of natural use values with 'wealth' I would agree with this passage which captures very well the essence of the argument in this chapter.
20 *Grundrisse*, Notebook VII, p.705 (emphasis added).
21 ibid., p.705 (emphasis added).
22 *Capital*, I, pp.379–86.
23 Just how remote can be seen vividly in Raphael Samuel, 'Workshop of the world: steam power and hand technology in mid-Victorian Britain' *History Workshop Journal*, no.3 (Spring 1977), pp.6–72.
24 For one gloomy view of the future, see B. Sherman and C. Jenkins, *The Collapse of Work* (London, Eyre Methuen, 1979). For a more considered view of the same issues see C. Gill, *Work, Unemployment and the New Technology* (London, Polity Press, 1985).
25 Allen Oakley, *Marx's Critique of Political Economy: Intellectual Sources and Evolution, Vol II, 1861–1863* (Routledge & Kegan Paul, 1985) has a good account of this; see especially pp.74–81.

26 See, for example, *Capital*, I, p.423, 'By means of its conversion into an automaton the instrument of labour confronts the labourer, during the labour process, in the shape of capital, of dead labour, that dominates and pumps dry living labour power.'

27 P. Sraffa, *The Production of Commodities*, ch.2, pp.6–11. See also M. Dobb, *Theories of Value and Distribution since Adam Smith* (Cambridge University Press, 1973), especially pp. 65–120.

28 This point is also made in Joan Robinson's *An Essay on Marxian Economics*, pp.17–19.

29 On this, see my *Rethinking Socialism*, pp.22–3 and 31–2.

30 See for example *Capital*, I, p.57.

31 In this connection it should be noted that several recent attempts to reformulate the theory of exploitation to make it a theory about the coerced or dominated nature of the labour peformed under capitalism (Hodgson, *Capitalism, Value and Exploitation*, chs 17 and 18 is a good case) whilst they have much merit of their own, cannot be said to constitute a defence of *Marx's* theory of exploitation. Marx did of course stress that the working class only performed surplus labour, because, having sold its labour power, the use of that very 'particular commodity' was then controlled by the capitalist class through managers, overseers, etc. But it is clear, at least to me, that this is *not* the central point of Marx's own theory which was to demonstrate, as I have said, that 'profit comes only from the exploitation of the working class'. There is therefore no point in denying that Marx himself would have been dismayed by any disproof of this proposition, either the one advanced in this chapter or the (closely related) post-Sraffian critique of Steedman, Hodgson, *et al*.

CHAPTER 5: MARX ON REVOLUTION AND COMMUNISM

1 On this variability in Marx and Engels' use of the term revolution, see Victor Kiernan's entry on this topic in *A Dictionary of Marxist Thought* (Oxford, Basil Blackwell, 1983), pp.424–8.

2 This is the central theme of Eric Hobsbawm's fine book *The Age of Revolution: Europe 1789–1848* (London, Weidenfeld & Nicolson, 1962).

3 On this see David McLellan, *Karl Marx: His Life and Thought* (London, Macmillan, 1973), pp.2–3.

4 See McLellan, op. cit., pp.226–89.

5 See Hobsbawm, op. cit., pp. 109–31 and for the Chartists see Gareth Stedman Jones, *Languages of Class: Studies in English Working Class History 1832–1982* (Cambridge University Press, 1983), ch.3.

6 Some idea of the extent of Marx's influence at the time of his death can be obtained from the range of material included in Philip S.

Foner (ed.), *When Karl Marx Died: Comments in 1883* (New York, International Publishers, 1973).

7 For an overview of these changes, see, for example, *The New Cambridge Modern History*, vol.XI ('Material Progress and World-Wide Problems 1870–1898') (Cambridge University Press, 1962), chs I, II, III, and IX.

8 On this see Marx's review of Guizot's book entitled 'Why has the English revolution been successful?' originally published in 1850 and reprinted in *Marx and Engels on Britain* (Moscow, Foreign Languages Publishing House, 1953), pp.342–8. Christopher Hill, 'The English Civil War interpreted by Marx and Engels' (*Science and Society*, 12 (1948), pp.130–46) provides a good overview of Marx's conception of the 'bourgeois revolution' in Britain.

9 The two most important early texts for these ideas are Marx's *Contribution to the Critique of Hegel's Philosophy of Right* and *On the Jewish Question* in MECW, vol.3, pp.3–129 and pp.146–74. A good overview is in McLellan, op. cit., pp.69–77 and pp.80–6.

10 *Manifesto of the Communist Party*, Part 1 (MESW, pp.39–46), *The Eighteenth Brumaire of Louis Bonaparte*, Parts 1 and 2 (MESW, pp.96–113). See also Engels' Introduction to Marx's 'The Class Struggles in France' (MESW, pp.641–58).

11 See, for example, Marx to S. Meyer and A. Vogt in New York, April 1870, in MESC, pp.235–8. Also Engels to K. Kautsky in Zurich, September 1882, MESC, p.351; Engels to Marx in London, October 1858, MESC, p.110; Marx to L. Kugelmann in Hanover, November 1869, MESC, pp.229–30; Marx to Hyndman in London, December 1880, MESC, p.334; Engels to F.A. Sorge in Hoboken, December 1889, MESC, pp.407–8; and Engels to F.A. Sorge in Hoboken, April 1890, MESC, pp.411–12.

12 Marx, *The Civil War in France*, MESW, pp.248–309, especially pp.257–8.

13 A good account of these activities is found in McLellan, op. cit., especially pp.167–77, 189–97, 205–8, and 221–36.

14 Quoted in Michael Evans, *Karl Marx* (London, Allen & Unwin, 1975), p.137.

15 Engels' Introduction to an 1895 edition of Marx's 'The Class Struggles in France' (MESW, pp.641–58) takes a very constitutionalist position, but Engels later complained, in a letter to Kautsky of the same year, that this piece was 'trimmed in such a fashion that I appear as a peaceful worshipper of legality at any price' (MESC, p.486).

16 MESW, p.36.

17 Marx's clearest statements on the matter are in his *On the Jewish Question*, MECW, vol.3, especially pp.153–68. A good summary is in McLellan, op. cit., especially pp.81–4.

18 MESC, pp.338–9.

19 From Marx's Paris manuscript called 'Comments on James Mill's *Elements of Political Economy*', 1844. MECW, vol.3, pp.227–8.

20 From Marx's *Economic and Philosophical Manuscripts of 1844*. Excerpt from the third manuscript 'Private Property and Communism'. MECW, vol.3, pp.296 and 300.
21 *GI*, p.53.
22 *Manifesto of the Communist Party*, MESW, p.53.
23 I refer here to the practice, adopted in Communist China during the period of Mao-Tse-Tung's chairmanship of the Chinese Communist Party, of sending students and other intellectuals from the cities to the countryside to undertake periods of manual labour alongside the peasants. This was especially common during the period of the 'Cultural Revolution'. See, for example, Derek J. Waller, *The Government and Politics of the Peoples Republic of China* (London, Hutchinson, 1981) pp.59–70. For an imagined version of the same solution, see Ursula Le Guin's science fiction novel *The Dispossessed* (Granada, Panther, 1981).
24 *Grundrisse*, Notebook VII, p.706 (emphasis added).
25 See David McLellan, *Karl Marx: His Life and Thought*, pp.149–50.
26 On this debate see the excellent entry on 'Human Nature' by Mihailo Markovic in *A Dictionary of Marxist Thought*, pp.214–17.
27 MESW, pp.319–21.
28 Michael Evans, *Karl Marx*, pp.159–60.
29 *Grundrisse*, Notebook VI, p.611 and Notebook VII, p.712.
30 Michael Evans, *Karl Marx*, pp.159–60 (emphasis added).
31 For some of the philosophical problems involved in trying to make a watertight distinction between wants and needs, see Michael Ignatieff, *The Needs of Strangers* (London, Chatto & Windus, 1985), especially chs 1 and 2. A good account and critique of Marx's theory of human needs is found in Kate Soper, *On Human Needs: Open and Closed Theories in a Marxist Perspective* (Brighton, Haverster, 1981).
32 The best single account of the Paris Commune is probably still Frank Jellinek, *The Paris Commune of 1871* (London, Victor Gollancz, 1937) republished 1971.
33 MESW, pp.288–9.
34 MESW, pp.258–9.
35 See Jellinek, op. cit., chs IV and V.
36 Antony Pollan (*Lenin and the End of Politics*, London, Methuen, 1985, p.81) remarks, surely correctly, that in a modern state, if one individual were seriously to try and be a legislator, administrator and elected representative at one and the same time, then 'the only question seems to be of what such an individual would die, over-work or multiple schizophrenia'.
37 On this, see Philip J. Kain, *Schiller, Hegel and Marx: State, Society and the Aesthetic Ideal of Ancient Greece* (Kingston, Queens University Press, 1982), pp.101–13 and 145–51.
38 MESW, p.291.
39 I mean 'high cost' here, not in the sense of a high money price, but in the sense that in the 'internal' labour accounting of the entirely self-subsistent economy, the products of such machines would cost

each person much more *of their own labour time* to obtain than they would if they were produced in greater quantity. This would be the case in Marx's socialist stage, and the communist stage proper would never in fact materialize because even relative material abundance would not be created under such conditions.

40 On this, see for example, A. Nove, *The Economics of Feasible Socialism* (London, Allen & Unwin, 1983).

41 See Pollan, op. cit., pp.89–112, for a good discussion of this issue.

CHAPTER 6: MUCH ADO ABOUT COMPARATIVELY LITTLE: CLASS, STATE, AND IDEOLOGY

1 See David McLellan, *Karl Marx: His Life and Thought* (London, Macmillan, 1973), p. 293.

2 See for example *A Dictionary of Marxist Thought* (Oxford, Basil Blackwell, 1983), pp.74–7, 219–23. Also *GI*, pp.41 and 58–9 and MESW, p.37.

3 On the complexities and limitations of ostensive definition see G.P. Baker and P.M.S. Hacker, *Wittgenstein: Meaning and Understanding* (Oxford, Basil Blackwell, 1980), ch. V, pp.81–118. See also Hanna Pitkin, *Wittgenstein and Justice* (Berkeley, University of California Press, 1972), pp.175 and 195; P.M.S. Hacker, *Insight and Illusion: Wittgenstein on Philosophy and the Metaphysics of Experience* (Oxford University Press, 1972), pp.134–5, 156–8, and 235–8; Stanley Cavell, 'The Claim to Rationality' (PhD thesis, Harvard University, 1961), pp.90–4, 175, 205, 228–9, and 267; also Anthony Kenny, *Wittgenstein* (Harmondsworth, Penguin, 1973), pp.154–7.

4 I refer here to the two books by the Glasgow University Media Group, *Bad News* (London, Routledge & Kegan Paul, 1976) and *More Bad News* (London, Routledge & Kegan Paul, 1980) which purport to uncover and analyse ideological bias in the presentation of news on television.

5 This is not the only possible answer. Another, and very fashionable answer is that classes, states, ideologies are examples of entities which are not perceptible by the senses but which none the less 'really' exist. They really exist in the sense that if they do not then a mass of perceptible phenomena cannot be explained. For this 'realist' position see R. Bhaskar, *A Realist Theory of Science* (Hassocks, Harvester, 1978), and for its explicit application to Marxism see Ted Benton, *The Rise and Fall of Structural Marxism: Althusser and his Influence* (London, Macmillan, 1984). For some incisive criticisms of realism see Richard Rorty, *Consequences of Pragmatism* (Brighton, Harvester, 1982) Introduction and ch. 1, pp.3–18.

6 I am referring here to the Registrar General's 'classification of occupations' which 'forms the basis of all the commonly used social class classifications in Britain'. For details see Ivan Reid, *Social Class*

Differences in Britain (London, Grant McIntyre, 1981), pp.38–58, from which the above quotation comes.

7 Wittgenstein, *Philosophical Investigations*, paragraphs 154, 182, 199, 321–5, 527, and 531. See also Kenny, *Wittgenstein*, ch. 8 for a good general account of this point.

8 For a development of this point and its importance, see Cavell, 'The Claim to Rationality', chapter V, and the recapitulation of his argument in Pitkin, *Wittgenstein and Justice*, ch. IV. Also K.T. Fann, *Wittgenstein's Conception of Philosophy* (Oxford, Basil Blackwell, 1969), p.54.

9 Wittgenstein, *Philosophical Investigations*, paragraphs 291 and 421 ('Look at the sentence as an instrument and its sense as its employment'). For amplifications of the problems of seeing nouns purely as names or labels and of seeing language as essentially a device for naming or labelling objects in the world, see Cavell, pp. 58, 90, 94, 208, 211, and 295; Pitkin, pp. 122, 175, 191, and 226; Baker and Hacker, ch. VII, pp.125–43; and Hacker, pp. 128, 237–8, and 240. A work which takes this aspect of Wittgenstein's later philosophy as its central focus is John Danford, *Wittgenstein and Political Philosophy* (University of Chicago Press, 1978). See especially pp.23, 28, 46–56, and 108.

10 I have taken the phrase 'form of representation' from P.M.S. Hacker, *Insight and Illusion*; see especially pp.146–7.

11 On this see, among others, Fann, pp.46 and 94; Cavell, pp. 137, 200, 232, 239–40, 260–1; Pitkin, pp.20, 61, 135–6, 223; Danford, pp.28, 33–4, 58–9, 65–7, 106, 161–6; and Kenny, pp.154–6. David Bloor, *Wittgenstein: A Social Theory of Knowledge* (London, Macmillan, 1983), p.25, calls this doctrine Wittgenstein's 'finitism' which is 'the thesis that the established meaning of a word does not determine its future applications. Meaning is created by acts of use. Like the town, it is constructed as we go along. Use determines meaning; meaning does not determine use.'

12 On this see Cavell, ch. IV and the recapitulation and development of his argument in Pitkin, chs III and IV (especially pp.72–8). See also Fann, pp.76–8 and Hacker, pp.130 and 158–9. Richard Rosenbluth 'Learning to speak and learning to think' (*Language and Ontology*, Proceedings of the 6th International Wittgenstein Symposium, Kirchberg/Wechsel, Austria, 1981), pp.408–11 applies some of Wittgenstein's insights in this area to child psychology, and Fahrang Zabeeh, 'On language games and forms of life' in E.D. Klemke (ed.), *Essays on Wittgenstein* (Urbana, University of Illinois Press, 1971), pp.343–6 and 361–3, also has some interesting observations on the connections between language learning and meaning. For the interesting hypothesis that Wittgenstein's experience as an elementary schoolteacher in rural Austria was influential in changing his own philosophical ideas about language and meaning, see W.W. Barclay III, *Wittgenstein* (London, Hutchinson, 1981), ch. 3.

13 Wittgenstein, *Philosophical Investigations*, paragraphs 246–61 and 269–71, in which he develops his best known arguments against the possibility of a 'private language', that is a language which is only comprehensible to one speaker. This thesis alone has generated a vast secondary literature. Kenny, ch. 10, provides a clear introductory account of a difficult issue. Saul A. Kripke, *Wittgenstein on Rules and Private Language* (Oxford, Basil Blackwell, 1982) provides the most contentious modern interpretation of Wittgenstein's argument to which Colin McGinn *Wittgenstein on Meaning* (Oxford, Basil Blackwell, 1984) is a reply. David Rubinstein, *Marx and Wittgenstein* (London, Routledge & Kegan Paul, 1981) bases his whole account on the centrality of Wittgenstein's private language argument in overcoming the dualism of 'objectivism' (or behaviourism) and 'subjectivism' in social science. See Rubinstein, chs 1, 2, and 10. For a recent attempt to rebut directly Wittgenstein's argument that meanings in language must be socially or inter-subjectively guaranteed, see A.J. Ayer, *Ludwig Wittgenstein* (Harmondsworth, Penguin, 1986) ch. 6.

14 For the pragmatic or 'purpose dependent' strand in Wittgenstein's theories of meaning and knowledge, see Fann pp.46 and 84–91 and Hacker, pp.123–4 and 259, Danford, p.85, and Zabeeh, p.340. See also Jerry H. Gill, *Wittgenstein and Metaphor* (University of America Press, 1981), pp.157, 202, and 219–20. See also Bloor, pp.47–8 where it is suggested that Wittgenstein's later philosophy is incomplete in its failure to relate language change, pragmatically, to a conception of changing human needs. Richard Rorty, *Philosophy and the Mirror of Nature* (Oxford, Basil Blackwell, 1980) and *Consequences of Pragmatism* (Brighton, Harvester, 1982), provides the most thoroughgoing appropriation of Wittgenstein as a pragmatic philosopher.

15 Marx, letter to Weydemeyer (1852), MESC, p.69.

16 On this see Noel W. Thompson, *The People's Science: The Popular Political Economy of Exploitation and Crisis 1816–34* (Cambridge University Press, 1984), ch. 5.

17 Ronald Meek 'The Scottish contribution to Marxist sociology' in his *Economics and Ideology and other Essays* (London, Chapman & Hall, 1967).

18 See the quotation from the Introduction to his *Critique of Hegel's Philosophy of Right* at the beginning of this chapter.

19 For the kind of formless theorizing I have in mind, see for example Jorge Larrain, *Marxism and Ideology* (London, Macmillan, 1982) and Bob Jessop, *The Capitalist State* (London, Martin Robertson, 1982).

20 Rorty's *Philosophy and the Mirror of Nature* may be seen as an exhaustive exploration of this point. See also Derek L. Phillips, *Wittgenstein and Scientific Knowledge: A Sociological Perspective* (London, Macmillan, 1977), pp.61–8; also Hacker, pp.160 and 216, Danford, pp.34, 49, and 65–7, and Cavell, pp.274–313.

21 I have not yet come across a detailed Wittgensteinian analysis of the particularly bewitching capacities of the verb 'to be', but for some

Karl Marx and the Philosophy of Praxis

apposite comments, see Cavell, pp.71, 87, and 137 and in particular Hacker, pp.128–30 in which mention is made of the confusions which can result from the fact that in English we use 'is' as a sign of identity, as a copula, and as an 'existential quantifier'.

22 For Wittgenstein on 'aspect' see *Philosophical Investigations*, Part II, pp.194–6 and 206–8.

23 Baker and Hacker, chs I, IV and VIII provide an excellent detailed account of Wittgenstein's arguments on this point. See also Kenny, ch. 9 for an introduction to the voluminous literature on 'language games' most of which is related to this point in one way or another.

24 For Wittgenstein's ideas on the relationship between the meaning of a word or sentence and the 'contexts' or 'surrounding circumstances' in which it is both learnt and subsequently used, see Pitkin, chs III and IV; Cavell, ch. IV; Fann, pp.76–82; Zabeeh, pp.343–6 and 361–3; Gill, pp.219–27; and Rosenbluth, pp.408–11.

25 Chapter 3 of Rorty's *Philosophy and the Mirror of Nature* amplifies this argument brilliantly. See also Zabeeh, p.364 and the remark in Cavell, p.274,

> It is as though we try to get the world to provide answers in a way which is independent of our responsibility for *claiming* something to be so (to get God to tell us what we must do in a way which is independent of our responsibility for choice); and we fix the world so that it *can* do this ... And we take what we have constructed to be *discoveries* about the world ...

26 For an application of this idea to the Marxist 'mode of production' discourse, see my 'Modes of production: suggestions for a fresh start on an exhausted debate' in the *Canadian Journal of African Studies*, 19, no. 1 (1985), pp.116–26.

27 For a comprehensive discussion of this issue see Ali Rattansi, *Marx and the Division of Labour* (London, Macmillan, 1982).

28 For a rather confused discussion of causality in history which continually falls into the false problems outlined here, see Paul Q. Hirst, *Marxism and Historical Writing* (London, Routledge & Kegan Paul, 1985), especially ch. 3, pp.43–56. In *Culture and Value* (Oxford, Basil Blackwell, 1980, p.62e) Wittgenstein wrote, 'there is nothing more stupid than the chatter about cause and effect in history books; nothing is more wrong-headed, more half-baked – But what hope can anyone have of putting a stop to it just by *saying* it.'

29 MESW, pp.40, 45, and 167.

30 *PP*, p.173.

31 Althusserian Marxism was particularly ensnared in this picture of language. For an overview see Benton, *The Rise and Fall of Structural Marxism*, ch. 2, pp.35–51.

CHAPTER 7: MARX'S DUBIOUS LEGACY: A PICTURE OF REALITY

1 Wittgenstein, *Philosophical Investigations*, paragraphs 59, 115, 191, 251, 295, 352, 374, 422–7, 573, and Part II, p.184. See also G.P. Baker and P.M.S. Hacker, *Wittgenstein: Meaning and Understanding*, (Oxford, Basil Blackwell, 1980), ch. 1, pp.1–27.

2 *Capital*, I, p.72.

3 One of the earliest uses of this metaphor known to me is in John Millar's *Obervations Concerning the Distinction of Ranks in Society* (Edinburgh, 1771), but I am sure that systematic research would reveal earlier sources.

4 Pitkin remarks:

> In Wittgensteinian terms one might say that 'individual', 'society', 'culture', 'state' are, first of all, concepts; they are words in our language. This does not mean that society is not real but a mere concept. Individuals are real and so is society, and both are dependent on our conceptualisation. We are tempted to suppose that society is a mere concept while individuals are really real because individual persons have tangible, visible physical bodies. But deeper reflection easily reveals that our concept of the individual person is by no means equivalent to that of his physical body; rather it is every bit as complex, as abstract, as *conceptual*, as our concepts of society or culture. What an individual is depends as much on the grammar of 'individual' as what a society is depends on the grammar of 'society'. Once that fact has penetrated into our habits of thought, new ways of investigating old issues about individuals and social wholes become accessible.

Hanna Pitkin, *Wittgenstein and Justice* (Berkeley, University of California Press, 1973), p.195.

5 In Eisenstein's film *Strike* there is a scene in which the *lumpenproletarian* strike-breakers actually emerge from manholes in the ground.

6 See Christopher Hill, *The World Turned Upside Down: Radical Ideas during the English Revolution* (Harmondsworth, Penguin, 1975), especially the extract from Henry Denne's 'Grace, Mercy and Peace' of 1645 quoted at the beginning of chapter 1.

7 A colleague at PNL, Eileen O'Keefe, points out to me that this is no longer strictly correct with modern building techniques.

8 I am not saying: if such-and-such facts of nature were different people would have different concepts (in the sense of a hypothesis). But: if anyone believes that certain concepts are absolutely the correct ones, and that having different ones would mean not realising something that we realise – then let him imagine certain very general facts of nature to be different from what we are used to and the formation of concepts different from the usual ones will become intelligible to him. (Wittgenstein, *Philosophical Investigations*, Part II, p.230e)

9 Wittgenstein, *Tractatus Logico-Philosophicus* (London, Routledge & Kegan Paul, 1961), paragraph 5.6, p. 56.

10 Wittgenstein's *Blue Book* is a particularly important source of observations upon the way in which language may bewitch or mislead through visual and spatial analogies. Ludwig Wittgenstein, *The Blue and Brown Books: Preliminary Studies for the 'Philosophical Investigations'* (Oxford, Basil Blackwell, 1972). For some amplifications of Wittgenstein's *Blue Book* insights, see P.M.S. Hacker, *Insight and Illusion: Wittgenstein on Philosophy and the Metaphysics of Experience* (Oxford University Press, 1972), pp.119–32; and Fahrang Zabeeh, 'On language games and forms of life', in E.D. Klemke (ed.), *Essays on Wittgenstein* (Urbana, University of Illinois Press, 1971), pp.348–51.

11 For Wittgenstein on 'aspect', see the reference in note 22, p.250.

12 Pitkin makes a very similar point in her analysis of the differing functions of 'motive' versus 'cause' vocabulary in the description of human action. Pitkin, *Wittgenstein and Justice*, pp.264–74.

13 At first sight it may appear ... that ... we have two kinds of worlds, worlds built of different materials; a mental world and a physical world. The mental world in fact is liable to be imagined as gaseous, or rather, aethereal. But let me remind you of the queer role which the gaseous and aethereal play in philosophy – when we perceive that a substantive is not used as ... the name of an object, and when therefore we can't help saying to ourselves that it is the name of an aethereal object ... It seems to us sometimes as though the phenomena of personal experience were in a way phenomena in the upper strata of the atmosphere as opposed to the material phenomena which happen on the ground. (Wittgenstein, *Blue Book*, p.47)

14 See for example S.S. Prawer, *Karl Marx and World Literature* (Oxford, Clarendon Press, 1976), pp.281–2.

15 A metaphor employed, along with that of the volcanic eruption, in several disaster movies.

16 For a most interesting discussion of structure and agency in history, see Philip Abrams, *Historical Sociology* (Somerset, Open Books, 1982), especially chapters 1 and 8.

17 MESW, p.429.

18 *GI*, p.47.

19 For another application of this thesis see Angela Reidy and Gavin Kitching, 'Primary health care: our sacred cow and their white elephant' in *Public Administration and Development* 6 (1986), pp.425–33.

20 On this, see for example Herschel B. Chipp, *Theories of Modern Art* (Berkeley, University of California Press, 1968), especially ch. VI.

21 It is of course true that human beings are natural creatures dependent upon a certain natural environment and that both their own nature and their natural environment impose certain constraints upon what they can do. But since these constraints are to an

(unknowable) degree alterable by human knowledge and inventiveness, it is certainly misleading to conceive of them on the analogy of fixed boundaries or limits. On this, see Alfred Schmidt, *The Concept of Nature in Marx* (London, New Left Books, 1971), especially ch. 3, pp.95–126.

22 *Capital*, I, p. 20.

23 See for example the entry on 'Ideology' by Jorge Larrain in *The Dictionary of Marxist Thought* (Oxford, Basil Blackwell, 1983), pp.219–23.

24 *PP*, pp.104, 121; *Capital*, I, pp.76–81.

25 *GI*, p.51. And later in the same work there is another passage on language and philosophy which is extraordinarily reminiscent of the later Wittgenstein:

> For philosophers one of the most difficult tasks is to descend from the world of thought to the actual world. *Language* is the immediate actuality of thought. Just as philosophers have given thought an independent existence, so they had to make language into an independent realm. This is the secret of philosophical language, in which thoughts in the form of words have their own content. The problem of descending from the world of thoughts to the actual world is turned into the problem of descending from language to life.
>
> We have shown that thoughts and ideas acquire an independent existence in consequence of the personal circumstances and relations of individuals acquiring independent existence. We have shown that exclusive systematic occupation with these thoughts on the part of ideologists and philosophers, and hence the systematisation of these thoughts, is a consequence of the division of labour, and that, in particular, German philosophy is a consequence of German petty-bourgeois conditions. The philosophers would only have to dissolve their language into ordinary language, from which it is abstracted, to recognise it as the distorted language of the actual world, and to realize that neither thoughts nor language in themselves form a realm of their own, that they are only *manifestations* of actual life. (*GI*, p.118, emphasis added)

Compare this passage with Wittgenstein's analysis of 'idling language' in, for example, *Philosophical Investigations*, paragraphs 81–133. See also the comments on this passage in A.R. Manser, 'The end of philosophy: Marx and Wittgenstein' (inaugural lecture, University of Southampton, Department of Philosophy, May 1973), and in Susan M. Easton, *Humanist Marxism and Wittgensteinian Social Philosophy* (Manchester University Press, 1983), p.119.

26 *GI*, pp.48–9, 62, 86, 115–6.

27 . . . to the kind of consciousness – and this is characteristic of the philosophical consciousness – for which conceptual thinking is the real human being, and for which the conceptual world as such

is thus the only reality, the movement of the categories appears as the real act of production – which only, unfortunately, receives a jolt from outside ... This is correct in so far as *the concrete totality is a totality of thoughts, concrete in thought, in fact a product of thinking and comprehending*; but [it is] *not* in any way a product of the *concept* which thinks and generates *itself* outside or above observations and conceptions *into* concepts. The totality as it appears in the head, as a totality of thoughts, is a product of a *thinking* head, which *appropriates* the world in the only way it can, a way different from the artistic, religious, practical and mental [? *sic*] appropriation of this world. The real subject retains its autonomous existence outside the head just as before ... *as long as* the head's conduct is *merely,* speculative, *merely* theoretical. Hence, in the theoretical method, too, the subject, society, must always be kept *in mind* as the pre-supposition. (*Grundrisse*, Introduction, pp.101–2; emphases added)

This is Marx at his very best.

28 Compare this formulation with a similar passage in the *Communist Manifesto*:

Does it require deep intuition to comprehend that man's ideas, views, and conceptions, in one word, man's consciousness, *changes with* every change in the conditions of his material existence, in his social relations and in his social life? What else does the history of ideas prove, than that intellectual production *changes its character in proportion* as material production is changed? The ruling ideas of each age have ever been the ideas of its ruling class. (MESW, p.51, emphases added)

See also the comments on this passage in S.S. Prawer, *Karl Marx and World Literature*, p.143.

29 For some comments on reductionism, see my *Rethinking Socialism* pp.144–65.

30 Wittgenstein has some interesting comments on the word 'consciousness', most of them intended in one way or another to draw attention to its reificatory dangers. See *Philosophical Investigations* paragraphs 20, 149, 156, 159, 412–21.

31 On this see Abrams, *Historical Sociology*, pp.300–35.

32 Strawson calls Wittgenstein's later philosophy a 'philosophical anthropology' or a 'weak naturalism'. See P.F. Strawson, *Scepticism and Naturalism: Some Varieties* (London, Methuen, 1985). Essentially this final chapter has depended on a particular application of Wittgenstein's 'form of life' concept which is at the heart of his philosophical anthropology. On this, see Fahrang Zabeeh 'On language games and forms of life'. Also J.F.M. Hunter, '"Forms of life" in Wittgenstein's Philosophical Investigations' *American Philosophical Quarterly* (October 1968), 5, no.4, pp.233–43. See also Pitkin, ch. VI, especially pp.132–9; Derek L. Phillips, *Wittgenstein and Scientific Knowledge* (London, Macmillan, 1977), pp.80–86, 100

and 130–1; Stanley Cavell, 'The Claim to Rationality' (Harvard University PhD thesis, 1961), ch.4; David Rubinstein, *Marx and Wittgenstein* (London, Routledge & Kegan Paul, 1981), ch. 10; Hacker, *Insight and Illusion*, p.220; and Anthony Kenny, *Wittgenstein* (Harmondsworth, Penguin, 1973), p.166. Indeed this is an important point at which, in my view, the philosophies of Marx and Wittgenstein meet, a meeting signalled in the very vocabulary which commentators feel moved to use in characterizing both their philosophies. Thus Pears (David Pears, *Wittgenstein*, London, Fontana, 1971, ch. 9), characterizes Wittgenstein's later philosophy as 'anthropocentric', precisely the same term which Kolakowski uses to characterize that of Marx ('Karl Marx and the classical definition of truth' in *Marxism and Beyond*, London, Paladin, 1971, p.68), whilst Bernstein (*Praxis and Action*, London, Duckworth, 1972, p.77), finds the terms 'philosophical anthropology' as appropriate to Marx as Strawson does to Wittgenstein.

33 For some of the confusions which may arise from the attempt to think about time in the language of physical movement, see Wittgenstein's *Brown Book*, pp.107–9.

34 See G.H. von Wright, *Wittgenstein* (Oxford, Basil Blackwell, 1982) p.209, footnote 10.

35 I have in mind here such works as B. Hindess and P.Q. Hirst, *Pre-Capitalist Modes of Production* (London, Routledge & Kegan Paul, 1975); B. Hindess and P.Q. Hirst, *Mode of Production and Social Formation: An Auto-Critique of 'Pre-Capitalist Modes of Production'* (London, Routledge & Kegan Paul, 1977); A Cutler, P.Q. Hirst, and A. Hussein, *Marx's Capital and Capitalism Today* (London, Routledge & Kegan Paul, 1977). Perry Anderson, *In the Tracks of Historical Materialism* (London, Verso, 1983) deplores the intellectual aridity and political obscurantism of recent post-structuralist thought in France, but fails to acknowledge the degree to which he earlier encouraged intellectual trends whose latest developments he now deplores.

AN ANNOTATED SELECT BIBLIOGRAPHY ON MARX AND WITTGENSTEIN

The full range of primary and secondary sources consulted in the writing of this book can be found in the notes. The aim of this short and very selective bibliography is not to reproduce that mass of references, but to provide the reader with a brief guide to the readings which I have found most helpful in the study of Marx and Wittgenstein and which I believe that a reader anxious to explore these issues further would also find helpful.

I should add however that the literature on both Marx and Wittgenstein, in the English language alone, is voluminous and growing continuously, and I make no claim to have read all, or even most of it. The suggestions and comments below must therefore be treated as a temporary summary of work and reading which is still, and always, in progress and as an attempt to help anyone, who for reasons similar to or different from my own, might wish to go along the same paths.

MARX

Primary sources

As well as the 'Complete Works' of Marx and Engels which have long been available in German and are now in process of production in English (by Lawrence & Wishart), there are a large number of anthologies of his major writings. The three which I have found most useful are: *Karl Marx and Friedrich Engels: Selected Works in One Volume* (London, Lawrence and Wishart, 1970); T.Bottomore and M. Rubel (eds), *Karl Marx: Selected Writings in Sociology and Social Philosophy* (Harmondsworth, Pelican, 1963); and E. Kamenka (ed.), *The Portable Marx* (Harmondsworth, Penguin, 1983).

Secondary sources

MARX THE MAN

For an authoritative account of Marx's life, David McLellan *Karl Marx: His Life and Thought* (London, Macmillan, 1973) is without rival in the modern literature in English, and is an excellent place for any student to begin their secondary reading. McLellan not only covers the whole range of Marx's thought, but provides an account of him as an individual which, in the best traditions of biography, is at once sympathetic but clear-eyed.

MARX'S THOUGHT

S. Avinieri, *The Social and Political Thought of Karl Marx* (Cambridge University Press, 1968) and W.L. McBride, *The Philosophy of Marx* (London, Hutchinson, 1977) are both excellent introductions to Marx's philosophical formation and ideas. For his political ideas Michael Evans, *Karl Marx* (London, Allen & Unwin, 1975), Part III, is very clear, but this is only one of a vast number of texts dealing with this aspect of Marx's thought. The situation with regard to Marx's economics is however much less satisfactory. John Harrison, *An Introduction to Marxist Economics for Socialists* (London, Pluto Press, 1977) is the only text which I have felt comfortable in recommending to a beginning student with no background at all in economics, and it restricts itself entirely to an exposition of Marx's most basic ideas without any attempt at criticism. It is also out of print and unlikely to be reprinted. For students seeking to go further and master the more complex dimensions of Marx's economic theory and its principal weaknesses, I can still find nothing better to recommend, after Harrison, than the old text by Paul Sweezy, *The Theory of Capitalist Development* (New York, Monthly Review Press, 1942) which is regularly reprinted. In addition, of newer books, Angus Walker, *Marx: His Theory and its Context* (London, Longman, 1978) is good on the classical roots of Marx's economics and explains some of the principal weaknesses well. Antony Cutler, Barry Hindess, Paul Hirst and Athar Hussain *Marx's 'Capital' and Capitalism Today* (London, Routledge & Kegan Paul, 1977) two volumes, includes all the basic criticisms of Marx's economics, but is long and makes very few concessions to the beginning student either in content or expression. The same is true of the anthology edited by M.C. Howard and J.E. King, *The Economics of Marx* (Harmondsworth, Penguin, 1976) which is frequently recommended in this context. In fact for a student seeking a clear, non-technical statement of the most fundamental problems of Marx's economics I know nothing better than Geoff Hodgson's, *Capitalism, Value and Exploitation: A Radical Theory* (Oxford, Martin Robertson, 1982) which is very clearly written and should be readily comprehensible to anyone who has previously worked through Harrison and Sweezy.

MORE ADVANCED TEXTS ON MARX

Sidney Hook, *From Hegel to Marx* (Ann Arbor, University of Michigan Press, 1962) and regularly reprinted is still, in my view, one of the best accounts of the Hegelian strain in Marx's thought, closely rivalled by the first chapter of Richard J. Bernstein's *Praxis and Action* (London, Duckworth, 1972). The recently published *Dictionary of Marxist Thought* (Oxford, Basil Blackwell, 1983) is an invaluable work of reference, not only on Marx, but on the Marxist tradition as a whole, though like all works of this sort it is of uneven quality and has some major omissions. The first volume of Leszek Kolakowski's *Main Currents of Marxism* (Oxford University Press, 1978), dealing with the thought of Marx and Engels, is also extremely incisive, and it is only a pity that the later volumes of this work lack the balance and sobriety that the first volume shows. Finally, I must include a reference to the finest work on Marx in English known to me, S.S. Prawer's *Karl Marx and World Literature* (Oxford, Clarendon Press, 1976), a work of positively awesome scholarship which is an education in itself as well as – along the way – the deepest analysis of the fundamentals of Marx's thought which I have encountered to date. That it provides powerful, if oblique, support to the thesis of this book, is only a secondary reason for its inclusion here.

WITTGENSTEIN

Primary sources

Those who are approaching Wittgenstein's later philosophy from a background in history or social science will find three texts particularly useful. These are *The Blue and Brown Books* (Oxford, Basil Blackwell, 1958) and regularly reprinted; *On Certainty* (Oxford, Basil Blackwell, 1969), but also regularly reprinted, and of course the famous *Philosophical Investigations* (Oxford, Basil Blackwell, 1958) which is continually in print. In addition the two further collections of his later writings entitled *Zettel* (Oxford, Basil Blackwell, 1967) and *Culture and Value* (Oxford, Basil Blackwell, 1980) have some further observations based on the same philosophical perspective.

It should however be noted that of all of Wittgenstein's published writings, only two, the *Tractatus Logico-Philosophicus* of 1921, and the *Philosophical Investigations*, first published in 1953, are in a 'finished' form which he himself approved for publication. All of the other works bearing his name (not only those mentioned above, but a number of others) were published by Wittgenstein's literary executors after his death and compiled by them from the mass of manuscripts, typescripts and dictated material in the Wittgenstein collection (or *Nachlass*) held in the library of Trinity College, Cambridge. A description of the collection by G.H. von Wright (one of the executors) can be found in his *Wittgenstein* (Oxford, Basil Blackwell, 1982), chapter 2 ('The Wittgenstein Papers').

None the less, the *Philosophical Investigations* does contain the core of Wittgenstein's later philosophy, expressed in a way which he found satisfactory (or at least not too unsatisfactory), and is the single most important text which any student who wishes to come to terms with that philosophy must read. Its cover blurb claims that it 'may well be the most important and influential philosophical work of modern times' and for once this does not seem an exaggeration.

Secondary sources

WITTGENSTEIN THE MAN

As well as being a great philosopher, Ludwig Wittgenstein appears to have been an extraordinary man whose 'character and personality had a striking impact on all those who encountered him'. A great deal of this extraordinariness comes through in a book written by one of his former students, Norman Malcolm (*Ludwig Wittgenstein: A Memoir*, Oxford University Press, 1958) from whom the quotation above comes. It is also manifest in the *Recollections of Wittgenstein* (Oxford University Press, 1984) edited by another former student, Rush Rhees, and containing recollections by a number of Wittgenstein's students and colleagues from his years as a Fellow in Cambridge University.

However, Wittgenstein only spent a part of his life in Cambridge and some interesting light is shed on other aspects of his life, especially in his native Austria, in the book by W.W. Barclay III (*Wittgenstein*, London, Hutchinson, 1973). This work caused something of a furor when it was published because of its 'revelations' about Wittgenstein's homosexuality, a furor which this reader at least finds totally bizarre and utterly obscuring of the real merit of the book. This lies in its unique discussion of Wittgenstein's years as an elementary school teacher in the village of Trattenbach in lower Austria in the 1920s, and the possible role of this experience in the slow changing of his philosophical ideas. However, it is possible that the shock caused to Wittgenstein's admirers by Barclay's revelations about his sexuality is itself a product of the 'striking impact' he made upon them in Cambridge, an impact which seems to have led some of his more ardent followers to see him as a kind of secular saint. On this see Barclay's 'Afterword' to the 1985 edition of his book ('On Wittgenstein and homosexuality').

WITTGENSTEIN'S THOUGHT

I have found K.T. Fann's *Wittgenstein's Conception of Philosophy* (Oxford, Basil Blackwell, 1969) the most clear and useful of several short introductions to Wittgenstein's philosophy currently available. It is particularly useful to social scientists because of its insistent attempt to dispel some of the most common myths about the 'conservative' thrust of Wittgenstein's later philosophy, myths found especially among

Marxists. Chapter X of Fann's book ('Understanding Wittgenstein') is especially important in this respect. Fann's book is certainly more directly relevant to social scientists than either of the other two most readily available introductions, both of which are addressed much more narrowly to philosophers. These are David Pears, *Wittgenstein* (London, Fontana Modern Masters, 1971) and Anthony Kenny, *Wittgenstein* (Harmondsworth, Penguin, 1975). However the latter is interesting for its insistence on the deep continuities between Wittgenstein's earlier and later philosophy and can be contrasted with Fann's more orthodox account in this respect. K.T. Fann has also edited what in my view is the best single anthology on Wittgenstein, *Ludwig Wittgenstein: The Man and his Philosophy* (Brighton, Harvester, 1978).

The two most interesting applications of Wittgenstein's philosophy to social science which I have encountered to date are Hanna Pitkin's *Wittgenstein and Justice* (Berkeley, University of California Press, 1972) and David Rubinstein's *Marx and Wittgenstein* (London, Routledge & Kegan Paul, 1981). The latter had the most direct influence on this book, though the former is undoubtedly the more original and wide-ranging work. Indeed Pitkin's is a pioneering study whose many incisive suggestions for the rethinking of social and political theory have never really been followed up, certainly in Britain. Not the least of the merits of her book is the critique it provides of Peter Winch's *The Idea of a Social Science and its Relation to Philosophy* (London, Routledge & Kegan Paul, 1958) which is perhaps the *only* application of Wittgensteinian philsophy to social science familiar to social scientists, and which, along with Ernest Gellner's *Words and Things* (Harmondsworth, Penguin, 1968), has perhaps been most responsible for Wittgenstein's rather poor reputation among social scientists. Chapter XI of *Wittgenstein and Justice* (on 'Action and the problem of social science') is particularly important in providing an alternative Wittgensteinian perspective on the possibility of a social science to that found in Winch.

Pitkin's work was in turn heavily influenced by a (then) unpublished doctoral dissertation in philosophy from Harvard University ('The Claim to Rationality' by Stanley Cavell, completed in 1961). Cavell subsequently published this dissertation, in a much expanded and amended form, as *The Claim to Reason: Wittgenstein, Skepticism, Morality and Tragedy* (Oxford University Press, 1978) but with the addition of several long discussions of literary theory which, for this reader at least, made the book a much less focused and exciting work than the dissertation had been. However, the core of his original thesis remained, and Parts One and Two of the book in particular (chapters I–VIII) incorporate the discussions of epistemology which deeply influenced Pitkin. The original Introduction to Cavell's dissertation ('The availability of Wittgenstein's later philosophy') is one of the best short accounts of the later Wittgenstein available in the literature and has been republished in several places including Cavell's own *Must We Mean What We Say?* (Cambridge University Press, 1976) pp.44–72 and in George Pitcher (ed.), *Wittgenstein: The Philosophical Investigations* (New York, Doubleday, 1966) pp.151–85.

The interesting question of how far Wittgenstein's later philosophy amounts to a variety of pragmatism, a central issue for this book, has not yet been much discussed in the secondary literature. For two contrasting accounts, see Richard Rorty, 'Keeping philosophy pure: an essay on Wittgenstein' in his *Consequences of Pragmatism* (Brighton, Harvester, 1982), pp.19–36, and Thomas Morawetz, *Wittgenstein and Knowledge* (Brighton, Harvester, 1980), ch. 3, pp. 63–75.

Finally, it should be noted that R.J. Bernstein's *Praxis and Action* can appear equally appropriately in this section on Wittgenstein as in the earlier section on Marx. Part 4 of the book, devoted to 'The concept of action' in modern 'analytic philosophy' has some most important observations both on Wittgenstein and on modern Wittgensteinian philosophy, observations which link directly to themes in his essay on Marx earlier in the book.

INDEX